GETTING TO KNOW THE PRESIDENT

Second Edition
INTELLIGENCE BRIEFINGS OF PRESIDENTIAL CANDIDATES,

1952–2004

John L. Helgerson

Center for the Study of Intelligence
Central Intelligence Agency
May 2012

The Center for the Study of Intelligence (CSI) was established as an organization within CIA to "think through the functions of intelligence and bring the best intellects available to bear on intelligence problems." The center, comprising professional historians and experienced practitioners from throughout the Intelligence Community, attempts to document lessons learned from past activities, to explore the needs and expectations of intelligence consumers, and to stimulate serious debate about current and future intelligence challenges.

To carry out this mission, CSI publishes books and monographs addressing historical, operational, doctrinal and theoretical aspects of the intelligence profession. It also administers the CIA Museum and maintains the CIA's Historical Intelligence Collection of published literature on intelligence. The center also houses the Emerging Trends Program, which seeks to identify the impact of future trends on the work of US intelligence.

The center also manages the quarterly journal *Studies in Intelligence*.

Past unclassified publications produced by CSI include:

ARCHANGEL: CIA's Supersonic A 12 Reconnaissance Aircraft (Second Edition, 2011), by David Robarge, CIA Historian

The Agency and the Hill: CIA's Relationship with Congress, 1946–2004, by L. Britt Snider (2008)

Directors of Central Intelligence as Leaders of the U.S. Intelligence Community, by Douglas F. Garthoff (2005)

Psychology of Intelligence Analysis by Richards J. Heuer, Jr. (1999)

Questions and comments may be addressed to:
The Center for the Study of Intelligence
Central Intelligence Agency
Washington, DC, 20505

*To Martha,
Katherine, and Paul*

JOHN L. HELGERSON

Mr. Helgerson was the Central Intelligence Agency's inspector general from 2002 until his retirement in 2009. Previously, he served as chairman of the Intelligence Community's National Intelligence Council and deputy director of the National Imagery and Mapping Agency.

Mr. Helgerson began his career in government as an analyst of African politics at the CIA. At varying ponts he headed units responsible for coverage of Africa, Latin America, and Europe. He served in a number of senior management posts, including deputy director for intelligence and director of congressional affairs.

Prior to his government service, Mr. Helgerson was an assistant professor of political science at the University of Cincinnati and a research affiliate of the University of Zambia in Lusaka. He specialized in international relations and African politics.

A native of South Dakota, Mr Helgerson graduated from Saint Olaf College in Northfield, Minnesota, and received M.A. and Ph.D degrees from Duke University in Durham, North Carolina.

He is the author of *Getting To Know the President: CIA Briefings of Presidential Candidates, 1952–1992*.

Mr. Helgerson has received a number of awards and commendations, including the National Intelligence Distinguished Service Medal, CIA's Distinguished Career Intelligence Medal, and NIMA's Distinguished Civilian Service Award.

Contents

Foreword ix

Foreword to First Edition xi

Preface xv

Introduction 3

CHAPTER 1: Truman and Eisenhower: Launching the Process 7
   Strained Relations Complicate the Arrangements 11
   Preelection Briefings 14
   Support to the President-Elect 16
   The New President as an Intelligence Consumer 20
   Briefing Governor Stevenson in 1952 23
   The Challenger Briefed Again in 1956 25

CHAPTER 2: Into Politics with Kennedy and Johnson 29
   The Presidential Debates 29
   Preelection Briefings: What Really Was Discussed? 34
   The Missile Gap 36
   Postelection Briefing on Cuba 40
   Other Covert Programs 42
   The Mystery Briefing of Late November 44
   Kennedy Visits the CIA 46
   Origins of the *President's Intelligence Checklist* 47
   The Transition to President Johnson 50
   Vietnam 53
   Evolution to the *President's Daily Brief* 56

CHAPTER 3: Nixon and Ford - Uneven Access 61
   Supporting Nixon's Team in New York City 65
   The Key Player: Henry Kissinger 67
   Nixon Remains Aloof 72
   A Closer Relationship With Ford 76
   Discussing Operations and Intelligence 79
   Political Problems Undermine the Briefing Process 82

CHAPTER 4: In-Depth Discussions with Carter 87
   Extended Preelection Briefings 88
   Operational and Political Issues Arise 97
   Carter's Use of the *President's Daily Brief* 104

CHAPTER 5: Reagan and Bush - A Study in Contrasts 111
   Postelection Briefings 114
   A Higher Level of Daily Support 118
   After the Inauguration 122
   The Transition to President Bush 124

CHAPTER 6: Briefing Governor Clinton in Little Rock 131
   The DCI Visits Little Rock 131
   Establishing a "Permanent" Presence 132
   Substance of Discussions 136
   Other Opportunities To Help 141
   Great Support Made It Work 144
   What Was Accomplished 147

CHAPTER 7: George W. Bush: Demanding Consumer 151
   The Presidential Debates 155
   Postelection Briefings 156
   Vice President-elect Cheney 160
   Covert Action Briefing 161
   Strong Supporting Cast 162
   Impact of Austin 166
   President Bush as a Customer 168
   Intelligence and Politics 170
   Kerry and Edwards Briefed in 2004 171

CHAPTER 8: Concluding Observations 177
   Patterns of Support 178
   What the Presidents Recommend 180
   Keeping Out of Politics 185
   The Arrangements Make a Difference 186
      Material That Was Welcome 189

Index 193

Foreword

The Central Intelligence Agency is more of a presidential service organization than perhaps any other component of the US government. Since 1952, CIA, and now the Intelligence Community, have provided presidential candidates and presidents-elect with intelligence briefings during their campaigns and transitions. These briefings have helped presidents be as well informed as possible on international developments from the day they take office.

In addition to their central, substantive purpose, these briefings usually have also served as the IC's introduction to the "First Customer," the individual who, more than any other, determines what place intelligence will have in the national security hierarchy. They have been crucial in giving an early sense of the personalities of the candidates and presidents-elect, their knowledge of world affairs, and their views of how intelligence and the IC can best support national security decisionmaking.

Getting To Know the President by John Helgerson makes a singular contribution to the literature of intelligence by describing this important process of information sharing between the IC and the chief executive. First published in 1996 and now revised and updated to include accounts of intelligence support to candidates and presidents-elect in the three elections between then and 2004, Helgerson's study provides unique insights into the mechanics and content of the briefings, the interaction of the participants, and the briefings' effect on the relationships presidents have had with their intelligence services. His observations on how and what to brief during the campaign and transition periods are essential reading for members of the community charged with that responsibility in the future and seeking to learn from the best practices of their predecessors.

In his 1996 foreword to the first edition of this book, Christopher Andrew took note of the "simple but important fact that each president is different." From that point flows another explanation for this second edition. Prepared then, as now, under the sponsorship of the Center for the Study of Intelligence, this work reflects CSI's and the CIA's commitment to the examination, and continual reexamination, of the profession of intelligence in the United States. This effort has been manifest in products of many kinds, unclassified and clas-

FOREWORD

sified, with many of the latter eventually released wholly or in part to the public. As with other dimensions of the IC's and CIA's work, service to policymakers and presidents demands both the scrutiny of today's practitioners of intelligence and the perspective of historians to follow. While this book is primarily intended to serve those who must consider the IC's role in a presidential election year, it is also hoped that it will help illuminate as much as possible for others the nature of CIA and IC service to past presidents, while at the same time keeping faith with the essential confidentiality to which sitting presidents are entitled.

David Robarge
Chief Historian
Central Intelligence Agency

FOREWORD
TO FIRST EDITION

GETTING TO KNOW THE PRESIDENT

This is an important and original book. How world leaders understand or misunderstand, use or fail to use, the intelligence available to them is an essential but still under-researched aspect both of modern government and of international relations. The making of the American intelligence community has transformed the presidency of the United States. Before the First World War, the idea that the United States might need a foreign intelligence service simply did not occur to most Americans or to their presidents. After the war, Woodrow Wilson publicly poked fun at his own pre-war innocence: "Let me testify to this, my fellow citizens, I not only did not know it until we got into this war, but I did not believe it when I was told that it was true, that Germany was not the only country that maintained a secret service!" Wilson could scarcely have imagined that, less than half a century later, the United States would be an intelligence superpower. Though the intelligence nowadays available to the president is, like all human knowledge, incomplete and fallible, it probably exceeds—at least in quantity—that available to any other world leader past or present.

The starting point for the study of relations between presidents and their intelligence communities since the Second World War are the briefings they receive from the CIA before their inauguration. John L. Helgerson is well equipped to write this path-breaking study of these briefings. A political scientist before joining the CIA, he served as the Agency's deputy director for intelligence during the Bush administration and was head of the team that briefed Bill Clinton in Little Rock after the 1992 election. In addition to having access to classified files, Mr. Helgerson has interviewed previous Agency briefers and all surviving former presidents.

Both briefers and former presidents are agreed on the simple but important fact that each president is different. Presidents differ more widely in their previous knowledge and experience of intelligence than in their grasp of most other areas of government. Harry Truman entered the Oval Office in April 1945 almost wholly ignorant of intelligence matters. His determination that no future president should take office as uninformed as he had been is partly responsible for the intelligence briefing offered to all presidential candidates since 1952. Unlike Truman, Dwight D. Eisenhower did not need to be persuaded of the importance of intelligence. Ike was the first president since George Washington already experienced in the use of intelligence when he took the oath of office. He wrote after the Second World War that 'intelligence had been of priceless value to me...and, in no small way, contributed to the speed with which the enemy was routed and eventually forced to surrender."

Recent presidents have varied almost as greatly in their experience of intelligence as Truman and Eisenhower. Agency briefers found Presidents Reagan and Bush, in Mr. Helgerson's words, "virtual polar opposites." Despite Ronald Reagan's membership in 1975 of the Rockefeller Commission on CIA activities within the United States, he had no previous experience as an intelligence consumer and felt the need for generality. Bush, by contrast, was the first former director of central intelligence, with the arguable exception of George Washington, to be elected president. He had a closer working relationship than any previous president with the CIA. Like Reagan, President Clinton had no previous experience as an intelligence consumer.

Mr. Helgerson provides the first detailed account of the way in which Agency briefers have attempted, with varying success, to adapt briefings to the differing experience, priorities, and working patterns of successive presidents. One of the earliest changes in the new administration is usually the format of the *President's Daily Brief*, probably the world's smallest circulation, most highly classified, and—in some respects—best informed daily newspaper. Some presidents, it appears, like it to include more humor than others. On average, about 60 percent of the items covered in the *President's Daily Brief* do not appear in the press at all, even in unclassified form.

The most important lesson of this book is that, if the CIA is to provide effective intelligence support to policymakers, there is no substitute for direct access to the president. There is the implied lesson also that, if presidents are to make the best use of the CIA, they need to make clear to the Agency at regular intervals what intelligence they do and do not want. As a result of his own experience as DCI, Bush plainly took this lesson to heart. Some presidents, however, have provided little feedback.

Most good books leave the reader wanting more. *Getting To Know the President* is no exception. As well as holding the interest of his readers, Mr. Helgerson will also increase their curiosity. What, for example, were the exotic and closely-held methods or the sensitive human-source and technical collection programs on which DCI George Bush briefed President-elect Jimmy Carter? Just as it is reasonable for readers to ask questions such as these, so it is also reasonable on some occasions for intelligence agencies to avoid precise replies in order to protect their sources and methods.

There is an inevitable tension between the curiosity of readers and scholars on the one hand and the security-consciousness of intelligence agencies on the other. Historians and intelligence officers are unlikely ever to reach complete agreement on how much of the past record can be declassified without compromising current operations. In recent years, however, the CIA Center for the Study of Intelligence has gone further than most of the world's major intelligence agencies in opening up some of its records to historical research, publishing important volumes of documents on subjects such as the Truman administration, the Cuban missile crisis, Soviet estimates, and spy satellites. All historians will hope that these documents will be followed by many more.

It is also to be hoped that *Getting To Know the President* will set a precedent for intelligence agencies in other countries. Until similar volumes are available on the briefing of, among others, British prime ministers, German chancellors, French and Russian presidents, and leading Asian statesmen, the use made of intelligence by world leaders will continue to be a major gap in our understanding of both modern government and international relations.

Christopher Andrew
Corpus Christi College
Cambridge

PREFACE

The first edition of this book, *Getting To Know the President: CIA Briefings of Presidential Candidates, 1952–1992,* was produced while I served a one-year assignment with the CIA's Center for the Study of Intelligence in the mid-1990s. This updated and expanded second edition was made possible through a contract with the Center in 2011. I am grateful for these opportunities. The resulting study is my work alone; the opinions offered are not those of the Central Intelligence Agency, the Office of the Director of National Intelligence (ODNI), or the US government.

To the maximum extent feasible, contemporaneous written records have been used to construct the account of developments presented. For the earlier presidential transitions, it has proved possible to declassify all relevant documents. Among the numerous individuals who helped search for source materials, a few were especially helpful and deserve special thanks: ODNI officers John Moseman and Richard Fravel; CIA officers David Robarge, Peter Clement, Janet Platt, Becky Rant, Emma Sullivan, and Michael Warner; Andrea Mehrer at the Library of Congress; and Dwight D. Eisenhower Library archivist David Haight.

Interviews with former presidents, CIA directors, and numerous others involved in the 10 presidential transitions provided invaluable additional material with which to flesh out the sometimes sparse written record. I deeply appreciate the honor and time granted me by Presidents George H. W. Bush, Ronald Reagan, Jimmy Carter, and Gerald Ford in agreeing to be interviewed. Similarly, I am grateful to the DCIs and DNIs who were most involved in the transitions—Richard Helms, William Colby, Stansfield Turner, Robert Gates, Michael Hayden, and Michael McConnell—for sharing their recollections. Former Agency officer Meredith Davidson provided invaluable assistance in reconstructing the events of the early 1950s.

The Intelligence Community (IC) protects carefully the confidentiality of comments made to its officers by serving presidents, and I have continued that tradition in this account. Readers will find neither exposés of our presidents' private moments nor specific descriptions of what they said during briefing sessions, especially regarding sensitive policy issues of continuing relevance

PREFACE

and importance. Similarly, it would not be appropriate to use this volume to offer judgments about how well the various presidents used the intelligence they were provided. Nevertheless, I have been able to recount in unclassified form the circumstances under which the Community established its relationships with successive presidents and to discuss, in general terms, the subjects about which they were briefed.

I thank David Robarge, Andres Vaart, Bruce Wells, David Peterson, Richard Kovar, Judith Van Roy, and Harriet Malone for their assistance in editing and producing the original study and this updated version.

John L. Helgerson

INTRODUCTION

It was President Harry Truman, in whose administration the Central Intelligence Agency and the postwar Intelligence Community (IC) were created, who instituted the custom of providing candidates for the presidency classified briefings on foreign developments. In 1952 he authorized the CIA to brief Gen. Dwight Eisenhower and Governor Adlai Stevenson so that the successful candidate would be as well informed as possible on the world situation when he took office. The briefings would also position the CIA to develop a close working relationship with the new president and his advisers. These two objectives have guided the efforts of the Agency and the IC during presidential transition periods ever since.

Thus it was, after Arkansas Governor Bill Clinton won the 1992 election, that CIA moved quickly to establish a presence in Little Rock to provide intelligence support to the new president-elect. As CIA's deputy director for intelligence, I was sent to meet with the governor and his staff to describe the materials the Agency proposed to make available and to elicit the governor's agreement to receive regular briefings from the CIA. Events unfolded in such a way that I became the head of a team that spent most of the period from November 1992 through January 1993 in Little Rock providing daily intelligence updates to the president-elect.

In keeping with President Truman's initiative, the Agency wanted to help the new president-elect prepare for his foreign policy responsibilities and acquaint him and his staff with IC's capabilities for collecting, analyzing, and delivering intelligence that would be vital to them when they took office. As we made arrangements for briefing Governor Clinton, we attempted to learn as much as possible from the Agency's experience in previous transition periods. What we discovered was that the CIA had provided pre-inaugural intelligence support to all eight presidents elected since the Agency was founded, but had no systematic records of those efforts. There was no body of organized information to indicate what had worked before and what had not. Such records and memories as we did have, however, made clear that we needed to make decisions quickly on how to proceed in a number of areas that would have an important bearing on whether we met our two primary goals.

INTRODUCTION

Author John Helgerson reviews materials for his briefing of Governor Bill Clinton at the Arkansas governor's mansion. Helgerson was CIA's deputy director for intelligence at the time.

The key variables that seem to determine whether the IC is successful in serving a new president fall into four general categories. The first of these relates to the level and type of person or persons the Community puts forward to represent it. In some transitions the director of central intelligence (DCI), and now the director of national intelligence (DNI), has been personally and extensively involved; in others the DCI took no active role. Sometimes the IC has fielded very senior officers as its briefers but in other instances relied on much more junior representatives. When senior officers do the briefings they generally give the Community's product and approach greater credibility and access, but their selection also increases the likelihood that the exercise will be seen as political.

A second category of key variables concerns other political considerations to which the Intelligence Community must be sensitive to ensure that it and a new president come to work together well. Foremost among these is the background of the president-elect himself, particularly as it relates to his familiarity with the IC and its products. It is quite a different matter, for example, to establish a relationship with an individual who has moved up from the vice presidency in the way that Presidents Gerald Ford and George H. W. Bush did, as contrasted with individuals who have come to the position with no Washington experience in the manner of Presidents Ronald Reagan, Bill Clinton, and George W. Bush. Similarly, the IC's experience has varied significantly depending on whether or not the new president has come from the same political party as his predecessor.

The DCI's or DNI's own political or career ambitions have sometimes raised delicate political problems. It is not unlikely, for example, that during a transition period the interests of the leader of the IC as an individual would not correspond with those of the IC itself. A most important political variable is the attitudes of the outgoing president and the national security advisor. Their support for the Community's efforts to establish an early and effective relationship with a new administration facilitates matters immensely.

The third group of key variables concerns logistic arrangements for the briefings. Should briefings be given prior to the election to both, or even multiple, candidates? Alternatively, should they be postponed until after the vote and provided exclusively to the single president-elect during the transition? How many briefings should be given and with what frequency? Experience shows that it matters, too, where the briefings are given and whether only the candidate is briefed or staff assistants are included as well.

Finally, concerning the substance of the information provided, there have been considerable variations in the amount and the type of material made available. All presidents-elect in recent years have valued receiving the *President's Daily Brief* (PDB), the intelligence summary created exclusively for the president. Some have wanted to receive additional, supplementary intelligence publications during the transition period. A few have wanted oral briefings by a number of substantive experts as opposed to hearing from a single Agency briefer each day; others have found multiple briefers confusing or overwhelming.

An important issue to be faced by the IC during each transition concerns how much information derived from sensitive human sources and technical collection efforts and regarding covert action programs should be included in the material given a president-elect, and when. Presidents in office are always informed of such programs, and careful attention is given to the timing, level of detail, and content of the presentation. And finally, concerning the substance of the support provided, there have been dramatic variations in the amount of tailored assistance the IC has provided presidents-elect and their national security teams to prepare them for pre-inaugural planning and policy deliberations, speeches and press conferences, and, in particular, their meetings and communications with foreign statesmen.

Given the importance of these variables in determining whether the IC will come to work well with a new president during the transition period and beyond, it seemed desirable for the Community's own purposes to create a record of what we have done in the past, noting what has worked and what has not. Even a cursory examination of the IC's experience over the past half century reveals that it is often not intuitively obvious or self-evident what approaches will translate into success. In preparing this study I have been pleased to discover, or confirm, that certain of the intelligence briefings provided to incoming presidents have turned out to be of genuine and lasting historical importance in their own right. To use one example, the DCI and the CIA's deputy director for plans (operations) provided President-elect Kennedy information on the Agency's plans for what would become the Bay of Pigs operation in Cuba. This occurred at a meeting with only the three of them present. A great deal of what has subsequently been written by others about what Kennedy was told, when he was told it, and what he said in response, is substantially wrong. I hope this account can clarify the circumstances of this and other important briefings provided to presidents over the years.

Finally, because the IC's role during transitions is unique, the Community seems to me to have an obligation to record what it has done and to make its account as widely available as possible. Perhaps this material will be of use not only to intelligence officers charged with meeting the Community's briefing responsibilities in the future, but also to others interested in IC contributions during these important chapters of our national history.

John L. Helgerson

CHAPTER 1

TRUMAN AND EISENHOWER: LAUNCHING THE PROCESS

On 22 November 1952, the newspapers reported that President Harry Truman, shortly after noon the previous day, had stolen away from the White House to give an "impromptu" speech at the Central Intelligence Agency. Truman had come to CIA at the invitation of the fourth director of central intelligence, Gen. Walter Bedell Smith, to address a training course of government officials. In that speech—delivered on a Friday afternoon almost two weeks after the national election—Truman revealed a great deal about his motives in founding the CIA and his aims in having the Agency provide intelligence briefings to the new president-elect, Gen. Dwight Eisenhower.

The president reminisced with his audience about how there had been no CIA when he had succeeded to the presidency in 1945. At that time, by many accounts, he had been surprised to discover how much information relating to intelligence and national security matters had been withheld from him. The most dramatic evidence of how ill-informed he was came on his 12th day in office when Secretary of War Henry Stimson briefed him for the first time on the Manhattan (atomic bomb) Project, about which Truman had heard only hints while serving as vice president and on key Senate committees.[1]

Truman also recalled how difficult it had been for him to obtain information from the various government departments, each of which seemed "walled off" from the others. On various occasions Truman had lamented to Smith that he "used to do all this myself." The president noted that this situation had been corrected over the intervening years, saying that the CIA's global intelligence operations and procedures for forwarding information had made it possible to "keep the President informed better than ever before." In a rather backhanded compliment, Truman said he believed that "we have an intelligence information service now that I think is not inferior to any in the world."[2]

Truman was responsible for the very existence of that intelligence service. Within a year of his becoming president, in January 1946, he formed the Central Intelligence Group (CIG). In the president's mind, its key responsibility

---

[1] David McCullough, *Truman* (New York: Simon and Shuster, 1992), 376–78.
[2] *New York Times*, 22 November 1952, 1,10.

CHAPTER 1

Gen. Walter Bedell Smith (left) relieves RAdm. Roscoe H. Hillenkoetter as Director of Central Intelligence in 1950.

was to ensure that he personally received intelligence reports on a timely basis. On 15 February 1946 the CIG launched the *Daily Summary*, and in June a counterpart *Weekly Summary* was produced for the first time. Both these publications were sent to the White House for the president. Both the daily and weekly publications continued to be published after CIG became the Central Intelligence Agency in September 1947.

There was much bureaucratic wrangling throughout the early years of the CIG and CIA about their proper role in the production of current intelligence. Virtually all key players involved with intelligence—in the military services, the War (later Defense) Department, and the State Department—had serious reservations about the new intelligence agency duplicating their work in current intelligence. The president was virtually alone in expecting to receive a daily, comprehensive current intelligence product, whatever the formal charters of the CIG and CIA might say. Needless to say, his expectations carried the day.

To consolidate the production of current intelligence, CIA in January 1951 formed the Office of Current Intelligence (OCI), which existed until the late 1970s when its functions were assumed by other offices. The CIA officers who formed OCI were already preparing a closely held, all-source weekly intelligence publication, the first of its kind, called the *Situation Summary*. This was a global review, built around the Korean situation and its worldwide implications that formed the basis for General Smith's weekly briefings of the president. Shortly after the establishment of OCI, two new publications were inaugurated for wider distribution. The daily publication became the *Current Intelligence Bulletin*, first issued on 28 February 1951; in August a companion weekly publication, the *Current Intelligence Weekly Review*, was begun.

Managers of OCI felt their early efforts had been rewarded when Truman, vacationing in Key West, Florida, wrote of the new publication, "Dear Bedel [*sic*], I have been reading the intelligence bulletin and I am highly impressed with it. I believe you have hit the jackpot with this one. Sincerely, Harry Truman."[3] The *Current Intelligence Bulletin* continued largely unchanged for the next 25 years.

While Truman received, read, and expressed his appreciation for the Agency's daily and weekly publications, it had become clear over the years that he especially valued the oral briefings delivered by the directors of CIA. The president experimented with various procedures for these briefings, and in the early years there were periods when he received them on a daily basis. What finally proved most satisfactory, however, were weekly worldwide intelligence updates.

The weekly briefings worked best during the extended period when "Beedle" Smith served as DCI. Smith briefed Truman each Friday, accompanied at the White House by a CIA officer, Meredith Davidson. Davidson would assist the director in the preparation of his material (a notebook was left behind with

---

[3] Harry Truman, letter to Bedell Smith, 8 March 1951.

CHAPTER 1

the president each week), but he did not normally go into the Oval Office. The briefing was based primarily on the *Situation Summary*, which was prepared with the president's needs in mind. Davidson's reward was to join the DCI and the president's special consultant for national security Affairs, Sidney Souers (who had served as the first DCI for a five-month period in 1946), for coffee and a postmortem on the president's reactions and follow-up requests.[4]

Mindful of how useful the weekly briefings were to him, Truman determined that intelligence information should be provided to the candidates in the 1952 election as soon as they were selected. In the summer of 1952, the president raised this idea with Smith. He indicated he wanted the Agency to brief Gen. Dwight Eisenhower and Governor Adlai Stevenson, remarking at the time, "There were so many things I did not know when I became President." Smith suggested to Truman that Davidson might be the proper individual to brief both Eisenhower and Stevenson to ensure they were receiving the same information.

Later, during his speech at the Agency on 21 November, Truman explained his rationale in providing briefings to the president-elect. The office of the president of the United States, he told his audience, "now carries power beyond parallel in history...that is the principal reason why I am so anxious that it be a continuing proposition and that the successor to me and the successor to him can carry on as if no election had ever taken place. I am giving this president—this new president—more information than any other president had when he went into office."

Referring to a widely publicized meeting he had held with Eisenhower at the White House to discuss foreign policy issues earlier that same week, Truman said, "It was my privilege a few days ago...to brief the General who is going to take over the office on the 20th of January." Truman did not mention in his address that on that occasion he had given Eisenhower a comprehensive *National Intelligence Digest* prepared by the CIA. Keyed to an NSC policy outline, the *Digest* summarized, in Smith's words, "the most important national intelligence on a worldwide basis."[5]

Eisenhower wrote in his memoirs more than a decade later that his meeting with Truman "added little to my knowledge." He recalled that Truman "received me cordially; however...the conversations...were necessarily general and official in nature. So far as defense affairs were concerned, under the instructions of the President, I had been briefed periodically by Gen. Walter

---

[4] Meredith Davidson, interviews by the author in Frederick, Maryland, 26 March and 25 October 1993. Unless otherwise indicated, the numerous references that follow concerning Davidson's briefings of Stevenson and Eisenhower come from these interviews.

[5] Walter Bedell Smith, memorandum for the president, 9 January 1953.

Bedell Smith and his assistants in the Central Intelligence Agency on developments in the Korean war and on national security."[6] According to Davidson, Truman told Smith he "had kept it general on purpose, for political reasons."

Strained Relations Complicate the Arrangements

In his remarks at the Agency, Truman could not bring himself to be completely deferential to his successor. In a mild dig, he observed that Eisenhower had been "rather appalled at all that the President needs to know in order to reach decisions." In private, Truman was bitingly critical of his elected successor. The press, for its part, was reporting that the meeting of the two men at the White House had been "coolly formal." The *New York Times*, for example, noted "there was some evidence of tension between Mr. Truman and his successor," observing also that "the President-elect looked serious and was somewhat brusque when he left the President's office."[7]

While Truman's motives appear to have been straightforward in providing information to enable Eisenhower to assume the presidency fully informed, the implementation left something to be desired and prompted suspicions on the part of Eisenhower and his staff. Indeed, tensions between the two came close to undermining the planned briefing process and with it the Agency's access to the president-elect during the important transition period. Ironically, the ultimate result was to elicit from Eisenhower a statement making clear he saw the CIA as a relatively apolitical provider of information. In the end he was willing to hear from the CIA things he was unwilling to hear from others.

A difficult private exchange between the president and his eventual successor had begun shortly after the Republican convention, when Truman sent telegrams to Eisenhower and Stevenson inviting them to lunch with his cabinet on Tuesday, 19 August. Truman proposed that he ask Smith and other CIA officers to brief "on the foreign situation" and have the White House staff report on other issues as well. In his telegram, Truman also extended an offer of weekly intelligence briefings for both candidates.[8]

Eisenhower declined the invitation. In reply, he told Truman he thought he should receive "only those communications from the outgoing Administration that could be known to all the American people." He added, "The problems which you suggest for discussion are those with which I have lived for many

---

[6] Dwight Eisenhower, *Mandate for Change, 1953–1956* (New York: Doubleday and Co., 1963), 85.
[7] *New York Times*, 19 November 1952, 1, 18.
[8] Harry Truman, telegram to Dwight Eisenhower, 14 August 1952. A similar telegram was sent to Adlai Stevenson.

years." The general concluded with a paragraph indicating he would welcome weekly reports from the CIA, but he wanted it understood that his possession of those reports "would not limit his freedom to discuss or analyze foreign programs as he wanted."[9]

The White House, obviously irritated that Eisenhower had declined Truman's personal invitation, released the texts of the telegrams from both men. What was not released to the public—nor, so far as I can tell, known to senior CIA managers at the time—was a very direct note that Truman had written by hand and sent to Eisenhower at his campaign headquarters in Denver on 16 August. In that note Truman indicated he was sorry if he had caused Eisenhower embarrassment with the luncheon invitation, but he underscored that his intention was to provide information that would permit a continuous, uninterrupted foreign policy despite the change of administrations.

In language only Truman would use, he wrote, "Partisan politics should stop at the boundaries of the United States. I am extremely sorry that you have allowed a bunch of screwballs to come between us." Truman added, "You have made a bad mistake, and I'm hoping it won't injure this great Republic. There has never been one like it and I want to see it continues regardless of the man who occupies the most important position in the history of the world. May God guide you and give you light."[10]

After reading Truman's note, Eisenhower obviously decided there was no point in responding in kind and sent back to Truman, on 19 August, a relatively conciliatory reply, also handwritten. Eisenhower reiterated the thought that, for political reasons and in the absence of any national emergency, he should not meet with the outgoing president and cabinet and thus had declined the invitation. He repeated his appreciation for the offer to send him weekly CIA reports, opined that those would be sufficient to keep him up-to-date on developments abroad, and assured Truman of his support for a bipartisan foreign policy.[11]

Although Eisenhower had taken a relatively moderate tone in his reply to Truman's outburst, he clearly was bothered by the overall exchange and indicated as much in separate correspondence with Smith. The general felt free to be open with Smith; they had worked closely together during the war in Europe when Smith served for an extended period as his chief of staff.

---

[9] Dwight Eisenhower, telegram to Harry Truman, 14 August 1952
[10] Harry Truman, letter to Dwight Eisenhower, 16 August 1952. Maintained in the holdings of the Dwight D. Eisenhower Library, Abilene, Kansas.
[11] Dwight Eisenhower, letter to Harry Truman, 19 August 1952. Eisenhower Library.

Following Eisenhower's nomination, Smith had sent a note of congratulations that Eisenhower had not acknowledged before the exchange with Truman over the briefings in mid-August. In a letter stamped "Personal and Confidential" dated 14 August, Eisenhower thanked Smith for his note of congratulations the previous month, but then launched immediately into some observations on his exchange with Truman. "The past two days my whole headquarters has been in a little bit of a steaming stew over an incident in which, according to the papers, you were at least briefly involved. It was the meeting that Governor Stevenson had with the president and the cabinet. According to the reports reaching here, you were brought in to help brief the Governor on the world situation."[12] Eisenhower expressed his understanding that the briefing of Stevenson had taken only a very few minutes but added, "To the political mind it looked like the outgoing administration was canvassing all its resources in order to support Stevenson's election." The general went on to stress the importance of doing what is right, recalling the challenges he and Smith had faced together in Europe during the war.

The lecture from Eisenhower caused great pain to his longtime friend and admirer (one former Agency officer recalls that "it upset the hell out of Beedle"). Nevertheless, in a reply to Eisenhower dated 18 August, Smith made no mention of the critical note. Rather, he offered in rather formal language the briefings that Smith had discussed with the president and which the president, in turn, had offered to Eisenhower. Smith proposed that he provide Eisenhower information on the world situation like that the president received each Friday morning, and that this information should be delivered by an officer of the CIA. Smith's letter was delivered to Eisenhower in Denver.[13] Fortunately for the Agency, in light of the tension that had developed, Eisenhower accepted the invitation to receive CIA briefings.

Eisenhower's "turning over of command" ceremony had been held at SHAPE (Supreme Headquarters Allied Powers Europe) in Paris on 30 May 1952. The following day the general, Mrs. Eisenhower, and Eisenhower's personal staff departed Europe for Washington. Although he had been on leave without pay from his post as president of Columbia University since early 1951, Eisenhower had continued to use the university home at 60 Morningside Drive in Manhattan when he was in the city. This residence became his headquarters for the next several months, and it was here that the first briefing by the CIA occurred.

---

[12] Dwight Eisenhower, letter to Walter Bedell Smith, 14 August 1952. Eisenhower Library.
[13] Walter Bedell Smith, letter to Dwight Eisenhower, 18 August 1952.

CHAPTER 1

Preelection Briefings

The first briefing was on Saturday morning, 30 August, by Melvin Hendrickson, then head of the military branch in OCI's "Indications Staff." Like many Agency officers at the time, Hendrickson had several years of Army experience; his last post had been assistant military attaché in Oslo.[14] With military precision, Eisenhower entered the library of his residence exactly at 7:45 to receive Hendrickson and an accompanying security officer, the two being introduced as "the gentlemen from CIA." Eisenhower suggested that they move to an adjoining smaller room.

The general took about 20 minutes to read carefully through the briefing material but paid scant attention to the information on the disposition of Soviet and satellite armed forces after confirming with Hendrickson that there had been no significant changes in their deployment since his briefings by the US Army in Europe some months earlier. There was more extended discussion of the situation in Iran, of France's growing difficulties in North Africa, and regarding trade between Japan and China. The latter subject was discussed in the context of the war in Korea and the ongoing armistice talks. Eisenhower commented specifically, "Since trade is one of our most powerful weapons, it seems to me that we should employ it to its maximum. Where are the Japanese going to get their materials if they can't get them from China?" Concerning the North African situation, the general's bottom line was a cryptic, "If the French don't do something fairly soon, they will have another Indo-China on their hands." At the conclusion of this first substantive discussion, Eisenhower indicated that he would like to receive future similar briefings.[15]

During the remaining weeks before the election on 4 November, Eisenhower received three additional briefings from CIA. The second in the series took place on 25 September when the general was in the midst of an extended

---

[14] Melvin Hendrickson, interview by the author in McLean, Virginia, 23 March 1993. Unless otherwise indicated, the references to his briefings of Eisenhower come from this interview. In discussing that first briefing, Hendrickson said his most vivid memory was of Eisenhower's powerful welcoming handshake, saying, "You had to be careful or he would squeeze your fingers off."
[15] Melvin Hendrickson, "Briefing of General Eisenhower—30 August 1952," memorandum for the record, 5 September 1952. As a reminder of how things change in 40 years, one cannot help noting that the Agency's New York office provided the visiting CIA team a chauffeur-driven Cadillac for their 20-minute trip from midtown to Columbia University on the upper west side. Conversely, some things never change. The team reported in their memorandum for the record that, when they returned later that day to New York's LaGuardia Airport for their flight to Washington, they discovered their reservations were for a flight departing from Idlewild (now JFK) Airport. They changed their reservation and arrived back at CIA's "Que" building in Washington by midafternoon. Among the stories Hendrickson told his colleagues was an account of his pleasure at having met not only General Eisenhower but also Mrs. Eisenhower and their grandchildren.

whistle-stop campaign tour. He had flown from New York to Moline, Illinois, and from there had traveled virtually nonstop through numerous small towns in Illinois, Iowa, Nebraska, Missouri, West Virginia, and finally Maryland. CIA's Hendrickson boarded the train in Silver Spring, Maryland, and briefed Eisenhower during the short trip into Baltimore.

During a subsequent period of almost nonstop campaigning, Eisenhower blocked out two weekends for rest. One was when the Eisenhowers were staying at the Brown Palace Hotel in Denver, Mrs. Eisenhower's hometown. Hendrickson provided the third preelection briefing at the couple's Brown Palace suite on 11 October, again a Saturday morning. On this occasion, Eisenhower, in turn, provided Hendrickson one of the more unusual experiences intelligence officers have had. Hendrickson recalls being invited to join the general and Mrs. Eisenhower at a rodeo in Denver that weekend. The Eisenhowers were driven around the rodeo grounds in a stagecoach. Hendrickson rode shotgun, up top with the driver.

The fourth and final preelection briefing was on 25 October, 10 days before the election. Eisenhower had been campaigning in Detroit and had taken an overnight train to New York. This time Hendrickson boarded the campaign train in the early morning at Harmon Station, New York, and briefed Eisenhower as they traveled to Grand Central in New York City.

During each of the briefings during the preelection period, Eisenhower spent 15–20 minutes studying the written material and, typically, another 10–15 minutes discussing that material and other items on his mind. He asked few specific factual questions but did make comments on a wide spectrum of issues, primarily the Soviet, Korean, and Iranian situations, which were at the forefront of US government attention in 1952. Eisenhower also read carefully and commented on Agency materials relating to security arrangements for the prospective Middle East collective security alliance then under consideration.[16]

The package of written briefing materials presented to Eisenhower (and Stevenson) at each meeting typically included 20 or more short items—one or two paragraphs in length—summarizing the current situation in a specific country of interest. Events in the USSR, Iran, Korea, Egypt, Yugoslavia, and Japan were included in almost all sessions, but in the course of the briefings more than 50 countries were addressed. In addition, there was normally one longer article on a priority country, Iran being the most common. Each package also contained the "Conclusions" of one or two recently published

---

[16] Hendrickson prepared very brief memorandums for the record concerning the second and fourth briefings, dated 29 September and 28 October, respectively; no written record has been found of the third briefing, held in Denver.

national intelligence estimates. The latter typically assessed the prospects for communist expansionism in different regions of the world.

The general, while a candidate, was appreciative of the preelection briefings, commenting that they had been very helpful. At the conclusion of the fourth session, however, he added—clearly referring to the Soviet Union and Korea—that he "missed the G-3 information" (US military plans and operations) that he observed "was essential for a complete understanding of those situations." Eisenhower also commented that "if he got the job, some other arrangement would have to be made for the briefings." He mentioned specifically securing clearances for some of his staff so that they, too, could benefit from the information being provided.

In an intriguing parting comment, Eisenhower mentioned to Hendrickson, "When you get back to Bedell Smith, tell him if I get elected I've got a job for him." Decades after the fact, it has proved impossible to establish whether this comment was passed to the DCI personally. In an interesting coincidence of timing, however, Smith, less than a week later on 1 November, forwarded to President Truman a written request to resign his post as DCI and to retire from active military service.[17]

Support to the President-Elect [18]

One day after he was elected president, Eisenhower on 5 November 1952 traveled to Augusta, Georgia, for two weeks' vacation. When the CIA briefings resumed late in the month, the most significant thing that had changed was that they were no longer given by Hendrickson but by General Smith, accompanied by Davidson. The first session following the election was held on 21 November, this time again on the train as the president-elect traveled from New York to Washington for a reunion dinner of his US Military Academy classmates at the Army-Navy Club. The train stopped at Baltimore to permit Smith and Davidson to board and talk with the president-elect on the remaining leg into Washington.

By coincidence, Davidson, while still working in Army Intelligence, had briefed Eisenhower on a couple of occasions at the Pentagon just after the war.

---

[17] Walter Bedell Smith, letter to Harry Truman, 1 November 1952. Eisenhower Library.
[18] Memorandums for the record have not been found in CIA files regarding the postelection briefings of Eisenhower, and there is reason to doubt that any exist. Davidson, who accompanied Smith to the first two sessions, remembers asking the DCI after the first meeting "whether there was anything he wanted me to write. He said no. Beedle would have been happy if nothing had been written." This attitude of the DCI also explains why the memorandums written by Davidson and Hendrickson, even about briefings in which Smith did not participate, were so cryptic.

To Davidson's astonishment, when he was escorted into the president-elect's car, Eisenhower immediately brightened as he recognized him and extended a warm greeting. In a jocular exchange, Davidson explained that he had not served in Europe as Eisenhower had, rather he had been fighting "the big war in the Pacific."

Smith cautioned Eisenhower that "you had better watch out, he has been briefing the opposition," referring to Davidson's sessions with Stevenson in Springfield, Illinois. This joking remark caused Eisenhower to turn deadly serious. Davidson was impressed that Eisenhower wanted to hear no jokes about Stevenson and was very positive about the Agency's briefings of the governor. Eisenhower observed that he thought very highly of Stevenson because he had kept the campaign on a high plane and demonstrated mastery of foreign affairs.

The relaxed social exchange with the Eisenhowers (both General and Mrs. Eisenhower were in dressing gowns) continued almost until the train had completed its late-evening run to Washington. The substantive part of the briefing, therefore, continued while they were parked at Union Station. Subjects of particular interest again included events in Korea and the negotiations under way to bring the conflict to an end. But Smith also provided an overview of the general world situation.

Because the DCI himself was now conducting the briefings, and because of the preexisting relationship between Eisenhower and Smith, the session involved substantially more give-and-take than had been the case before the election. A more serious analysis of the issues was also to be expected because Eisenhower, like all presidents-elect, realized he would have to grapple with the world's problems within a matter of weeks. Eisenhower asked a number of questions, particularly about the political aspects of the Korean quagmire. He especially wanted to clarify in his own mind what China was up to and to understand better that country's role and motivations in the conflict. Eisenhower asked, for example, "I never did know why we let the Chinese call themselves volunteers?" In reply, Smith explained the nuances of the situation, concluding by saying, "We didn't have to bomb Peking—that's why we acquiesced."

Well after midnight, Smith and Davidson took their leave of the president-elect at Union Station. General and Mrs. Eisenhower spent the night in their Pullman car on the train. Mrs. Eisenhower had been an active participant throughout the discussions. Davidson recalls that "she gave me the impression of being much more political than Ike."

In his memoirs Eisenhower recalled, "In a Detroit speech on October 24, I announced my intention, if elected, to go to Korea before the following January and to determine for myself what the conditions were in that unhappy country." For some days Eisenhower and his closest advisers had been discussing the wisdom of making this dramatic proposal public.[19] Once it was announced, the idea was very well received and, in fact, has been cited by many observers as having clinched the Eisenhower victory 10 days later.

After the election, while preparing for his trip to Korea, Eisenhower telephoned Smith to inform him that he was not comfortable relying exclusively on US Army information regarding what was going on in Korea; he wanted the DCI to come to New York to give him the Agency's independent assessment. The president-elect called at virtually the last moment and emphasized that their visit should be given no publicity.

In keeping with their interpretation of Eisenhower's instructions, Army security officers took Smith and Davidson to the briefing location in New York via a circuitous route. The two were led in the front door of a drugstore and out the back, for example, in a counterintelligence maneuver that served only to enrage the always-impatient Smith. Ironically, they reached Eisenhower's office in the Commodore Hotel for an afternoon appointment that had been wedged into a day filled with a dozen other well-publicized visitors. Smith and Davidson were waiting in an outer office as a luncheon group hosted by Eisenhower broke up. Smith was surprised to see Gen. William Donovan, the founder of the Office of Strategic Services, among those leaving the general's office.

Because the president-elect had requested Smith's frank and personal assessment of the situation in Korea, the two generals were alone for most of the briefing session. Near the end of the session, Davidson was called in to answer two or three factual questions. Eisenhower departed secretly for Korea early the following day, 29 November.

Smith took very seriously his responsibility to provide an independent assessment. He had insisted that his CIA staff derive facts about military developments from the US Army and Navy but jealously guarded his prerogatives as DCI to make assessments and estimates based on those facts. By chance, Smith and Davidson ran into John Foster Dulles in the lobby of the Waldorf Astoria Hotel shortly after they had seen Eisenhower at the Commodore. Dulles elicited confirmation that they had seen Eisenhower and asked what they told him. Smith responded with a curt, "That's between him and me."

The late-November visit to the president-elect's office also created a bit of momentary tension with the Secret Service. Smith was sometimes reluctant to have a protective officer from the Agency's Office of Security accompany him and would override vigorous recommendations to the contrary by CIA's director of security, Sheffield Edwards. In this case, the DCI adamantly opposed

---

[19] Eisenhower, *Mandate for Change*, 72.

having additional people accompany him to New York given the ground rules Eisenhower had set regarding secrecy. Edwards earlier had approached Davidson, insisting that he become weapons-qualified so he could protect the DCI. On the train from Washington to New York, the DCI learned that Davidson was carrying a weapon and challenged, "Edwards got to you, didn't he?" The DCI's reaction was mild, however, compared with that of Secret Service officers when they discovered that Davidson was carrying a weapon during incidental conversation in the president-elect's outer office.

The private meeting between Eisenhower and Smith on 28 November went on for more than an hour and allowed the two to conduct some intelligence business beyond their discussion of Korea. During that session Smith secured Eisenhower's approval of a proposal that CIA should establish a briefing facility in New York City to provide continuous support to Eisenhower and his staff. The facility was subsequently set up, but not as close to Eisenhower's as Smith would have liked. Agency officers recall that Sherman Adams, who was to become Eisenhower's chief of staff, intervened to ensure that the CIA office was "a broom closet some distance from the President's office." Adams obviously did not want Smith to have the same access to the new president that he enjoyed with Truman.

The Agency maintained its office in the Commodore from 28 November through the end of the transition period in January 1953. A CIA briefing officer representing the DCI was present at all times. For most of the period the officer was Ed Beatty, a former newsman who was editor of CIA's *Current Intelligence Bulletin*. Each day a courier from Washington would bring to the New York office the latest current intelligence products for use by the president-elect and his staff. Eisenhower's staff did utilize this facility, and Adams himself came by seeking information on at least one occasion. Eisenhower, however, relied exclusively on the briefings provided by the DCI.

During the transition period in late 1952 the press occasionally wrote of the DCI's "weekly" briefings of the president-elect. But, in fact, the general's schedule did not permit briefings on any regular schedule. His trip to Korea and the Pacific took more than two weeks, with the result that the next CIA briefing did not occur until 19 December. Eisenhower was accompanied at that meeting by Adams and Smith by Deputy Director for Intelligence Robert Amory. Specifically labeled "off the record" on Eisenhower's calendar, it was a session Smith would rather not have attended. He entered Eisenhower's office in high spirits but came out crushed. Sitting in morose silence all the way back to Washington, he finally muttered, "And I thought that it was going to be great." Smith never explained what had happened.

He had offered his resignation in writing to President Truman some six weeks before, obviously hoping for a challenging appointment from his old friend and colleague. It was widely known at the time that Smith aspired, perhaps unrealistically, to be chairman of the Joint Chiefs of Staff. Agency historians have surmised that Eisenhower informed Smith he would not be appointed chairman of the Joint Staff, asking him instead to serve as under secretary of state.

Smith did, in fact, serve in the number-two job at the Department of State during the first year and a half of Eisenhower's first term. But it was no secret that he did not enjoy being the under secretary. He felt uncomfortable with the nonmilitary way the Department functioned, he did not like John Foster Dulles, and he was uneasy about Allen Dulles's appointment as DCI.

The last occasion on which Smith is known to have met with Eisenhower while serving as DCI was on 14 January 1953 in New York City. There Smith joined John Foster Dulles and other Eisenhower advisers and appointees for an extended foreign policy conference with the president-elect. Less than a week later, on 20 January, Eisenhower was inaugurated.

The New President as an Intelligence Consumer

To no one's surprise, Eisenhower's preferences on how he should receive intelligence support did not change once he became president. CIA histories indicate that the day after his inauguration in 1953 the Agency's director of current intelligence, Huntington Sheldon, sent to James Lay Jr., the executive secretary of the National Security Council, a list of publications the Agency could furnish the White House. It quickly became apparent, however, that the president did not want to receive written intelligence materials on a regular basis and had no interest in frequent briefings by CIA experts. As had been his preference during the transition period, the president relied instead on periodic high-level briefings.

The practice that developed and continued throughout the eight years of the Eisenhower presidency involved the DCI, Allen Dulles, providing weekly briefings to the National Security Council. Eisenhower chaired these NSC meetings, and under his leadership they were more regular and more formal than under any president before or since. He told President-elect Kennedy in 1960 that the NSC "had become the most important weekly meeting of the government."[20]

---

[20] Dwight Eisenhower, *Waging Peace* (New York: Doubleday and Co., 1965), 712.

The NSC met every Thursday morning at 9:00 a.m. and with rare exceptions opened its meetings with an intelligence briefing by the DCI. The briefing addressed subjects mutually agreed with Lay of the NSC staff, representing the interests of the president's special assistant for national security affairs, Gen. Robert Cutler. If the president, Cutler, or Lay did not have specific subjects they wanted addressed, the CIA was free to propose its own agenda, although the Agency's ideas were always vetted with Lay before the briefing.

Agency veterans remember a wide variety of subjects being addressed at the NSC meetings, reflecting the president's broad interests. He was intrigued with matters ranging from Italian elections, to the battle of Dien Bien Phu, to periodic updates on Agency covert action operations. Eisenhower would interrupt periodically with questions and, within limits, permit questions from others as well. When his patience ran out, however, he was not at all reluctant to cut off discussion, saying "OK Allen, let's go ahead."

According to Gen. Andrew Goodpaster, who served as secretary of the White House Staff, Eisenhower expected Dulles to provide the latest intelligence on the crisis of the moment but, more important, to concentrate primarily on providing the intelligence background to whatever larger or longer term planning issue was on the agenda. Because of this long-term focus, most of the briefing materials used by the DCI were prepared by CIA's Office of National Estimates. Goodpaster recalls that Eisenhower frequently would ask, "How solid is that information—where does it come from?" Dulles was reluctant to answer "with fourteen people in the room." Eisenhower, Dulles, and one staff aide (sometimes Goodpaster and sometimes Senior Staff Assistant Gordon Gray) would then hold a smaller, follow-on meeting after the regular NSC to answer the president's more probing questions.[21]

The briefing process during the 1950s had several important advantages from the Agency's point of view. Among these was the fact that the DCI was able to provide intelligence on important matters on a predictable schedule in a forum that included not only the president, but also the chairman of the Joint Chiefs of Staff, the secretaries of state and defense, and other key players in the foreign policy decision making process. The single-most-important advantage of the system, however, was that it was unambiguously obvious each week whether the president was interested in, and well served by, the intelligence he was receiving. With this feedback, CIA was able to be responsive to his needs and those of the NSC. Senior Agency officers believed the system worked well. Sheldon summed it up by saying, "The Director got used to the

---

[21] Andrew Goodpaster, interview by the author in Washington, DC, 26 September 1993. Unless otherwise indicated, all references to Goodpaster's observations come from this interview.

procedure and was happy with it, and everybody was happy with it; it simply remained that way until the next administration."

The DCI himself provided the vast majority of the briefings of the NSC. It was clear to all involved, however, that Dulles was much more comfortable with political and economic subjects than with scientific and military issues. Quite often the director would permit a specialist to brief on such subjects, always designating personally the individual he wanted to do the job. Herbert Scoville Jr., the assistant director for scientific intelligence, gave many of the briefings on scientific subjects, and the Agency's nuclear specialist, Herbert Miller, distinguished himself with briefings in that specialized field. Amory, the Agency's DDI, from time to time would brief on military matters.

White House records make clear that attendees at the NSC meetings noticed the difference between briefings delivered by the DCI and those delivered by the substantive experts. Gray addressed this subject in a meeting on 11 January 1961 when he discussed transition matters with McGeorge Bundy, representative of President-elect John Kennedy. Responding to questions by Bundy about whether the president should have daily briefings and, if so, who should deliver them, Gray wrote in his memorandum for the record, "I had made a note several months ago to discuss with my successor intelligence briefings in the Council. I believe that these should be crisper and should be conducted by more junior officers with a special briefing competence.... I acknowledged to Mr. Bundy that this would cause serious personal problems and I was not sure I would advise him to tackle it. It was simply a question I left with him." In that same conversation, however, Gray asserted that the practice of having the DCI brief the NSC every week was "a very useful device."[22]

Goodpaster recalls that Eisenhower "had a lot of respect for Allen Dulles growing out of Dulles's work during the war. The president thought he was very skilled at top-level intelligence—collecting it and analyzing it." Eisenhower would read enough of the Intelligence Community's estimates to get the point and the highlights and, according to Goodpaster, "felt the formal estimates and papers were the genuine view," meaning they were not politicized.

But there were some problems. Eisenhower had been struck, for example, at how the "bomber gap" of the mid-1950s turned out to be a false alarm. When the Intelligence Community and the US military began writing of the Soviets' great progress in missile production during the late 1950s, "Eisenhower was more than skeptical; he was unconvinced, challenging repeatedly, 'what do they base this on?'"

---

[22] Gordon Gray, memorandum for the record, 17 January 1961. Eisenhower Library.

According to Goodpaster, Eisenhower believed there were at least two reasons why the bomber and missile issues turned into serious political problems. One difficulty was that there was a lot of contact between elements of the Intelligence Community, particularly the Air Force, and Capitol Hill, in which Congress "heard this continual drumbeat about how we were falling behind." The other problem, in Eisenhower's view, was that "there was a lot of self-interest in the intelligence assessments of the military services—they were out to promote their own programs."

Throughout his presidency, Eisenhower avoided reading daily intelligence reports from any one agency. In fact, he normally read no daily reports. Instead, Goodpaster, with the help of the president's son, Lt. Col. John Eisenhower, each morning would review the separate reports from CIA, State, Defense, and the Joint Chiefs. They would meld this material into one early morning oral briefing. In those sessions, Eisenhower occasionally would ask to see a specific raw report or analytic paper, or task additional work.

Agency veterans recall that Sheldon and Deputy Director for Intelligence Loftus Becker in early March 1953 did discuss the idea of producing a brief, all-source, daily current intelligence publication exclusively for the president. As the Agency came to understand Eisenhower's preferences, however, this idea was never followed up. In any event, no such publication was actually produced until the Kennedy administration. One innovation that was begun in the early Eisenhower years and continued throughout his administration was the practice of cabling a daily intelligence report to the president while he was traveling abroad. That practice has continued to the present.

Briefing Governor Stevenson in 1952

During the 1952 presidential campaign, it proved considerably easier to arrange briefings of Governor Adlai Stevenson than it was to arrange the briefings of Eisenhower. For a start, the governor accepted President Truman's invitation to lunch and an initial round of discussions on 19 August at the White House. Thereafter, he was briefed every two to three weeks by the CIA at the Governor's Mansion in Springfield, Illinois. Those sessions took place on 30 August, 15 September, and 1 and 20 October.

In the initial division of labor, it was decided that Davidson would travel to Springfield to brief Stevenson. The plan had been for him to brief both candidates, but as luck would have it they requested their first briefing on the same day. The material Davidson took to Illinois was almost exactly the same as that provided Eisenhower. The exception—a distinction not observed in subsequent years—was that Eisenhower received material that included information derived from communications intelligence. Stevenson lacked experience with this sensitive material and did not receive it.

Stevenson was an even more gracious host and careful reader than Eisenhower. During their Saturday afternoon sessions, he invariably offered his CIA visitor refreshments and had numerous questions and comments about the material he read. It was clear from the outset that Stevenson had the background and the intellect to take full advantage of the intelligence the Agency was providing. Thinking back on the briefings more than four decades later, Davidson still commented with awe, "I was impressed with the questions he asked. He was well ahead of all of us."

Of the many substantive issues that arose during the intelligence briefings in 1952, the single one in which Stevenson was most interested was Iran. Mohammed Mossadeq had become prime minister in April 1951, and shortly thereafter he had secured passage of a law nationalizing the Anglo-Iranian Oil Company. In the succeeding months, relations between Iran and the United Kingdom steadily worsened and approached the crisis point during the fall of 1952. Diplomatic relations were severed in October.

The United Kingdom was concerned about oil, prestige, and compensation, and the United States was worried that Mossadeq might be deposed by the Tudeh (Communist) Party. Stevenson, like Eisenhower, wanted to follow the situation very carefully. Fortunately for the Agency, it was not until after the election that serious discussions began between the United States and the United Kingdom about a covert action program to remove Mossadeq. Whether to brief a presidential candidate on a covert action program as important as the one that was implemented in Iran the following year was a question that did not arise.

Supplementing the briefings he received during the 1952 campaign, Stevenson asked a number of questions to which the Agency responded with written memorandums. In one case, for example, DCI Smith personally sent a memorandum to the governor analyzing Josef Stalin's address to the 19th Communist Party Congress, held on 15 October. In addition to a factual account of the points Stalin had made, Smith included an analysis that comes across in retrospect as a policy lecture to the candidate. The memorandum concluded with the observation, "It is extremely unwise to underestimate the importance of any of Stalin's statements, although sometimes it is not as easy as in the present instance to highlight their actual meaning. The significance of the above is unmistakable."[23]

---

[23] Walter Bedell Smith, memorandum for Governor Stevenson, 16 October 1952.

The Challenger Briefed Again in 1956

During the 1956 presidential campaign, President Eisenhower continued to receive routine intelligence briefings at NSC meetings just as he had for the previous four years. Without hesitation, Eisenhower authorized the resumption of support to Stevenson during the 1956 campaign along the lines of the briefings he and the governor had received four years earlier.

The responsibility for keeping Stevenson informed in 1956 fell primarily to the Agency's deputy director of current intelligence, Knight McMahan. This time the logistics of the briefings were not as simple as they had been in 1952 when the candidate worked out of one location in Springfield. McMahan briefed Stevenson on 10 September at the Biltmore Hotel in New York City, on 17 September and 1 October at the Sheraton Park Hotel in Washington, and on 29 October in Boston. McMahan conducted these briefings alone, except that on 17 September in Washington he was joined by the deputy director of central intelligence, Gen. Charles Cabell.

Like his predecessor four years earlier, McMahan observed, "One could not help being impressed with Stevenson; he was a very informed man, but what he read brought him up to date and included things he didn't know anything about."[24] Much of the information provided Stevenson in 1956 addressed the crisis in Hungary. Beyond that issue, the governor studied very carefully material presented to him on Soviet disarmament policy. He was also interested in developments in India and in the warming relationship between India and China. He had questions on the Sino-Burmese relationship, developments in Malaysia and Singapore, the disputed islands off the China coast, and Russia's threatening activities in the vicinity of Sakhalin and the Kuril Islands.

Stevenson's interests in Hungary and the Asian issues, however, were secondary to his primary concern, which was the developing Suez Crisis, caused by Egyptian President Gamal Abdel Nasser's refusal to allow Israeli shipping access to the Canal, in violation of longstanding agreements. Agency memorandums for the record show that during the first three briefings Stevenson asked a number of questions about the Suez situation.[25] He cross-examined McMahan closely on such details as the convention of 1888 that governed Canal operations, Israeli shipping, developments in the UN, the attitudes of the nonpermanent members of the Security Council, possible solutions to the controversy, the status of international funding for Nasser's Aswan Dam project, and the failure

---

[24] Knight McMahan, interview by the author in Hanover, New Hampshire, 18 April 1993. Unless otherwise indicated, all references to McMahan's briefings of Stevenson come from this interview.
[25] McMahan drafted memorandums for the record following his first three sessions with Stevenson, dated 12 September, 18 September, and 2 October 1956. No record is available of his fourth session, held on 29 October in Boston.

of Britain's blue-ribbon negotiating mission. As the crisis continued to build, Stevenson probed the legal aspects of Nasser's position and the Egyptian leader's ability to maintain his government against expected economic sanctions. And he was interested in regional aspects of the problem, including tensions between Israel and Jordan and the buildup of British forces on Cyprus.

On 29 October, McMahan was, in his own words, "caught in the worst situation possible for an intelligence briefer: briefing Stevenson in Boston on the day Israel attacked Egypt." McMahan had taken the train from Washington to Boston the previous day while the interagency "Watch Committee" was reviewing newly available intelligence confirming that Israel, with British and French support, was completing its mobilization and would attack Egypt. Because the evidence came from intercepted communications, this sensitive material was not included in the written briefing materials prepared for Stevenson. Instead, McMahan intended to handle this breaking story orally.

To McMahan's chagrin and embarrassment, he had no more than settled into a chair to begin his briefing of Stevenson when one of the governor's aides burst in to inform him that the press was reporting that Israel had attacked. McMahan had not yet said anything. In 1993, McMahan still remembered this encounter clearly, recalling, "Stevenson took the news in stride, surprised that he had heard it first from the media rather than from us. But he reacted with consternation and concern." Stevenson was more gracious than his running mate, Senator Estes Kefauver. According to McMahan, "Kefauver [who was briefed separately] gave me a very hard time—he couldn't believe that the French and the British had shut us out of the planning process."[26]

Looking back on the Agency's exchanges with Stevenson in 1956, it is clear that he asked the right probing questions concerning the Suez Crisis as it unfolded. He wanted to know not only about the situation in Egypt but also about developments in Israel, Jordan, and Cyprus that were key to understanding the intentions of the parties involved. McMahan discussed with Stevenson all aspects of the intelligence reporting but was not at liberty to review with Stevenson the politics of intelligence collection and policy support that had been unfolding as well. Agency officers had noted, for example, that Secretary of State Dulles gave the impression that he did not want to receive detailed information regarding the UK buildup on Cyprus lest the knowledge of the US government, accompanied by its silence, represent approval. Particularly in the early stages of the crisis, there had been a clear assumption by key policymakers that Israel and its backers, knowing of Eisenhower's opposition to a military move, would somehow hold back.

---

[26] Memorandums for the record, dated 1 and 8 October 1956, are available for only two early briefings of Kefauver.

Although the US Intelligence Community was, in fact, not aware of all of the details of the Israeli, French, and British cooperation, it did not report some of the details it did have. The increase in tensions had been well documented in the intelligence reporting but clear warnings of coming hostilities were issued only a week ahead. When the attack occurred, the president and the Democratic candidates were furious with the European allies and less than proud of their own handling of the crisis.

From the Agency's point of view, thanks to the problems with the Suez Crisis, the briefings for Stevenson in 1956 ended on an awkward note. In all other respects, however, the sessions with Stevenson and Kefauver were a great success. Stevenson personally wrote Acting DCI Cabell to thank him for the briefings provided by McMahan, observing that they were "excellent and I found him very well informed."[27]

Agency officers who met with Stevenson during his two campaigns came away deeply impressed with his knowledge of foreign affairs and his interest in and appreciation of the intelligence product. More than that, it had been a great personal pleasure to deal with him. McMahan recalls, "He was a very courteous, polite man. I remember thinking it was a blessing he was not elected, in light of the public and personal attacks to which our presidents are subjected."

⌘ ⌘ ⌘

---

[27] Adlai Stevenson, letter to C. P. Cabell, 11 September 1956

CHAPTER 2

INTO POLITICS WITH KENNEDY AND JOHNSON

The CIA's early relationship with presidential candidate John Kennedy could hardly have been more different from the one it had established eight years earlier with General Eisenhower. In 1952, the Agency's briefings in the preelection period had been undertaken by working-level officers who, for the most part, delivered current intelligence summaries in written form. With few exceptions, the reports and analyses offered by the briefers steered clear of policy issues. In 1960, by contrast, the briefings were handled personally by DCI Allen Dulles and included extended discussions of sensitive matters.

In 1960, the CIA and its programs for the first time became involved in the political campaign, sometimes within public view and sometimes behind the scenes. Issues arose relating to the need for, and the protection of, US intelligence capabilities, specific intelligence collection programs such as the U-2 aircraft overflights, and substantive analytic findings related to Soviet economic and strategic capabilities. Charges were made regarding the allegedly selective use of intelligence information by the White House and the Agency. And, for the first time, CIA faced the question of what obligation it might have to brief a presidential candidate on a major covert action program.

The Presidential Debates

Many of these issues were on display during the presidential debates, held for the first time in 1960. The first debate, in Chicago on 26 September, focused exclusively on domestic issues, but in the second debate, on 7 October in Washington, Republican candidate Richard Nixon attacked Senator Kennedy's earlier statement that the United States should have apologized to the Soviets for the incident in which Francis Gary Powers's U-2 aircraft was downed over the USSR during a CIA reconnaissance mission. "We all remember Pearl Harbor," the vice president began. "We lost 3,000 American lives. We cannot afford an intelligence gap. And I just want to make my position absolutely clear with regard to getting intelligence information. I don't intend to see to it that the United States is ever in a position where, while we are negotiating with the Soviet Union, that we discontinue our intelligence effort, and I don't intend ever to express regrets to Mr. Khrushchev or anybody else."[1]

CHAPTER 2

In the third debate on 13 October, featuring Kennedy from New York and Nixon from Los Angeles, Kennedy cited the DCI as his authority for an invidious comparison of US and Soviet achievements: "The economic growth of the Soviet Union is greater than ours. Mr. Dulles has suggested it is from two to three times as great as ours."[2] In that debate and in the fourth and final encounter in New York on 21 October, Kennedy pursued the theme that the Soviets were surpassing the United States economically and militarily, a topic that headed the list of CIA intelligence production priorities.

Perhaps the most crucial foreign policy issue raised in the 1960 debates, which derived directly from US intelligence analyses, was the alleged gap between US and Soviet intercontinental missile production. Kennedy charged that the Soviets had "made a breakthrough in missiles, and by '61-2-3 they will be outnumbering us in missiles. I'm not as confident as he [Nixon] is that we will be the strongest military power by 1963." Kennedy added, "I believe the Soviet Union is first in outer space. We have made more shots but the size of their rocket thrust and all the rest. You yourself said to Khrushchev, you may be ahead of us in rocket thrust but we're ahead of you in color television, in your famous discussion in the kitchen. I think that color television is not as important as rocket thrust."[3]

During three of the debates, Nixon attacked Kennedy for his lack of willingness to defend Quemoy and Matsu, the small Nationalist-held islands off the coast of Communist China. The extensive discussion of the Quemoy-Matsu issue did not create any direct problem for the CIA, but it led directly to a controversial dispute between the candidates over policy toward Cuba, where a popular revolution had established a Soviet-supported communist government. The politically charged clash had a number of repercussions in the White House and at the CIA.

Kennedy adviser Arthur Schlesinger Jr. later described the relationship of these China and Cuba issues and the sequence of events in his memoir of the Kennedy administration, *A Thousand Days*: "The Kennedy staff, seeking to take the offensive after his supposed soft position on Quemoy and Matsu, put out the provocative statement about strengthening the Cuban fighters for freedom."[4] The controversial press release, crafted late one evening in the Biltmore Hotel in New York City by speechwriter Richard Goodwin, said, "We must attempt to strengthen the non-Batista, democratic, anti-Castro forces in exile, and in Cuba itself, who offer eventual hope of overthrowing Castro."

---

[1] *New York Times*, 8 October 1960, 10.
[2] *New York Times*, 14 October 1960, 21.
[3] *New York Times*, 22 October 1960, 8, 9.
[4] Arthur Schlesinger, Jr., *A Thousand Days* (Boston: Houghton Mifflin, 1965), 225.

According to Goodwin, the policy statement was not shown to the sleeping Kennedy because of the late hour; it was the only public statement of the campaign not approved by the candidate.[5]

The ill-considered statement on Cuba received wide press play and was immediately attacked. The *New York Times* the next day ran the story as the lead item on the front page with the headline: "Kennedy Asks Aid for Cuban Rebels to Defeat Castro, Urges Support of Exiles and Fighters for Freedom." James Reston wrote in the *Times* that Kennedy had made "what is probably his worst blunder of the campaign."[6]

Coming the day before the fourth presidential debate, the statement from the Kennedy camp put Nixon in what he found to be an extraordinarily awkward position. Many years later Nixon wrote in his memoirs, "I knew that Kennedy had received a CIA briefing on the administration's Cuba policy and assumed that he knew, as I did, that a plan to aid the Cuban exiles was already under way on a top secret basis. His statement jeopardized the project, which could succeed only if it were supported and implemented secretly."[7]

Throughout the campaign the two candidates had engaged in a spirited exchange about whether the Eisenhower administration had "lost" Cuba, and Nixon knew that the issue would be revived in the final debate, which was to be devoted solely to foreign affairs. Nixon has written that to protect the security of the planned operation he "had no choice but to take a completely opposite stand and attack Kennedy's advocacy of open intervention." And he did attack, saying, "I think that Senator Kennedy's policies and recommendations for the handling of the Castro regime are probably the most dangerously irresponsible recommendations that he has made during the course of this campaign."[8]

Former Kennedy advisers have underscored over the years that the statement on Cuba was released without Kennedy's knowledge by staffers ignorant of the covert action planning under way at the time and was crafted solely to ensure that Kennedy would not again be put on the defensive about communist expansionism. These same advisers differ among themselves, however, on the key question of whether Kennedy himself knew of the covert action plans. Kennedy speechwriter Theodore Sorensen said in 1993, "I am certain that at the time of the debates Kennedy had no knowledge of the planned operation. His reference to more assertive action regarding Cuba was put in by one of my assistants to give him something to say."[9]

---

[5] Richard Goodwin, *Remembering America* (Boston: Little, Brown and Co., 1988), 125.
[6] *New York Times*, 23 October 1960, E10.
[7] Richard Nixon, *The Memoirs of Richard Nixon* (New York: Grosset and Dunlap, 1978), 220.
[8] *New York Times*, 22 October 1960, 9.

CHAPTER 2

The assistant was Richard Goodwin, whose memory is quite different. He asserts that as a presidential candidate, Kennedy "had received secret briefings by the CIA, some of which revealed that we were training a force of Cuban exiles for a possible invasion of the Cuban mainland."[10] Goodwin and Sorensen have both made clear that they were not in attendance at any CIA briefings.

The US government's planning for a covert action program intended to undermine Castro had been approved by President Eisenhower in March 1960 and was in progress throughout the period of the presidential campaign. The question of when and to what extent Kennedy—or any presidential candidate—would be informed of the covert action deliberations was important to CIA because it raised the delicate question of informing individuals outside the normally restricted circle in CIA, the Congress, and the executive branch.

In 1960 this was uncharted territory. In subsequent presidential campaign years, the Agency's practice came to be one of delaying briefings even on established covert action programs, as well as on sensitive technical and human-source collection programs, until after the election had determined who would be president. This meant denying such briefings to presidential candidates, creating the risk that they would inadvertently make statements during the campaign that might embarrass themselves and the Agency, or—more important—complicate the future execution of US foreign policy.

Well before the Cuba liberation issue came to a head in October, the outgoing Eisenhower administration had realized that covert action planning on Cuba could be a political bombshell. Following one of Allen Dulles's briefings of the National Security Council in early August, for example, the vice president pulled the DCI aside to ask him whether Kennedy and his running mate, Senator Lyndon Johnson, were being provided information on covert action projects, specifically those related to Cuba. Dulles gave a carefully crafted answer to the effect that Kennedy was being told a little but not too much. According to former Agency officials familiar with the exchange, Nixon reacted strongly to Dulles's reply, saying, "Don't tell him anything. That could be dangerous."[11]

In his own account of these events, published in 1962, Nixon charged that Kennedy, before the election of 1960, had knowledge of covert action planning "for the eventual purpose of supporting an invasion of Cuba itself."[12] This

---

[9] Theodore Sorensen, telephone interview with the author, 19 May 1993. Unless otherwise indicated, all references to Sorensen's comments come from this interview.
[10] Goodwin, *Remembering America*, 125.
[11] Knight McMahan, interview with the author in Hanover, New Hampshire, 18 April 1993.
[12] Richard Nixon, *Six Crises* (New York: Doubleday and Co., 1962), 354.

Senator John F. Kennedy and DCI Allen Dulles prepare to meet the press.

charge prompted a formal press release from the White House on 20 March 1962 denying that Kennedy had been told of any plans for "supporting an invasion of Cuba" before the election. The White House denial was backed up by Dulles, by then a former DCI, who explained that Nixon's comments were apparently based on a misunderstanding of what was included in the briefings he had given Kennedy.

CHAPTER 2

Preelection Briefings: What Really Was Discussed?

As early as 30 March 1960, Edward P. Morgan of the American Broadcasting Company used the occasion of a presidential press conference to ask Eisenhower if the presidential nominees to be selected in the summer would be given high-level intelligence briefings. At that early date the DCI had not yet raised the subject with the president, but Eisenhower did not hesitate, saying "We always do that. They did it for me in 1952 and I did it in '56, as quick as the nominees are named they begin to get it."[13] Indeed, on 18 July, Eisenhower sent telegrams to the Democratic nominees offering them briefings by the CIA. Undoubtedly recalling his own difficult exchange with President Truman eight years earlier, Eisenhower included in his telegram a paragraph saying, "Because of the secret character of the information that would be furnished you, it would be exclusively for your personal knowledge. Otherwise, however, the receipt of such information would impose no restriction on full and free discussion."[14]

Senator John F. Kennedy, the Democratic presidential nominee, immediately accepted the offer, and the first intelligence briefing was held five days later, on Saturday, 23 July. The briefing was conducted at Kennedy's vacation home in Hyannisport, Massachusetts, by the DCI alone in a session that lasted approximately two and a quarter hours. Dulles then briefed Senator Lyndon Johnson, the vice-presidential nominee, at his ranch in Texas on 28 July.

In that first round of briefings, the DCI put heavy emphasis on Soviet issues, including Soviet progress in strategic delivery capabilities, missiles, and bombers, and discussed the nuclear testing issue. He also reviewed Soviet statements on Berlin and Sino-Soviet cooperation. Dulles went over the latest intelligence on the Taiwan Straits situation; Middle East politics, particularly events in Iran; France's anticolonial problems in Algeria and Belgium's in the Congo; and Cuba. The Johnson briefing differed from that of Kennedy only because the Texas senator was also interested in discussing Mexico.[15]

Dulles recorded that both wanted to know what developments might arise during the campaign, especially in Berlin, Cuba, and the Congo. Kennedy asked Dulles's opinion about the likelihood of an early Chinese attack on the offshore islands in the Taiwan Straits and inquired about the status of the conference on limiting nuclear testing. Johnson, in addition to his interest in Mex-

---

[13] Dwight Eisenhower, in comments recorded by Allen Dulles, memorandum for the president, 9 July 1960.
[14] Dwight Eisenhower telegrams to John Kennedy and Lyndon Johnson, *Public Papers of the Presidents*, 1960, 582.
[15] Allen Dulles, memorandum for the president, 3 August 1960.

ican and Caribbean matters, asked about Soviet missile developments, reflecting his position as chairman of the Senate Preparedness Committee.

At the conclusion of the first briefing, Kennedy stated that in future briefings he wanted the DCI to cover potential trouble spots all around the world, but subsequent scheduling difficulties delayed the next (and, as it turned out, the last) preelection briefing session almost two months. On 17 September, a Saturday night, Dulles was dining with friends in Georgetown when he was surprised by a telephone call from a member of the Kennedy staff at about 9 p.m. Could the DCI meet with the senator on Monday morning, 19 September, at the Kennedy home in Georgetown?[16]

When the DCI arrived with his hastily prepared briefing package, he found Kennedy engaged in discussion with Senator Albert Gore Sr. while various other people, including Prince Sadruddin Khan, uncle of the Aga Khan, waited their turns. When the other visitors had departed, the DCI had approximately 30 minutes with Kennedy to give him an update on world trouble spots. Dulles's memorandum for the record notes that he discussed Cuba, the Congo, Berlin, Laos, Jordan, Syria, the Sino-Soviet dispute, and the Soviet space program.

During this second briefing Kennedy was interested in learning what Khrushchev's objectives would be in his coming visit to the UN and what the Agency believed the Soviet leader was likely to say or do. The senator said he wanted to be alerted to any critical areas that CIA thought might blow up over the next six or seven weeks before the election, but Dulles apparently took no specific action at the time to meet this request.

More than a month later, with the election looming, Robert Kennedy contacted Acting DCI Gen. Charles Cabell to repeat the request for information on possible trouble spots. This brought a response within 24 hours. On 2 November, Cabell traveled to California, where Kennedy was campaigning, to deliver a memorandum that discussed a number of potentially troublesome developments. These included the Soviets' October Revolution anniversary, Sino-Soviet developments, tensions in Berlin and the Taiwan Straits, possible Chinese nuclear tests, a Soviet space spectacular, the French-Algerian impasse, events in Southeast Asia, King Hussein's delicate position in the Middle East, the unsettled situation in the Congo, and possible action by Cuba against Guantanamo Naval Base. In this review of explosive international situations, the Agency cautioned that, in fact, "we do not estimate any of them are likely to occur prior to 8 November."[17]

---

[16] Allen Dulles, memorandum for the record, 21 September 1960.
[17] CIA, untitled list of significant developments in response to Kennedy's request; no date.

CHAPTER 2

A search of CIA records has failed to confirm that Dulles briefed Kennedy on the status of Cuban covert action planning in either of their two sessions held before the election in 1960. The DCI's memorandums recording the sessions in July and September mention Cuba only as one of many trouble spots around the world. Taken alone, this would suggest that their discussion concerned what was going on in Cuba rather than what the United States might be planning to do about it.

An internal CIA memorandum of 15 November 1960 discussing an anticipated postelection briefing mentions that "the following draft material is much more detailed and operational than that prepared for the candidates in July."[18] This formulation suggests that the message on Cuba Dulles conveyed in July was at least a bit "operational," even if not detailed. Such an inference would be consistent with Dulles's answer to Nixon's question in early August that he had told Kennedy, in effect, a little but not too much.

When Dulles met with Kennedy in July (their only meeting before the exchange between Dulles and Nixon in early August), the planning on Cuba and the limited operational activities already launched related almost entirely to propaganda and political action. Paramilitary planning at that point envisaged the deployment of extremely small (two or three men) guerrilla units. Contingency planning within the Agency for more forceful action intensified over the next several months, but the idea of a conventional assault by Cuban exile forces was not put before the interagency Special Group until 3 November and was rejected.

The Missile Gap

In the two preelection briefings in 1960, the most challenging issue the DCI is known to have discussed at length was that of Soviet strategic capabilities. Without intending to do so, Dulles had created a considerable political problem for himself by giving a number of public speeches in which he asserted that Soviet capabilities were growing and raised the question of what the US response ought to be. He had highlighted the USSR's progress in basic science, in training large numbers of scientists, and its research and development efforts as well as its demonstrated achievements in building spacecraft and missiles.

In early 1960 the United States was aware of the Soviet missile flights from the Tyuratam test site, but did not know with certainty if any operational Soviet missiles had been deployed. In the search for deployed missiles, among other priority missions, U-2 aircraft had been flown over the Soviet Union

---

[18] CIA, "Draft Cuban Operational Briefing: President-Elect," 15 November 1960.

since July 1956. On 1 May 1960, Gary Powers was shot down. In the United States, the West Virginia primary election campaign was at its peak; there was no doubt that the U-2 incident would figure in the impending general election campaign.

In his formal memorandums for the record, Dulles did not provide much detail regarding exchanges he may have had with Kennedy about the U-2 shootdown. He did note that the senator, in the September briefing, had asked him about a book by Maj. Gen. John Medaris, entitled *Countdown for Decision*. The Medaris book had criticized the US government for its failure to replace the U-2 with a more sophisticated aircraft or an invulnerable satellite reconnaissance system.

In a memorandum sent to Gen. Andrew Goodpaster, the staff secretary of the White House, on 25 September, Dulles recorded that Kennedy and Johnson had separately inquired about intelligence techniques or capabilities to replace the U-2.[19] Dulles was clearly uneasy about the security hazards in these questions and noted that he had replied only in a general way, indicating that research and development work on advanced aircraft and satellites were progressing "with reasonably satisfactory prospects." Dulles added, "Unless I hear from you to the contrary, I shall not give any more detailed briefings on this subject." In fact, the first US satellite reconnaissance system was being used in an experimental way in the late summer of 1960; it was launched in August. Significant amounts of analytically useful imagery did not become available from the new system until December 1960, after the election.

During the preelection period, Dulles was also in an awkward position owing to a minor dispute or misunderstanding between the White House and the Kennedy team about whether the senator should receive a briefing from Secretary of Defense Thomas Gates. During the preelection period, in the interest of fairness to each candidate, Eisenhower wanted Kennedy to receive general overview briefings on the world situation from the CIA, and these were being provided. On the other hand, the president initially declined the Kennedy team's request that he receive a briefing from the secretary of defense. By the end of August, however, the White House had changed its mind and approved a briefing by Gates.

Dulles had weighed in with the White House on at least two occasions, including once with Eisenhower personally, to urge that Gates brief Kennedy. The DCI knew that he would be courting political trouble if he answered what had been Kennedy's first question: "Where do we ourselves stand in the missile race?" As he had done on innumerable occasions in congressional appear-

---

[19] Allen Dulles, memorandum for Gen. Andrew J. Goodpaster, 25 September 1960.

CHAPTER 2

ances, Dulles insisted that the Defense Department "was the competent authority on this question."

The White House was obviously uneasy that Kennedy would hear several versions of the story concerning Soviet strategic capabilities. Democrats on the Preparedness Committee, led by the uniquely well-informed Senator Stuart Symington, were attacking the White House with claims that the Soviets were outdistancing the United States. Gates had been trying to play down the importance of the issue, but the chairman of the Joint Chiefs, Air Force Gen. Nathan Twining, was emphasizing the more alarmist views of the Air Force. As DCI, Dulles had been charged with pulling together a collective view of this intractable problem of collection and analysis, but everyone, including Eisenhower, knew the Agency did not have the detailed technical intelligence or the bureaucratic clout to referee the contentious issue.[20]

In responding to Kennedy's questions about Soviet strategic capabilities, Dulles did not improvise. On this critical and technical subject he stuck very closely to the findings laid out in numerous national intelligence estimates. During the period from 1957 to 1960, the Intelligence Community published from two to four NIEs annually evaluating Soviet progress on space and ballistic missile programs. In December 1957, the Community had published one of its most ominous NIEs, referring to the Soviets' "crash program." That estimate had projected that the USSR sometime during calendar year 1959 would probably have its first operational capability with 10 prototype ICBMs.[21] The same estimate projected that the Soviet Union probably would have "an operational capability with 100 ICBMs about one year after its first operational capability date, and with 500 ICBMs two, or at most, three years [that is, 1963] after first operational capability date."

By early 1960, the Community as a whole was using somewhat more moderate language to discuss probable Soviet missile capabilities, but, nevertheless, early that year three separate NIEs were published whose findings were sufficiently alarmist to fuel the missile gap debate. The bottom line of an estimate published in February was especially important because it came as close as the US Intelligence Community ever did to a net assessment. It stated: "Our analysis leads us to believe that if the US military posture develops as presently planned, the USSR will in 1961 have its most favorable opportunity to gain a decided military, political, and psychological advantage over the United States by the rapid deployment of operational ICBMs."[22] The February esti-

---

[20] Andrew Goodpaster, interview by the author in Washington, DC, 26 September 1993. Unless otherwise indicated, all references to Goodpaster's observations come from this interview.
[21] Special National Intelligence Estimate No. 11-10-57, *The Soviet ICBM Program - Conclusions*, 10 December 1957, 1, 2.

mate went on to observe that the Soviet ICBM program did not appear to be a crash program but was designed to provide a substantial ICBM capability at an early date. A separate NIE, also published in February, stated flatly: "The single-most-important development affecting the structure of Soviet military power during the period of this estimate will be the buildup of an ICBM force. Long-range missiles will enable the USSR to overcome its inferiority to the United States in nuclear strategic attack capability, as it was unable to do with bomber aircraft."[23]

In terms of the political debate on the issue, an even larger problem was posed by the Air Force conclusion that leaders of the Soviet Union were endeavoring to attain a decisive military superiority over the United States. This superiority, the Air Force assessed, would enable the USSR "to launch such devastating attacks against the United States that at the cost of acceptable levels of damage to themselves, the United States as a world power would cease to exist." This extremely ominous Air Force view was repeated in several NIEs—often referred to inaccurately as CIA products—published during the period. It was shared widely with the Congress and leaked to the press.

The findings of these Intelligence Community estimates were having a significant impact on the White House, the Congress, and the voters. In the words of Howard Stoertz, a senior CIA officer who often accompanied Dulles to his briefings of the Congress and the NSC, "Our findings were sufficiently scary that those who wanted a new administration to be elected were finding support in our Estimates."[24]

One interesting index of the impact of this intelligence was provided by former President (and Congressman) Gerald Ford in September 1993. Responding to an open-ended question about whether he remembered occasions when intelligence findings had created particular policy dilemmas, Ford volunteered, "Mostly I remember the period from 1953 to 1964 when I was on the Defense Appropriations Subcommittee that provided the CIA's budget. Allen Dulles and others from the CIA would come in and paint the most scary picture possible about what the Soviet Union would do to us. We were going to be second rate; the Soviets were going to be Number One. I didn't believe all that propaganda."[25]

---

[22] National Intelligence Estimate No. 11-8-59, *Soviet Capabilities for Strategic Attack through Mid-1964*, 9 February 1960, 2.

[23] National Intelligence Estimate No. 11-4-59, *Main Trends in Soviet Capabilities and Policies, 1959-1964*, 9 February 1960, 4.

[24] Howard Stoertz, interview by the author in McLean, Virginia, 27 September 1993.

[25] Gerald Ford, interview by the author in Beaver Creek, Colorado, 8 September 1993.

CHAPTER 2

The same material that was briefed to the House had been provided to the Senate Foreign Relations Committee and, therefore, to one of its most prominent junior members, John Kennedy. Kennedy made effective use of this intelligence in his presidential campaign, to the discomfort of the CIA, the White House, and Vice President Nixon—the Republican candidate. Goodpaster remembers that the politics of the issue became sufficiently awkward that Eisenhower sent him to the Agency to meet personally with Dulles and Symington to get to the bottom of the problem. Howard Stoertz remembers well that "Allen Dulles had us prepare a chart to prove we had not cooked the books for the election."

Postelection Briefing on Cuba

Once Kennedy had won the election, the CIA felt free to provide him a systematic briefing on the Agency's covert action programs worldwide, and—most important—to inform him in detail about the deliberations under way on Cuba. This took place at the Kennedy residence in Palm Beach, Florida, on 18 November, some 10 days after the vote. Reflecting the importance and sensitivity of the subject, there were two high-level briefers: Dulles, whom Kennedy had announced he would keep on as DCI the day following the election (along with FBI Director Hoover, his first appointments); and Richard Bissell, the Agency's deputy director for plans (operations). Like Dulles, Bissell knew Kennedy from the Washington social scene and, in his own case, from a shared New England background.

In discussing the briefing more than 30 years later, Bissell recalled that "Allen and I felt great pressure to inform the new president. The [Cuban] operation had acquired a considerable momentum and could not just be turned off and on. We settled outside on the terrace at a table and I gave him an abbreviated but fairly complete briefing on the state of the operation. I went on at least 30 minutes, maybe 45. I was fairly detailed in outlining the plan of what we hoped would happen."[26]

A review of the briefing papers used by Dulles and Bissell suggests that they gave Kennedy a careful overview of the Cuba plans as they existed in mid-November 1960. Their review included an explanation of the presidential authorization, signed by Eisenhower on 17 March, for the Agency to undertake planning. The briefing described the political action initiatives already under way in which the Agency was providing support to various anti-Castro groups and individuals inside and outside Cuba. They described the propa-

---

[26] Richard Bissell, interview by the author in Farmington, Connecticut, 17 April 1993.

ganda operation in place at the time, including the preparation of publications and radiobroadcasts aimed at weakening Castro's rule. These included broadcasts from Swan Island, which years later came to play a prominent role in the Agency's activities against the Sandinista government in Nicaragua.

The briefing of 18 November occurred in the midst of a fundamental review, back in Washington, of the scope of the paramilitary aspects of the anti-Castro program. At that time, everything was in flux. Nothing had been decided, let alone finally approved. In these circumstances, Dulles and Bissell planned to brief Kennedy carefully on a range of possible paramilitary operations.

The first option envisaged the development and support of dissident groups by the Agency's Cuban assets to undertake antiregime guerrilla action inside Cuba. A group of instructors had been trained who would, in time, oversee the instruction of up to 500 additional men, and radio and flight training were being provided Cuban pilots. The two briefers were to describe all these preparations, as well as the role of a few small groups already placed inside Cuba and the airdrops of supplies and equipment that were sustaining them.

The potential second phase of the paramilitary plan to be covered by the briefers was a combined sea-air assault by trained Cuban exiles coordinated with the guerrilla activity generated on the island. This undertaking would attempt to establish a close-in staging base for future anti-Castro military operations. A last phase, should it be needed, would be an air assault on the Havana area in support of guerrilla forces in Cuba moving on the ground into the capital. Mention was to be made of a contingency plan for overt US military intervention that would include the use of Agency assets.

Bissell remembers emphasizing particularly the plans for the possible movement of exile ground and air forces to Cuba both by sea and by air. He recalls that he "put a lot of emphasis on the timing aspects, and the numbers [of men and equipment] involved." Dulles and Bissell intended to inform Kennedy that it did not appear that in-country guerrilla actions alone would be successful in sparking a successful revolt against the regime. It is unclear whether they intended to brief the president-elect on the even more pessimistic assessment expressed by some in the Agency that even an invading force of exile Cubans would be unsuccessful without direct US involvement.

Press accounts of the briefing of Kennedy in Palm Beach indicate that it went on for two hours and 40 minutes. Bissell remembers that throughout the extended session the president-elect "was almost entirely a listener—although a very good listener. Kennedy had a number of questions that grew out of the briefing, but he had no prepared list of questions ahead of time."

Available CIA records do not suggest that Kennedy volunteered any opinion regarding the wisdom, or lack thereof, of the plans presented to him. Noth-

CHAPTER 2

ing in the documentation suggests that he either authorized the operation or urged restraint. To the contrary, Dulles stated in a memorandum sent to Gen. Maxwell Taylor, the president's special adviser on military affairs, on 1 June 1961 that "the purpose of the briefing was not to solicit the president-elect's approval or disapproval of the program but merely to acquaint him of its existence."[27] This implies, obviously, that Dulles had not previously informed Kennedy of the plans.

As Bissell put it, "We were in an absolutely untenable position until the new president knew what was going on, but we avoided seeking a yea or nay." He added that "Kennedy was favorably interested, but extremely careful to avoid a commitment, express or implied. We didn't get any negative reaction—I was interested above all in his studious neutrality. Allen Dulles and I talked about the Kennedy reaction after the fact. We had the same impression—on the whole Kennedy's attitude was favorable." This shared impression obviously cleared the way for continued Agency planning for what ultimately became the Bay of Pigs operation.

Other Covert Programs

Dulles intended to have the briefing of the president-elect in Palm Beach cover worldwide intelligence operations, of which Cuba was only one. His records indicate he wanted to establish that the Agency was fully supportive of the new president. "We made it clear to him that from this time on any information he desired was at his immediate disposal and would be willingly given."[28] In fact, Dulles was also working hard to solidify his personal standing with Kennedy. Senior Agency officers undoubtedly had mixed feelings when Dulles announced at a special staff meeting on 10 November that "all liaison with the new Administration by CIA would be conducted by the Director."[29]

According to handwritten notes prepared by Bissell, he and Dulles also were prepared to brief Kennedy on a variety of issues, large and small.[30] For example, one planned topic was the question of clearances. Although the president would be told that he possessed all clearances automatically, he should be advised of what was involved in providing special compartmented clearances that would enable his staff to receive intercepted communications and other sensitive material. Dulles also intended to discuss with Kennedy the legal basis for CIA's worldwide special operations. On the substantive side, in

---

[27] Allen Dulles, memorandum for Gen. Maxwell D. Taylor, 1 June 1961.
[28] Allen Dulles, *My Answer on the Bay of Pigs*, unpublished draft, October 1965.
[29] Lyman Kirkpatrick, Diary, 10 November 1960.
[30] Richard Bissell, untitled and undated notes for briefing President-elect Kennedy.

addition to Cuba, Dulles was prepared to brief Kennedy on operations in Venezuela, the Dominican Republic, and elsewhere in Central America. Agency activities in Tibet were also a discrete item.

The majority of the items to be raised did not address specific countries or regions. Rather, Dulles planned a thematic discussion of Agency propaganda and political action programs, with illustrative successes from around the world. Dulles was primed to provide examples of where the Agency had succeeded in reducing the power of communist parties abroad and in supporting the growth of constructive opposition parties. In a review of what was, at that time, still recent history, Dulles intended to inform Kennedy of CIA actions related to coups in Guatemala, Laos, and South Vietnam.

Regarding technical collection, Dulles was undoubtedly relieved to be able to discuss with Kennedy more fully the progress that had been made with aircraft and satellite systems to replace the U-2. The DCI's notes suggest he intended to discuss the existing U-2 program and two follow-on programs. One was the SR-71 aircraft, then under development, and the other the first imaging satellite, a film-return system.

Thirty years after the fact, there is no way to know with certainty how much of the material Dulles and Bissell prepared was actually discussed with Kennedy. Bissell remembers that the bulk of the time he and Dulles spent with Kennedy in Palm Beach was used to discuss Cuba. After that discussion, Bissell remembers that "Allen Dulles and John Kennedy drifted off to the end of the terrace and talked for some time about matters having nothing to do with Cuba." Bissell recalls that their conversation lasted at least 15 but certainly no more than 30 minutes. When shown several pages of his own handwritten notes concerning the issues the two had intended to raise, Bissell laughed and asserted that "nobody had time to cover everything that is on this list at any time prior to inauguration."

Records of the Eisenhower White House suggest that Dulles discussed, or at least was authorized to discuss, only a narrow agenda with the president-elect at the Palm Beach meeting. On 17 November, the day before Dulles traveled to Florida, Goodpaster recorded that he had informed the president that he had discussed the agenda with the CIA director and with Gen. Wilton Persons, the White House chief of staff. Goodpaster had informed Dulles that CIA operations were to be disclosed to Kennedy only as specifically approved on a case-by-case basis by President Eisenhower. Goodpaster's memorandum confirms Eisenhower had approved Dulles's plan to inform Kennedy of operations relating to Cuba as well as to "certain reconnaissance satellite operations of a covert nature." No other subjects were specifically approved.[31]

Dulles's notes state not only that Eisenhower authorized the Palm Beach briefing but also that the briefing was given at his suggestion and that it covered "worldwide intelligence operations." Bissell recalls that the scheduling of the briefing came up rather quickly. To his knowledge, Dulles received no guidance or suggestion from the White House on what the subject matter should be.

In discussing the politics of these briefings in 1993, Goodpaster remembered clearly the conflicting views the president and others in the White House had about them. On the one hand, some of Eisenhower's preelection reservations had evaporated by mid-November. He had issued a directive that, because Kennedy was to be the next president, "We must help him in any way we can." On the other hand, Goodpaster also remembers that Eisenhower had some uneasiness about how far Dulles should and would go in his discussions. The president believed ongoing deliberations by him and his advisers should remain confidential, and he worried about the inherent problems of protecting that confidentiality while at the same time briefing Kennedy fully.

Goodpaster's records indicate he discussed with the president and Senior Staff Assistant Gordon Gray the "special problem" of Dulles's continued attendance at NSC meetings once he had been designated by Kennedy to serve in the next administration. Goodpaster informed Dulles that while the president wanted him to continue to attend NSC meetings, the proceedings of those sessions were not to be disclosed outside the NSC room. According to the records, he had the impression that "Mr. Dulles had not understood that this matter was a delicate one." In 1993, Goodpaster reiterated that "there was a feeling that all this had to be explained pretty carefully to Allen Dulles."

The Mystery Briefing of Late November

A number of books and articles written about the Bay of Pigs contain the assertion that Kennedy was informed in detail of the planned operation and gave his approval in a briefing by Dulles in late November 1960. A review of the chronology of these publications suggests that most authors picked up this piece of information from the widely read account of events contained in Schlesinger's *A Thousand Days*. Schlesinger opened chapter 10, entitled "The Bay of Pigs," with the statement: "On November 29, 1960, 12 days after he had heard about the Cuban project, the president-elect received from Allen Dulles a detailed briefing on CIA's new military conception. Kennedy listened with attention, then told Dulles to carry the work forward."[32]

---

[31] Andrew Goodpaster, memorandum for the record, 17 November 1960.

If this briefing occurred, it would be by far the most important in the series Kennedy received. This would place on the president-elect an earlier and more direct responsibility for the development of the operation than would otherwise be justified. In fact, however, the Dulles-Kennedy meeting of 29 November cited by Schlesinger appears not to have occurred at all. Available CIA records contain no mention of such a briefing. Dulles's personal desk calendar shows that he had a very full day, with 10 different appointments running from 9:00 a m. to 5:45 p m., none of which was with the president-elect. It would be most extraordinary if the director's calendar or other CIA records failed to note a meeting of the DCI with the president-elect. Similarly, there is nothing in information available about Kennedy's activities to indicate that he met with Dulles that day. The *New York Times* of 30 November reported, "The Senator worked at home throughout the day [of 29 November] leaving only to visit his wife Jacqueline and son John F. Jr. in Georgetown University Hospital." The newspapers also reported that Kennedy had met at home that day with prospective cabinet appointee Chester Bowles, and with Terry Sanford, the latter visiting to recommend Luther Hodges for a cabinet position. Other visitors to the Kennedy home in Georgetown included his father, Joseph P. Kennedy, Edward Foley of the Inaugural Committee, and Senator Dennis Chavez of New Mexico.[33]

In thinking back on the briefings Kennedy received on the controversial Cuban operation, Ted Sorensen, his speechwriter and confidant, recalls, "President Kennedy did tell me, much later, that he had been briefed on the operation by the CIA while he was president-elect. CIA told him what they had in mind and why in some detail. That was the Palm Beach briefing." Sorensen doubted that Kennedy received a more detailed briefing by Dulles on 29 November, adding, "I saw him every single day and we discussed the whole range of policy matters—the foreign issues as well as 500 domestic ones."

Schlesinger was amused that he may have described a critical briefing that appears not to have occurred. In a letter to the author in 1993, he recommended that the original draft manuscript of his *A Thousand Days* be reviewed to ascertain whether the controversial assertion was footnoted. "If nothing turns up I must take Rick's way out," he wrote, referring to the character in *Casablanca* played by Humphrey Bogart. "Bogart: 'I came to Casablanca for the waters.' Claude Raines: 'What waters? We're in the desert.' Bogart: 'I was misinformed.'"[34]

---

[32] Schlesinger, *A Thousand Days*, 233.
[33] *New York Times*, 30 November 1960, 1,30.
[34] Arthur Schlesinger Jr., letter to the author, 23 June 1993.

CHAPTER 2

An important meeting concerning the Cuba operation, in fact, was held on 29 November at the White House at 11:00 a m. with the president (Eisenhower) in the chair. The president-elect was not included. Schlesinger and other authors, writing a few years after the fact, had obviously learned that on that date "the president" was briefed on Cuba and, being oriented to president Kennedy, assumed that it was he who was involved. Indeed, the meeting of 29 November was an important one. On that date, Eisenhower underscored that he wanted to continue active planning for the project. Eisenhower was pushing ahead vigorously; Kennedy was not yet responsible in any degree.

Soon after his inauguration on 28 January 1961, Kennedy did receive a full briefing on the planned Cuban operation. At that meeting the new president authorized the Agency to continue its preparations and asked that the paramilitary aspects of the plan be provided to the Joint Chiefs for their analysis. Even in late January, however, Kennedy withheld specific approval for an invasion, with or without direct US involvement.

Kennedy Visits the CIA

One unique aspect of Kennedy's familiarization with the CIA was the president-elect's decision to visit CIA Headquarters during the transition period. He was initially scheduled to visit the Agency's South Building, at 2430 E Street in downtown Washington, on 16 December. In preparation for the visit, Dulles asked Huntington Sheldon, the director of current intelligence, to prepare a book for the DCI containing material he and senior Agency officials should use in discussions with Kennedy.

The ambitious agenda that was prepared for the visit envisaged presentations by the DCI and eight other senior officers.[35] Briefings were prepared on the Agency's mission, organization, and budget, and on the legal basis for its activities. Dulles and others would describe the Agency's relationship with the Congress; the functions of such organizations as the Watch Committee and the President's Board of Consultants; and the functions of the several agencies that made up the Intelligence Community. The assistant director for national estimates would describe the estimates process and brief one specific paper, a recently published estimate of the world situation.

The chiefs of the Agency's key directorates were primed to explain their roles and activities. The clandestine services portion of the briefing included a description of clandestine intelligence collection and the covert action func-

---

[35] CIA, "Agenda for President-elect," 16 December 1960.

tions. In the latter discussion, the chief of operations was to update "Cuban operations since the Palm Beach briefing."

Owing to scheduling difficulties, Kennedy was unable to visit the Agency on 16 December. The visit was delayed until after the inauguration and finally occurred on Thursday, 26 January 1961. Dulles's desk calendar notes that the briefings were to run from 2:40 until 4:10 p m. In reality, they had to be abbreviated considerably, much to the consternation of the participants, because an unintended opportunity came to the president's attention.

For reasons having nothing to do with Kennedy's visit, the Agency, a few weeks before, had put together an attractive exhibit of materials relating to the history of intelligence that was located just inside the entrance of South Building. A number of exhibits were displayed under a sign that read, "These letters loaned courtesy of the Houghton Library of Harvard University." The newly elected Harvard man immediately noticed the reference to his alma mater. He stopped and read thoroughly the entire case of historical materials, much to the chagrin of Dulles and other waiting CIA executives.

Kennedy was already frustrated at press leaks from his new administration and, therefore, was especially taken with one of the letters in the display case. Written by General Washington to Col. Elias Dayton in July 1777, that letter included the observation that "The necessity of procuring good Intelligence is apparent and need not be further urged—All that remains for me to add is, that you keep the whole matter as secret as possible. For upon Secrecy, Success depends in Most Enterprizes of the kind, and for want of it, they are generally defeated." Kennedy asked Dulles if he could have a copy of the letter, which, of course, was sent promptly. The president wrote the CIA director thanking him and the creator of the exhibit, Walter Pforzheimer, saying, "The letter is both a fine memento of my visit with you and a continuing reminder of the role of intelligence in national policy."[36]

Origins of the *President's Intelligence Checklist*

Within days of his election, President Kennedy sent word to the White House that he would like to receive daily briefings on the same material that was being furnished to President Eisenhower.[37] The request from Kennedy came by way of one of his assistants for transition matters, Washington attorney Clark Clifford. Eisenhower approved the passage of this material to Kennedy on 17 November, the eve of Dulles's trip to Florida. There is no record

---

[36] John Kennedy letter to Allen Dulles, 10 February 1961.
[37] Goodpaster, memorandum for record, 17 November 1960.

that Dulles discussed this matter with Kennedy the next day, however, and some weeks were to go by before there was any organized follow-up.

When Kennedy visited CIA Headquarters after his inauguration, Sheldon described the current intelligence products that were available to him. Kennedy reiterated that he wanted to read the publications and designated his military aide, Brig. Gen. Chester Clifton, who was present at the meeting, to receive the material. Clifton had taken over Goodpaster's role of providing daily briefings to the new president, although Goodpaster continued to serve in the White House for a few weeks to help with the transition.

For the first few months of the Kennedy administration, Agency couriers each morning would deliver CIA's *Current Intelligence Bulletin* to Clifton. Clifton or MacGeorge Bundy would then take the material to the president, reporting back his questions or comments if there were any. Unfortunately, the intelligence report was part of a large package of material Kennedy received each day and was often not read. This left the new president less well informed than he thought he was, a situation that was soon driven home to him during his unfortunate encounter with Soviet Premier Nikita Khrushchev in Vienna, when he found himself unprepared to respond to his adversary's boasting and bullying.

From the start of the Kennedy administration, Dulles had few opportunities to present intelligence directly to the president. In large part, this was because Kennedy did not hold regularly scheduled NSC meetings as Eisenhower and Truman had done. In addition, however, there was a problem of personal chemistry and a generational gap between the new president and the CIA director. Agency veterans at the time had the feeling that Dulles may have been patronizing to Kennedy in his early briefings and, thus, was not warmly welcomed to the White House.[38] Along the same lines, Sorensen remembers Kennedy "was not very impressed with Dulles's briefings. He did not think they were in much depth or told him anything he could not read in the newspapers." In these awkward circumstances, Dulles's practice was to prepare written memorandums for the president on items that he deemed to be of particular significance, delivering them personally when possible. He also made personal deliveries when he wanted to bring certain important national estimates to the president's attention.

The fiasco at the Bay of Pigs in April 1961, reinforced by Kennedy's frustration at the meeting with Khrushchev in early June, changed everything. General Clifton informed current intelligence director Sheldon that the president was reluctant to continue receiving intelligence in the normal way. Clifton sug-

---

[38] Richard Lehman, interview by the author in McLean, Virginia, 10 March 1993.

gested the Agency would have to come up with some entirely different way of presenting its information if it were to regain the president's confidence. He volunteered that there was no point in the DCI discussing the matter directly with the president as that would be counterproductive. Dulles took this implicit criticism calmly, possibly foreseeing that the president's disappointment with the Agency on this and other scores would lead, as it did in November 1961, to his own removal.

Dulles gamely soldiered on in his attempts to bring the new president the fruits of the Agency's collection and analysis in the traditional manner, but it was largely the unauthorized efforts of his subordinates that opened a new and less formal channel to the White House that would satisfy Kennedy and most of his successors. In mid-1961 Huntington Sheldon and other managers of the Office of Current Intelligence—working with Clifton but without the knowledge of their superiors either at the White House or the Agency—came up with a new intelligence briefing publication designed exclusively for the president. Longtime current intelligence specialist Richard Lehman worked up a dry run of the proposed *President's Intelligence Checklist* and Sheldon took it to Clifton for his approval. Clifton was pleased with the trial document, which eliminated the bewildering array of source classifications and restrictions common to intelligence publications and presented facts and analysis in short, vernacular paragraphs.

The first issue of the new publication was delivered to Clifton on Saturday, 17 June, and carried by him to the president at his country home near Middleburg, Virginia. The first *Checklist* was a small book of seven pages, measuring 8-1/2 by 8 inches, that contained 14 items of two sentences each with a half-dozen longer notes and a few maps. Agency managers spent a nervous weekend; they were immensely relieved the following Monday morning to hear Clifton's "go ahead—so far, so good."

Quickly it became clear the president was reading the *Checklist* regularly and issuing instructions based on its contents. Not infrequently he asked to see source materials, estimates of developing situations highlighted for his attention, texts of speeches by foreign leaders, and occasional full-length Agency publications that provided more depth, details, and explanations. Within a few months, the secretaries of state and defense asked to see what the president was reading. In December, six months after publication had begun, Clifton passed the word to the Agency that those two cabinet members should be added to the subscriber list.

No Agency officer sat with the president while he read the *Checklist*, but Clifton was careful to pass back to the Agency the president's reactions and questions. CIA officials regarded the new system as the best possible daily

CHAPTER 2

channel to a president. The relationship with Kennedy was not only a distinct improvement over the more formal relationship with Eisenhower, but would only rarely be matched in future administrations.

Meanwhile, in November 1961, Allen Dulles had been replaced by John McCone, who served Kennedy as DCI for almost two years. In the early part of this period, McCone succeeded in rebuilding the Agency's relationship with Kennedy. McCone saw Kennedy frequently, and the president—more than any other before or since—would telephone even lower level Agency officers for information or assistance. Interestingly, McCone's prescience in alerting the president to the possibility that the Soviets would place missiles in Cuba backfired for him personally. Although McCone was right when most others were wrong, the president did not like the DCI's public references to this fact, and their relationship cooled noticeably.

Editors of the *Checklist* were especially heartened in September 1963 when Clifton passed back the president's personal expression of delight with "the book." A month later, on a morning when Clifton, McGeorge Bundy, and the Agency's briefing officer were huddled in the basement of the West Wing going over the *Checklist*, President Kennedy called down asking where they were and when they were going to bring it to him. Clifton and his Agency contacts were also heartened by Secretary Rusk's comment that the *Checklist* was "a damned useful document."

President Kennedy's *Checklist* was published daily for two and a half years, capturing the regular attention of the president and serving his needs. Created out of an almost desperate desire to please a president who had found the Agency wanting, it proved to be the forerunner of the *President's Daily Brief*, the publication that was to serve all presidents from 1964 to the present.

The Transition to President Johnson

The transition to President Johnson was as abrupt for the US Intelligence Community as it was for the rest of the country. In some respects, it was also as uncertain. Johnson had received a number of intelligence briefings as chairman of the Senate Aeronautical and Space Sciences Committee and later as Senate majority leader. He had met on one occasion with Allen Dulles in July 1960 while a vice-presidential candidate, but neither Dulles nor his successor, John McCone, had paid much attention to keeping Johnson informed during the intervening years.

Johnson, in turn, had paid relatively little attention to the products of the Intelligence Community while he was vice president. Each day his office received the Agency's *Current Intelligence Bulletin*, a widely distributed

Attorney General Robert Kennedy and new DCI John McCone.

product that contained less sensitive and less highly classified information than was included in the *Checklist*. Although the *Checklist* at the end of the Kennedy presidency was being sent also to the secretaries of defense and state and to the chairman of the Joint Chiefs of Staff, Johnson was unaware of its existence. For reasons undoubtedly growing out of the earlier political rivalry between Kennedy and Johnson, Kennedy's intelligence assistant, Bromley Smith, early in the administration had ordered that "under no circumstances should the *Checklist* be given to Johnson."[39]

On Saturday morning, 23 November 1963, the day following Kennedy's assassination, McCone instructed his executive assistant, Walter Elder, to telephone the new president's secretary and inform her that the DCI would, as

---

[39] Lehman interview, 10 March 1993.

usual, be at the White House at 9:00 a.m. to give the president the regular morning intelligence briefing.[40] In reality, there was nothing usual or regular about the DCI's involvement in a morning briefing, but McCone obviously believed he needed to take an extraordinary initiative to establish a relationship with the new president.

McCone was waiting in Bundy's office in the basement of the West Wing when Johnson entered at approximately 9:15. Johnson had been an infrequent visitor to those quarters, which also included the White House Situation Room, but he was forced to come there for the meeting because Kennedy's office had not yet been cleared out. R. Jack Smith, CIA's director of current intelligence, was present and talked briefly with Johnson in Bundy's outer office, writing later that the president looked "massive, rumpled and worried."[41]

Despite the irregular and strained nature of the circumstances, McCone accomplished his mission during that first meeting with President Johnson. The president expressed his confidence in McCone, who, in turn, reassured the new president that he and the Agency stood ready to support him in every way. McCone introduced the president to the *Checklist* and reviewed with him the unspectacular substantive items in the publication that day. Johnson had few questions during their 15-minute session, but he did agree that McCone should brief him personally each morning at least for the next several days. He asked that the director bring any urgent matters to his attention at any time, day or night.

The *Checklist* shown to Johnson on that first occasion was a bulky publication containing five unusually long items and six additional notes. R. Jack Smith explained to Bromley Smith that the Agency had tried to provide, as unobtrusively as possible, a bit of extra background for Johnson. Bromley Smith approved the strategy but added that he hoped the Agency would not be too obvious in its tutorials. In his memoirs, Johnson wrote of his relief to discover "on that sad November morning" that the international front was relatively peaceful and that there was nothing in the material McCone brought to him that required an immediate decision.[42]

McCone met with Johnson almost every day for the next two or three weeks, briefing him on virtually all the world's trouble spots and providing information from CIA files and collection efforts on President Kennedy's assassin, Lee Harvey Oswald. The president told the director to make sure that

---

[40] Walter Elder, interview by the author in McLean, Virginia, 21 April 1993.
[41] R. Jack Smith, *The Unknown CIA My Three Decades with the Agency* (Washington: Pergamon-Brassy's, 1989), 163.
[42] Lyndon Johnson, *The Vantage Point* (New York: Holt, Rinehart and Winston, 1971), 22.

CIA gave the FBI all information and support necessary to its investigation of Oswald's background.

McCone also used these opportunities to inform the president of a variety of CIA covert action and technical collection programs, including the successful effort to build what became known as the SR-71 reconnaissance aircraft to augment the U-2. McCone brought the president up to date on the status of the program (by that time a number of aircraft had been built) and to brief him on McCone's discussions with President Kennedy about the advisability of making the program public. Secretaries Rusk and McNamara had urged Kennedy to announce the aircraft's existence and Kennedy was inclined to do so. But a discussion of the political and security issues involved prompted Johnson to postpone any public announcement of the program. He ordered McCone to get as many aircraft produced and deployed to the operating site as possible and eventually revealed the existence of the aircraft at a press conference in February 1964.

Vietnam

The most significant issue Johnson and McCone discussed during this period undoubtedly was Vietnam. McCone was straightforward in providing the Agency's analysis of the course of the war there. Initially, this won him favor with the new president, who had not favored certain of the steps taken in Vietnam by his predecessor, but it was to lead ultimately to a falling out between McCone and Johnson.

On 24 November, a mere two days after Kennedy's assassination, Johnson met at 3:00 p.m. in the Executive Office Building with Rusk, McNamara, George Ball, Bundy, McCone, and Ambassador to South Vietnam Henry Cabot Lodge. According to McCone, Lodge informed the group that the United States had not been involved in the recent coup against President Ngo Dinh Diem.[43] In fact, Lodge had instructed a CIA liaison officer to tell the South Vietnamese generals that the US government had lost confidence in President Diem, and he was kept aware of events before and during the coup on 1 November. During the course of the military takeover, Diem was captured and then killed.

Lodge maintained that the population of South Vietnam was very happy as a result of the coup, showing the group assembled at the Executive Office Building some pictures of crowds in Saigon. Lodge argued that the change in government in South Vietnam had been an improvement and that he was

---

[43] John McCone, "South Vietnam Situation," memorandum for the record, 25 November 1961.

CHAPTER 2

hopeful about the course of the war, expecting "marked progress" by February or March 1964. He also stated, without elaboration, that there were indications that North Vietnam might be interested in reaching mutually satisfactory arrangements with the United States. McCone wrote in his memorandum for the record that Lodge's statements were "optimistic, hopeful and left the president with the impression that we were on the road to victory."

McCone presented the group with a much more pessimistic CIA assessment. He cited the continuing increase in Viet Cong activity over the previous month, predicting more and sustained pressures from the guerrillas. The director pointed out that the South Vietnamese military was having considerable trouble organizing the government and was receiving little help from civilian leaders, who seemed to be staying on the sidelines. McCone said the Intelligence Community could not give an optimistic appraisal of the future.

Johnson stated that he approached the situation in Vietnam with misgivings and was anxious about calls in the Congress for a US withdrawal. While recognizing he would have to live with the results of the coup, he was particularly doubtful the United States had taken the right course in upsetting the Diem regime. He was critical, even harsh, about the divisions within the ranks of US advisers about the conduct of the war. He made clear his desire to replace several key figures in the US country team in Saigon and dictated that he "wanted no more divisions of opinion, no more bickering, and any person that did not conform to policy should be removed."

During McCone's daily discussions of the *Checklist*, the president regularly raised the question of Vietnam. Despite his strictures against differences of opinion, he appeared to appreciate the fact that McCone's assessments did not correspond to what he was hearing from others. The president repeatedly asked for the director's appraisal of the situation, but the continuing exchange between the two ultimately proved troublesome for the director. In large part this was because Johnson sought McCone's advice on the sensitive issue of who should "run the show" in South Vietnam and discussed his thoughts on possible personnel changes among his advisers and ambassadors.

Johnson remarked to McCone that, although he appreciated the work the DCI was doing in intelligence, he did not want him to confine himself to that role. The president invited the director to come to him personally with suggestions for courses of action on policy that McCone thought wise, even if his ideas were not consistent with the advice others were providing. Johnson mentioned specifically that he was not satisfied with the advice he was receiving on nuclear testing, Cuba, and particularly South Vietnam. The president questioned McCone closely about the prospects in South Vietnam, underscoring his desire for an "objective appraisal." Johnson specifically asked for any recommendations McCone might have for modifying his Vietnam policy.

Johnson's confiding in McCone during the first two weeks of his presidency clearly flattered the CIA director but also put him in an awkward position with other key players in the government, as well as with regard to his obligation provide objective intelligence assessments. Within months, events were to reveal that McCone probably took the president more literally than he should have. The DCI's candor in providing advice to the president eventually strained their relationship.

The president was not so completely preoccupied with Vietnam that he did not remember to focus on another enduring problem—the Castro regime in Cuba. Within a week of becoming president, he asked McCone how effective US policy was regarding Cuba and what the CIA projected to be the future of that country. Johnson was especially interested in the effectiveness of the economic embargo of Cuba and wanted to know what the Agency planned to do to dispose of Castro. The president said he did not want any repetition of "the fiasco of 1961," the CIA-planned rebel invasion, but he felt the United States could not abide the existing Cuban situation and wanted the CIA to propose a more aggressive strategy. Johnson informed McCone that he looked to the CIA for firm recommendations.

Initially, it was unclear whether Johnson would return to a system of regular NSC meetings or continue the more casual Kennedy approach. There was, therefore, much interest in the NSC meeting the president called for 5 December 1963. At that meeting, McCone was to brief the group on the Soviet military and economic situation. He prepared thoroughly for this first NSC meeting with the new president, bringing one assistant, Clinton Conger, and a number of large briefing charts to the meeting.

To McCone's surprise, Johnson had invited to the meeting the chairmen and ranking minority members of the leading congressional committees. The director accommodated this novel approach by quickly briefing the congressional leaders on the fact of, and restrictions related to, communications intercepts, which were to be mentioned during the briefing. Just as the meeting began, however, there was another surprise when the president gave a nod and in came his White House photographer. McCone was aghast as the photographer began shooting pictures left and right. He turned around with a start to confirm that Conger had managed to turn over a map of Soviet ICBM sites before the first pictures were taken of that end of the room. In the subsequent months, it was to become clear that Johnson was no more enamored of weekly NSC meetings than Kennedy had been. When a rare meeting was held, however, it normally began with an intelligence briefing by McCone.

CHAPTER 2

With few formal NSC meetings, much of the Agency's relationship with the new president came to rest on the briefings McCone was providing Johnson privately. Unfortunately, these soon became a casualty of the differences emerging between the two men regarding Vietnam. The momentum of McCone's contacts with Johnson was interrupted by a trip the director took in December 1963 to review the Vietnamese situation. It was his second trip to Saigon since becoming DCI, and McCone was discouraged by what he found. His pessimism made him skeptical of proposals Defense Secretary McNamara made for an extended program of clandestine raids against North Vietnam in early 1964. During a subsequent trip to Vietnam in March 1964, McCone's reservations deepened, and he concluded that the war effort, even with McNamara's enhancements, was not succeeding.

McCone recommended to the president a six-point program to reverse the deteriorating situation that would involve an escalation of US military actions significantly beyond anything McNamara and Johnson had considered. Johnson refused to accept the DCI's recommendations. As the president came to side with McNamara's approach to the conduct of the war, he became increasingly impatient with McCone and with the continuing differences between the DCI and the secretary of defense. By the end of March 1964, Johnson clearly had lost confidence in McCone and interest in his regular intelligence updates. In the succeeding months McCone attempted periodically to restart his briefings of the president, at least on an occasional basis, but Johnson turned him aside.

In June 1964 the director informed the president for the first time that he would like to resign as soon as Johnson had decided on a successor.[44] Despite his growing disenchantment with McCone, Johnson insisted that he remain in his post until after the presidential election in November 1964.

Evolution to the *President's Daily Brief*

Providing the *Checklist* to President Kennedy had worked so well that CIA naturally hoped the arrangement would continue with Johnson, but this was not to be. In his first weeks as president, Johnson read the *Checklist* and seemed interested in discussing its contents during his meetings with McCone. After those meetings stopped, however, Johnson tended not to read the daily publication.

Observing that Johnson was no longer reading the *Checklist*, General Clifton (who had stayed on from the Kennedy administration as military aide to the president) proposed the idea of a twice-weekly intelligence report. CIA

---

[44] Elder interview, 21 April 1993.

managers thought this strategy was worth a try. In truth, they thought that anything that would catch the president's eye was worth a try; several formats were offered during this period. They had been dismayed by Bromley Smith's assessment that Johnson was probably disinclined to read the Kennedy-tailored *Checklist* that had been denied him as vice president.

On 9 January the first issue of the semiweekly was taken to Clifton at the White House. The next morning Clifton called Lehman at CIA to report that he had shown the new publication to the president at breakfast and it had "worked like a charm." At the end of January, Clifton again made a point of seeking Johnson's reaction to the *Intelligence Review*. The president observed at that point that he found it a valuable supplement to the intelligence briefings he received and wanted the publication continued without change.

Although the president read primarily the semiweekly review, his staff requested that the *Checklist* continue to be published daily to enable them to answer the president's frequent spur-of-the-moment questions. With the president not reading the *Checklist* most days, McCone decided he would expand its readership; he obtained permission to send it to four additional officials in the State Department, two more in Defense and in the Joint Chiefs, and to the offices of the secretary of the treasury and the attorney general.

The practice of producing two presidential intelligence publications worked well through the election year of 1964. The president typically read the *Review* on the return leg of campaign trips, and his staff felt well supported with the daily *Checklist*. As the election neared, however, Secretary of State Rusk expressed to McCone his concern about the security of the *Checklist* as a result of its expanded dissemination. Rusk was worried about possible leaks regarding sensitive policy issues during the campaign. The DCI was more concerned about the basic question of whether it made any sense to publish a "presidential" *Checklist* when the president himself almost never read it, but agreed something should be done.

Meanwhile, during the 1964 electoral campaign, Johnson's opponent, Senator Barry Goldwater, set a precedent by declining to receive intelligence briefings. In July, after consulting with the president, McCone had telephoned Goldwater to offer the customary briefings. According to his assistant, Walter Elder, Goldwater replied only that he would consider it. Within hours, an assistant called to decline, explaining that the senator appreciated the offer but felt he had all the information he needed to conduct his campaign. McCone, reflecting a frustration he and Johnson shared, mused, "He probably does; the Air Force tells him everything he wants to know."

Responding to the concerns of the secretary of state and the DCI about the circulation of the *Checklist*, R. Jack Smith proposed that the most graceful

CHAPTER 2

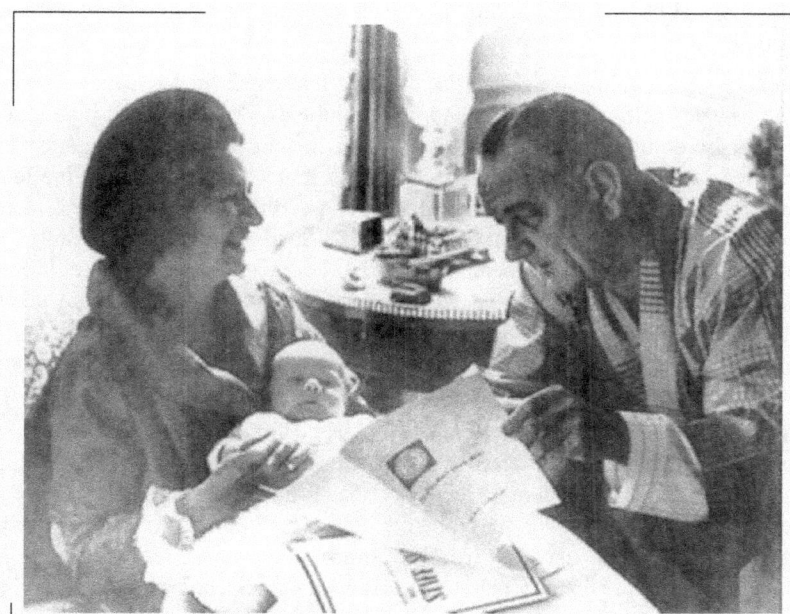

President and Mrs. Lyndon Johnson pose with their grandchild and a copy of the President's Daily Brief.

way for the Agency to drop a number of the readers of the *Checklist* would be to discontinue the publication and produce a new one. Smith observed that the Agency would maximize the likelihood that Johnson would accept a new publication and read it regularly if it were produced to conform as much as possible to his work habits. Because Johnson did much of his reading at night, in bed, Smith recommended that the publication be published and delivered in the late afternoon as the *Review* had been, rather than in the morning like the *Checklist*.

Smith's proposal was accepted, and after the election both the *Checklist* and the *Review* were dropped. The new *President's Daily Brief*, designed specifically for President Johnson, was delivered to the White House on 1 December 1964. Its fresh appearance obviously appealed to the president. His assistant, Jack Valenti, sent the first issue back to Bundy with word that the president read it, liked it, and wanted it continued. Quite apart from the packaging of the current intelligence, President Johnson—like other presidents—was becoming a closer reader of the daily products as he became increasingly enmeshed in foreign policy matters. By mid-February 1965, for example, he was reading not only the PDB but also CIA's daily Vietnam situation report, which Bromley

Smith insisted be delivered at 8:00 a m. each day so that it could be sent to the president early.

In early 1965, Johnson agreed that the time had come for McCone to return to the private sector. That understanding undoubtedly was furthered by a letter the director delivered to Johnson on 2 April in which he argued against an expanded land war in Vietnam and concluded that US bombing was ineffective.[45] By coincidence, the day that McCone passed the directorship of CIA to his successor, VAdm. William Raborn—28 April—was also the day US Marines landed in the Dominican Republic to deal with the crisis there. It was during the Dominican crisis that word was received that the PDB had taken firm root in the White House. Presidential spokesman Bill Moyers said on 21 May, approximately six months after the PDB had been launched, that the president read it "avidly."

The PDB process that was in place in early 1965 continued more or less unchanged throughout the Johnson administration. CIA did not receive from Johnson the steady presidential feedback that it had received from Kennedy. The Agency knew, however, that the president was reading the PDB regularly, and Johnson's aides, usually Bromley Smith, were consistently helpful in passing back the president's reactions, criticisms, and requests. The only significant change made in the PDB process came when the president again reversed himself and indicated he wanted to receive the PDB early in the morning rather than in the evening. He had decided that he wanted to see the PDB at 6:30 a.m., before he began reading the morning newspapers.

Those newspapers later provided conclusive evidence that the publication was reaching the president. Agency personnel were surprised one morning to see a photograph in the papers showing President and Mrs. Johnson sitting in the White House in dressing gowns. Mrs. Johnson was holding their first grandson while the president was reading a copy of the *President's Daily Brief*.

⌘ ⌘ ⌘

---

[45] Ibid.

CHAPTER 3

NIXON AND FORD - UNEVEN ACCESS

During his eight years as vice president in the 1950s, Richard Nixon had had broad exposure to the activities of the civilian US Intelligence Community. He was aware CIA had briefed the presidential candidates in every election since 1952 and undoubtedly harbored mixed feelings about the way the process had worked in 1960, when his narrow defeat by John Kennedy might well have hinged on the candidates' different perceptions of the intelligence process. This familiarity with the IC's capabilities and practices made him willing, at the outset of his new campaign for the presidency in 1968, to accept briefings from CIA Director Richard Helms. It also led him to decline to receive routine briefings from lower level officers, opening the way for Henry Kissinger, his national security advisor, to play a central and expanding role.

Nixon won the Republican Party nomination on 8 August 1968. Two days later the nominee and his running mate, Governor Spiro Agnew of Maryland, flew to Texas to hear a "general review of the international situation" from President Johnson and his key foreign policy advisers. In addition to the president, the group included Secretary of State Dean Rusk, Cyrus Vance (the number-two negotiator in the Vietnam peace talks in Paris), and DCI Helms. The president welcomed the Republican candidates with a tour of his ranch in an open convertible, but when the time came for the substantive briefing, he made only a few introductory remarks and then gave the floor to Helms.

Helms's memorandum for the record indicates that he focused on the handful of international developments that were at a critical stage during the late summer of 1968, including the confrontation between Czechoslovakia and the Soviet Union, events in the Middle East, and the military situation in Vietnam.[1] The director also discussed Cuba, including Castro's support for revolutionary efforts in Latin America, and events in the Dominican Republic and Haiti. Following Helms's briefing, Vance continued with a review of developments in the Paris peace negotiations that included details of the private talks under way between the United States and North Vietnam.

---

[1] Richard Helms, "Briefing of Former Vice President Nixon and Governor Agnew," memorandum for the record, 12 August 1968.

CHAPTER 3

President Richard Nixon greets CIA employees as DCI Richard Helms looks on.

Helms recorded that Nixon and Agnew were interested, in particular, in the effects of the Soviet-Czechoslovak confrontation on Poland and Yugoslavia. He also noted that they were surprised to hear the North Vietnamese were demanding that the Saigon government negotiate directly with the communist shadow administration in South Vietnam, the National Liberation Front. During the course of the briefing, Nixon directed a number of policy questions to Rusk. The Republican candidate made clear he had no intention of saying or doing anything that would complicate the job of the US negotiators in Paris.

Looking back on his first briefing of candidate Nixon 25 years after the fact, Helms recalled that, in his view, it was not a particularly well-organized or useful session.[2] After his own 15-minute overview of key worldwide developments, he recalled, the politicians' instincts took over for the balance of the discussion in the sitting room at the LBJ ranch and during the one-hour lunch that followed. Johnson was on a liquid diet, recovering from a bout of diverticulitis, so he was free to do all the talking while the others enjoyed a meal of steak and corn on the cob. Helms recalled with some amusement that the president of five years and the candidate, with his eight years of vice-presidential experience, each wanted to demonstrate to the other his mastery of foreign affairs.

Nixon appears to have been pleased with the session; he later wrote positively in his memoirs about the "full-scale intelligence briefings ordered by Johnson for each of the nominees."[3] The session concluded with the president's assurance to Nixon that he could call on Rusk or Helms for any additional information he might require.

As it happened, the discussion in Texas on 10 August was the only briefing Nixon was to receive in the preelection period. That session had focused entirely on the facts of developments abroad and the status of negotiations in which the United States was involved. Unlike the situation that had developed in 1960, there was in the August briefing—and in the whole campaign in 1968—no effort by anyone to make a political issue of the Intelligence Community's programs or analysis. A key factor that helped ensure that did not happen was Helms's strict constructionist view of the CIA director's job. He was determined to stick to the facts and avoid involvement in policy discussions, unlike his predecessors Allen Dulles and John McCone.

Helms was aided in his determination to avoid any politicization of intelligence in 1968 by the fact that there were no presidential debates that year. Although there had been one debate during the primaries (between Robert Kennedy and Eugene McCarthy), once the nominations were final Nixon concluded that he could avoid debating his opponent, Vice President Hubert Humphrey, just as Johnson had declined to debate Goldwater in 1964. Nixon's judgment was buttressed by the results of polls showing, as early as the first week in September, that he was leading Humphrey by a substantial margin, which he was able to retain throughout the campaign.

---

[2] Richard Helms, interview by the author in Washington, DC, 16 March 1993. Subsequent comments of Helms come also from this interview.

[3] Nixon, *Memoirs*, 316. Nixon's Democratic opponent in 1968, Hubert Humphrey, routinely received intelligence reports by virtue of being the incumbent vice president. Two other candidates also received intelligence briefings in that unusual year: former Alabama Governor George Wallace on 26 July and Georgia Governor Lester Maddox on 21 August. Helms and others briefed each of these candidates in Rusk's office, generally on the same array of subjects they had covered with Nixon. Very brief accounts of these sessions can be found in Helms's memorandums for the record, "Briefing of Former Governor George C. Wallace," 26 July 1968, and "Briefing of Governor Lester Maddox," 22 August 1968.

CHAPTER 3

After a postelection vacation in Key Biscayne, Florida, President-elect Nixon and his wife returned to New York City on Monday, 11 November, stopping en route in Washington for lunch with the president and an impromptu afternoon of discussions with the president and his foreign affairs aides. In addition to the president, Rusk, and Helms, this time the group also included Secretary of Defense Clark Clifford, JCS Chairman Gen. Earl Wheeler, and National Security Advisor Walt Rostow. Helms remembers that the afternoon meeting in the cabinet room suffered from the short notice and complete lack of preparation given the participants. There was only a desultory exchange on substantive issues, inasmuch as "nobody knew what was wanted or expected."

Invigorated by his election and vacation, the president-elect was struck by the very different mood of the other participants as they concentrated on Vietnam.[4] He recalled that those assembled seemed very nearly worn out from dealing with the prolonged crisis and "had no new approaches to recommend to me." Nixon said he saw the war etched on the faces around him and found them relieved to be able to turn the morass over to someone else. He recorded that they emphasized to him that the United States must see the war through to a successful conclusion and that a negotiated settlement that looked like a defeat would have a devastating impact on US allies and friends in Asia and around the world.

From Helms's point of view, the meeting on 11 November was of significance for a reason unrelated to the discussion of Vietnam. Helms remembers that Johnson asked him to stay on for a private talk after the session adjourned. At that time, Johnson told Helms that Nixon had twice asked about him (Helms). Johnson said he told Nixon that he "had no idea how Helms had voted, but that his was a merit appointment."

Johnson's kindness in recommending Helms to the Nixon administration may have resulted from a lingering embarrassment over the way he had treated Helms at an earlier point. In 1965, Johnson had passed over Helms to appoint VAdm. William Raborn Jr. as DCI. At the time, Johnson informed Helms that, although he had heard good things about him, he was "not well enough known in this town," meaning on Capitol Hill. But Johnson went on to tell Helms that he "should attend every meeting Raborn did."

The director's only other meeting with Nixon during the transition period occurred later the same week when he was summoned to New York City on Friday, 15 November. Helms entered the Nixon suite on the 39th floor of the Pierre Hotel at 1:30 p m. to find the president-elect conversing with adviser

---

[4] Ibid., 336.

John Mitchell, who was to become attorney general. With virtually no preliminaries, Nixon indicated that he would like Helms to stay on as DCI. The public announcement would come some time later.

Supporting Nixon's Team in New York City [5]

Discussions between Johnson and Helms resulted in a decision that CIA should make available to the president-elect in New York City the same daily intelligence information being provided to the outgoing president in Washington. Helms assigned the task of providing this assistance to the Agency's deputy director for intelligence, R. Jack Smith. As a first step, he asked Smith to confer with Nixon's chief aide, former advertising executive Robert Haldeman.

Joined by Howard Osborn (CIA's director of security) and Richard Lehman (deputy chief of the Office of Current Intelligence [OCI]), Smith went to New York on the morning of 12 November.[6] Smith showed Haldeman a sample of the intelligence publications the Agency proposed to make available to Nixon—the *President's Daily Brief* (PDB), the *Central Intelligence Bulletin* (CIB), the daily *Situation in Vietnam*, the *Weekly Review*, and selected memorandums. In turn, Haldeman asked that the Agency initiate special intelligence security clearances for a number of staff members, including Richard Allen and Martin Anderson. They had been the president-elect's advisers on foreign affairs during the campaign and were to advise him during the transition period.

It was agreed that CIA should establish a reading room in a secure area to which members of the Nixon staff could come for security indoctrination and to read classified documents. Space was not available in the Pierre, so it was decided to locate the Agency's outpost, dubbed "DDI-New York," in the basement of the Nixon campaign headquarters at 450 Park Avenue, six blocks from the president-elect's office. This site, formerly the world headquarters of the North American Missionary Alliance and soon to be demolished, was chosen because it seemed unlikely to attract attention from the press and the public. Allen's office was also in the building.

Paul Corscadden, an 11-year veteran of OCI, was designated officer in charge. Kenneth Rosen, an intelligence officer who had served in the White House Situation Room under President Johnson and worked a year as a spe-

---

[5] The material that follows regarding the Agency's activities in New York City draws very heavily on the classified writings of the late Paul H. Corscadden; he is, in effect, the author of this section.
[6] They had planned to fly, but a heavy snowfall intervened, and the three men traveled by train instead, arriving at Pennsylvania Station in the storm-struck metropolis at the onset of the evening rush hour. They were provided a police escort to take them through the badly snarled traffic to the Central Park area and the Pierre Hotel.

CHAPTER 3

cial assistant to McGeorge Bundy, was second in command. Corscadden and Rosen moved into the Statler-Hilton Hotel at 7th Avenue and 33rd Street for the duration of the transition period. Because of the expense of living in New York City and the representational nature of the assignment, the executive director of CIA waived the standard per diem limitation and allowed each of them up to $30 per day.

The area selected to house the Agency's facility required extensive renovation, which, magically, the CIA's Office of Logistics accomplished in 72 hours, including one weekend. The construction activity did not go unnoticed by other occupants of the building. Reports soon circulated that the Secret Service, the FBI, or some other sensitive, top secret government agency had moved in and would, among other things, assume responsibility for the physical security of all the president-elect's staff offices and the protection of his family. The CIA's Office of Security had decided not to identify the operation as Agency sponsored but, rather, to allow those who learned of its existence to draw whatever conclusions they chose. This decision, reasonable on the face of things, led to unexpected consequences. Before long, Nixon staff secretaries were calling to ask that someone "behind the Black Door" investigate the disappearance of office supplies or solve the mystery of a purloined television set. On another occasion, the supervisor of the staff mailroom demanded that one of the Agency communicators "taste" and immediately remove from the mailroom a crate of canned hams sent to the president-elect as a Christmas gift.

Those who were curious about what was housed behind that Black Door enjoyed the unwitting support of the municipal health authorities. Occupants of nearby buildings along Park Avenue had complained of an infestation of black rats that had established colonies in the ground around the brightly lighted Christmas trees festooning the avenue from 59th Street to Grand Central Station. Within hours, health inspectors poured through all the nearby buildings. A team came to the door of the Agency facility, demanding admission. They were turned away with the assurance that there were no rats inside.

Beginning on 19 November, intelligence publications were wired to New York on a daily basis. The *Situation in Vietnam* report arrived the evening of its publication in Washington; the PDB came soon after 5 a.m. each morning. Nixon staff members who had access to the intelligence publications came to the facility at their convenience. A reading table contained all of each day's publications, along with appropriate national intelligence estimates, special memorandums, intelligence handbooks, and various graphic aids. Of the key staffers, Allen and Anderson visited most often.

Corscadden and Rosen delivered a complete set of publications each day in a sealed envelope marked "Eyes Only—The President-elect" to Rose Mary

Woods in Nixon's office. Woods had been granted the proper clearances, and the Agency had installed a safe in her office for the secure storage of classified materials. Initially, it was thought that she probably would return the publications after two or three days, during which time the president-elect would have had the opportunity to read at least a current issue of the PDB.

For the first 10 days of the operation, only intelligence analyses prepared for the outgoing administration were made available to the president-elect's staff. It soon became apparent, however, that the needs of the incoming administration did not coincide in every detail with those of the Johnson administration. To meet the emerging special needs of the new team, OCI on 29 November compiled the first "Nixon Special," an "Eyes Only" intelligence memorandum based on sensitive intelligence information that the Agency knew would be of interest to Nixon. The Foreign Broadcast Information Service (FBIS) soon afterward provided an additional service by transmitting directly to New York from its field bureaus foreign press and radio articles pertaining to the incoming administration.

The Key Player: Henry Kissinger

The appointment of Harvard Professor Henry Kissinger as assistant for national security affairs was announced by the president-elect at a news conference on 2 December. By prior arrangement with DDI Smith, who had telephoned him from Washington the morning of Nixon's announcement, Kissinger came to the Agency facility on Park Avenue for a briefing that same afternoon.[7] He was shown current issues of all the intelligence publications available in the facility and was told what had been delivered to the Pierre for the president-elect since the Agency support operation began. Kissinger was assured that the CIA was prepared to provide full support to him and the rest of the incoming administration.

During that first session, Kissinger expressed appreciation for the Agency's willingness to assist him and for the support it had so far provided the incoming administration. He promised to arrange his schedule to allow 15 minutes per day to read the intelligence publications. He also accepted a proposal that Corscadden and Rosen undertake during off-duty hours to advise him of any critical world developments requiring the attention of the president-elect. This precautionary arrangement had earlier been accepted by Allen and Anderson as well as Haldeman.

---

[7] A more detailed discussion of Smith's exchange with Kissinger can be found in his memoirs, *The Unknown CIA*, 201–203.

CHAPTER 3

Kissinger asked for time to become familiar with Nixon's reading habits and daily routine before advising the Agency of any recommendations he might have for changes. He did say—in what foreshadowed Nixon's style and his own, in the White House—that it had been made clear to him that the president-elect had no intention of reading anything that had not first been perused and perhaps summarized by one of his senior staff. Kissinger said he did not know what had happened to issues of the PDB already entrusted to Rose Mary Woods but that, without his prior approval, future deliveries would not reach the president-elect. Two days later, Kissinger underscored that the Agency should not provide intelligence support to anyone at the Pierre other than the president-elect and himself; Mr. Haldeman and others from the campaign might have access to classified publications after they had arrived in Washington, but they would have no need for them before that time.

Kissinger reacted none too favorably to the first few issues of the PDB that he read. At one time he expressed a preference for the CIB with its more complete text and greater detail. He complained that the prose in the PDB was too often elliptical and that the selection of topics was too random and lacked the continuity necessary for the uninitiated reader. Kissinger's points were well taken. The PDB was uniquely tailored to the needs of the outgoing administration—just as its predecessor had been shaped to the reading preferences of President Kennedy. Moreover, its authors could assume that President Johnson and his advisers were familiar with the background of the subjects covered each day. Nixon and Kissinger, however deep their background and however well read, lacked detailed familiarity with many of the ongoing, current issues addressed in the PDB.

The Agency had anticipated this situation, because it had come up in all prior transitions. OCI had already begun to devise a new version of the PDB for Nixon and his aides. Considerably expanded in length, the new brief had been circulated for comment to the DCI, DDI, and others of the Agency's principal officers. With their concurrence, it was decided to send the new PDB to New York. Kissinger approved its format and style at a meeting on the evening of 6 December. Thus, the Agency began to publish, in effect, two PDBs. The substance was the same, but the publication given to Johnson was significantly more concise than that given to Nixon.

To no one's surprise, it proved impossible to schedule daily briefings with Kissinger; he was seen frequently but unpredictably. His assistant, Lawrence Eagleburger of the Department of State, was seen every day and was notably more appreciative of the assistance he was provided.

On 9 December, Kissinger told Corscadden that he had been asked to brief the president-elect's "senior staff" and would need inputs for a 30-minute session on the Soviet intervention in Czechoslovakia, the state of US-Chinese relations, the US-USSR strategic arms balance, and the Arab-Israeli conflict. He asked especially for "tidbits, local color...things which will make these people think they're getting the inside story but which, if leaked, will not compromise or embarrass me or the president-elect or the United States Government." He promised to come to Park Avenue soon to review the drafts.

On the afternoon of 11 December, Kissinger paid his second visit to the basement suite on Park Avenue, arriving with Eagleburger. It was evident the two had discussed the format Kissinger preferred even before he had seen the materials prepared by the Agency. Eagleburger's assignment was to redraft CIA's contribution. After scanning the briefing book and posing one or two questions about France's nuclear program, Kissinger asked for still more material on Berlin, the problem of Nigeria's breakaway state of Biafra, the strategic arms balance, NATO, the Russian intervention in Czechoslovakia, and the prospects for a meeting in Warsaw of Chinese and American representatives. Kissinger delegated to Eagleburger responsibility for preparing "drafts" for his consideration the next evening in Washington, when the president-elect proposed to unveil his cabinet during a nationwide television broadcast from the Shoreham Hotel in Washington. Eagleburger worked in the basement at Park Avenue until three o'clock in the morning, returned to the Pierre for a few hours' rest, and then resumed the job of redrafting and editing the briefing Kissinger was to give.

Eagleburger's task was complicated by the fact that, except for Woods, none of the Nixon clerical staff, including Kissinger's secretary, had yet been granted special intelligence security clearances. Corscadden arranged to have Eagleburger's preliminary text typed by the Agency secretary assigned to DDI-NY and to have it taken to the Pierre. Eagleburger was then driven to LaGuardia Airport for his flight to Washington. CIA officers met Eagleburger at National Airport and took him to an improvised two-room office at the Shoreham Hotel. They remained with Eagleburger for much of the night of 12 December, calling on the Agency's analytical resources to provide substantive backup through the duty officer in the Operations Center.[8]

During his late-evening television appearance, the president-elect disclosed that he and his cabinet-to-be and top advisers would spend the following day, Friday, 13 December, in conference. One of the highlights of their all-day session would be an intelligence briefing by Kissinger. Agency officers received no direct feedback on the substantive discussions held on 13 December. They were interested that Kissinger, in their next meeting, directed that Attorney

---

[8] The CIA officers involved in this exercise were delighted later in the month when Kissinger sent Helms a letter of thanks for their extraordinary efforts.

CHAPTER 3

General-designate Mitchell receive the PDB and all other reports in which he expressed any interest. Before long, Mitchell was being briefed on a daily basis and proved to be "very helpful as a window into what Nixon wanted."[9]

In mid-December, Kissinger also directed that no national intelligence estimates were to go to the president-elect. Somewhat sharply, he explained that no one department or agency of the government would be permitted to present its views directly to Nixon to the disadvantage of any other. Corscadden pointed out that an NIE was the product of the Intelligence Community as a whole, that it was issued in the name of the United States Intelligence Board, and could not be considered "parochial." This rejoinder had no appreciable effect.

Toward the end of December, Kissinger began to meet more regularly with Corscadden and Rosen. By then Kissinger was able to read only the PDB with any regularity; DDI-NY was responsible for calling to his attention "critical items" in other publications. The balance of the 15-minute "daily" session was devoted to a capsule review of crucial international situations the new administration was likely to face during its first few months in office—"stressing the significance, not the facts"—and to discussion of whatever papers Kissinger had requested of the Agency. He directed that memorandums prepared for Nixon should contain a "statement of the problem and an assessment of its significance," as well as a summary.

Kissinger's reading of an estimate on Soviet strategic attack forces led him to ask for an oral briefing on the US-Soviet strategic balance. After consulting with his military aide, Gen. Andrew Goodpaster, and with Eagleburger, Kissinger decided that the J-3 section of the Joint Chiefs should take the lead. CIA's deputy director for science and technology and director of strategic research were also invited to participate in the briefing, which was held on Saturday, 21 December 1968. In addition to Kissinger, Mitchell, Eagleburger, and Goodpaster were present.

This was the most formal briefing Kissinger received during the transition; unfortunately, it did not go well. The J-3 team that had traveled from Washington to conduct the briefing used only the "high side" numbers regarding Soviet capabilities in their text and graphics. This prompted the CIA experts present to try to supplement the briefing and question some of its conclusions. In the discussion that followed, Kissinger, Goodpaster, and finally Mitchell asked ever-more probing questions, to the obvious chagrin of the briefers. Kissinger and Mitchell both made clear after the fact that they were not satisfied.

The issue of possible direct State Department involvement in the support process in New York arose as a result of a PDB item on coup reports in a cer-

---

[9] Richard Lehman, interview by the author in McLean, Virginia, 10 March 1993.

tain country. Kissinger asked about US contingency plans if a coup occurred. When the Agency officers replied that they were not normally privy to such contingency planning, Kissinger turned to Eagleburger and insisted that a representative of the State Department attend the morning briefing sessions. Eagleburger discussed the idea with CIA, but nothing came of it. Years later, describing how the system worked, Eagleburger recalled that he "occasionally called on the State Department to send specific written materials—I was from State, after all—but the Agency team was all we needed right there."[10]

As Kissinger became more and more active toward the end of December, his probing questions and his insatiable demands for assessments of the significance of isolated developments—even those in the low order of probability—meant that far more speculative, estimative analysis was required. This led CIA to the strategy of having its substantive officers prepare detailed backup pieces to complement the topics covered each day in the PDB. These reports provided the generalists who briefed Kissinger with additional information with which to field his queries.

Mindful of Kissinger's repeated requests for "problem papers," special briefings on emergent crises likely to confront the new administration during its first months in office, and "must reading" before Inauguration Day, the Agency in late December began appending to the PDB a series of special papers focused on critical issues. For more than 18 months, the PDB, at President Johnson's request, had carried special annexes on Vietnam and on North Vietnamese reflections on the US political scene. Kissinger decided that the annexes need not be sent to the president-elect and should not be published after Inauguration Day. The new "problem papers" were designed in part, therefore, to replace the Vietnam annexes in the New York edition of the PDB, which was by now being tailored for the incoming administration.

In the remaining days of the operation, Kissinger read the "problem papers" on such subjects as access to Berlin, the communist troop buildup in South Vietnam, the military balance between the two Koreas, and the French economic situation. For each of these subjects, CIA analysts with the appropriate expertise traveled to New York to accompany the regular briefers. Especially in the cases of Vietnam and Korea, Kissinger had numerous questions. He wanted to know the Agency's past track record in estimates on the subject at hand and pressed the analysts for "your personal opinion."

On 6 January, Kissinger, who initially became Nixon's national security advisor, turned to the question of intelligence support on Inauguration Day and

---

[10] Lawrence Eagleburger, telephone interview by the author, 1 November 1993. Other comments by Eagleburger also come from this interview.

thereafter. By this time, Nixon had expressed his intention to hold regular staff meetings with his key advisers at 9:00 a m. or 9:30 a m. each morning. Kissinger surmised that he would brief the president for 30 minutes each morning, immediately following these staff conferences. He did not want to give Nixon anything he and his National Security Council staff had not had time to mull over and was anxious to "preview" intelligence reporting each evening, with an eye to meeting the chief executive early the next day.

Kissinger proposed that the DCI change the PDB's publication time for the PDB from early morning to late afternoon, releasing the publication to him in the evening and to the president the following morning. This would, Kissinger admitted, introduce a lag of 12 hours in the reporting time, but he was not disturbed that the PDB would be less current; he was more concerned that he have time to prepare his own comments on anything the president would see.

With Inauguration Day less than a week away, the Agency proposed to introduce to the president-elect and Kissinger an entirely new PDB—redesigned to meet Kissinger's specifications for a briefing paper tailored to Nixon's preferences. The new publication was to consist of three sections—"Major Developments," "Other Important Developments," and occasional annexes—all double spaced and printed on legal-size paper bound at the top.

The first section, "Major Developments," was to be subdivided into sections on Vietnam, the Middle East, Soviet Affairs, and Europe. This was not a static listing. As developments warranted, some areas could be dropped, others added. The second section, "Other Important Developments," was intended to highlight problems which—though not yet critical—could in time engage US policy interests. The annexes were to fulfill the same role as the "problem papers" that were appended to the PDB sent to New York during the early part of January. Kissinger approved the new format on 15 January 1969.

Nixon Remains Aloof

The support operation mounted in New York constituted the most elaborate system yet designed to provide intelligence to a president-elect. Ironically, Nixon's aloof style resulted in a situation in which the Agency had no direct contact with him. Until mid-December, for example, Agency officers were uncertain whether he had been reading the PDB or the other publications deposited each morning with his secretary. On 18 December, Eagleburger confided that Nixon had informed Kissinger that Woods had been "stockpiling" the unopened envelopes containing the PDB, CIB, and memorandums on Vietnam. Nixon had asked Kissinger to send someone upstairs to retrieve these envelopes so that Kissinger could review the collection and decide whether there was anything in it that the president-elect should read. The question had been answered: Mr. Nixon had read no Agency publications during the first month of the New York operation.

Eagleburger observes that Nixon's handling of the intelligence material was a result of his management style rather than any disinterest in foreign developments. In fact, he says, "Nixon was very interested—but it was just him and Henry. That's why you didn't brief him directly." Eagleburger did not see Nixon either—briefings of the president-elect were the prerogative of Kissinger alone.

Other accounts, however, confirm more directly that Nixon's refusal to receive intelligence briefings personally stemmed from negative attitudes about the CIA that went well beyond an aloof and formal management style. Goodpaster, who worked with the transition staff to help organize the national security apparatus, remembers discussing with Nixon how the Eisenhower team had handled intelligence support. Goodpaster says Nixon "acknowledged the importance of intelligence, but also commented that when you needed it, it often wasn't there."[11]

Discouraging as it was to CIA officers not to have personal contact with Nixon, a great deal of Agency material did reach the president-elect through Kissinger's daily briefings. According to Eagleburger, "Henry made heavy use of the CIA material. I remember especially Korea and other Asian issues. Henry would go in and go over the material with Nixon; documents would be left behind that Nixon would read." Rosen remembers how pleased the Agency team was when it would occasionally receive back from Kissinger copies of the PDB initialed by Nixon, confirming that at least some of the material was being read.[12]

Throughout the two months of the operation in New York, there was some uneasiness among Agency managers because Kissinger levied heavy demands for analytic work in the president's name, and Eagleburger levied similarly heavy demands in Kissinger's name. Without direct access to the principal consumer, it was always unclear how much of this material was really wanted or read by Nixon himself. For the most part, however, it did not matter. CIA took pride in serving those who clearly would be the key foreign policy aides to the new president.

On one occasion the ambiguity about who was really speaking for whom was especially worrisome. A few days before the inauguration, Kissinger called Helms in Washington with a discouraging message. He said that the CIA

---

[11] Andrew Goodpaster, telephone interview by the author, 17 November 1993.
[12] Kenneth Rosen, interview by the author in McLean, Virginia, 22 March 1993.

CHAPTER 3

DCI Helms waits to deliver his intelligence briefing to the National Security Council.

director, following the inauguration, should brief the National Security Council on intelligence matters at the opening of its meetings but should then leave the meetings before the policy discussions. This scenario was represented by Kissinger as Nixon's idea, but Helms knew it was a ridiculous idea. Long experience had shown him that policymakers, during the course of their deliberations, frequently needed to turn to the representative of the Intelligence Community for factual updates.

Two days following the inauguration, the first NSC meeting was held. At the outset, Nixon invited the attendees to stay for lunch following the meeting. With this encouragement, Helms stayed through the meeting and lunch. And with the precedent established, he simply stayed throughout all subsequent NSC meetings. The scenario earlier raised by Kissinger never surfaced again.

CIA's direct access to Nixon was limited to the briefings by the Agency's directors—Richard Helms, James Schlesinger, and, finally, William Colby—at meetings of the National Security Council. In an interview in 1982, Helms offered a graphic account of how difficult those meetings could be, especially during the early period of the Nixon presidency:

From the very beginning of the Nixon administration, Nixon was criticizing Agency estimates, estimates done back when he was Vice

President. What he knew about estimates in the intervening years I don't know. But he would constantly, in National Security Council meetings, pick on the Agency for not having properly judged what the Soviets were going to do with various kinds of weaponry. And obviously, he was being selective, but he would make nasty remarks about this and say this obviously had to be sharpened up. The Agency had to understand it was to do a better job and so on. And I haven't the slightest doubt that Nixon's carping affected Kissinger, who after all was his national security advisor.

Despite this challenge to the estimates, the analysis and so forth of the Agency, the fundamental fact remains that if the things had not been read, if people were not paying attention to them there never would have been the challenge. So I don't think anybody needs to feel bad about a rocky period in the Agency's history. It was bound to be a rocky period with Richard Nixon as President, given the fact that he held the Agency responsible for his defeat in 1960. And he never forgot that and he had a barb out for the Agency all the time because he really believed, and I think he believes to this day, that that "Missile Gap" question was the responsibility of the Agency and that it did him in.[13]

When he was elected president in 1968, Nixon could hardly have imagined how US collection capabilities had improved since the end of his term as vice president eight years before. At the time he had left that office, several years of U-2 flights had given the United States an invaluable look at the Soviet Union. But the flights had been intermittent and covered only a portion of Soviet territory. As a result, the United States in 1960 was still dealing in conjecture, albeit informed conjecture, about possible deployed Soviet strategic systems. In 1968 it was dealing in facts. It was never clear that the cynical president appreciated what had changed. As the years passed, the NSC forum was less and less fruitful. Colby remembers that "Nixon didn't operate well in meetings—he liked to make decisions on the basis of written material. When you did brief him on something, he looked like his mind was on other things—he may have been thinking about Watergate, I guess."[14] Colby wrote in his memoirs that none of Nixon's three DCI's saw him outside formal or ceremonial meetings. "I remember only one private conversation with him; it occurred when he phoned to ask what was happening in China and I provided a quick summary off the top of my head."[15]

---

[13] Richard Helms, interview by R. Jack Smith, Washington, DC, 21 April 1982.

[14] William Colby, interview by the author in Washington, DC, 7 April 1993. Unless otherwise noted, subsequent comments by Colby also come from this interview.

CHAPTER 3

Throughout the Nixon presidency, a courier delivered the PDB to Kissinger's office. Each day Kissinger delivered to the president a package of material that included the PDB along with material from the State Department, the White House Situation Room, the Joint Chiefs, and others. Nixon would keep the material on his desk, reading it at his convenience throughout the day. Feedback to the Agency typically was provided by Kissinger directly to the DCI.

A Closer Relationship With Ford[16]

In the late spring of 1974, when it was becoming apparent that Nixon would not survive the Watergate scandal, the DCI saw a responsibility and an opportunity.[17] William Colby, who had been appointed director in September 1973, decided that CIA should help the new vice president, Gerald Ford, prepare for his probable elevation to the presidency. Colby's initiative was to afford CIA unprecedented direct and daily access to the resident when Ford moved into the Oval Office.

Colby modestly recounts that his decision to provide full intelligence support to Ford "had as much to do with good preparation in case something happened to the president—any president—as it did with Nixon's problems with Watergate." Colby remembers thinking at the time, "We should get the PDB to the Vice President so that he would know everything the President knew. We didn't want another situation like when Truman was unaware of the Manhattan project."

Whatever his mix of motives, Colby invited the vice president to visit CIA Headquarters. Ford came, on 12 June 1974, and was given wide-ranging briefings on intelligence operations and assessments. In response to Ford's request, Colby agreed to send him the PDB, in addition to the *National Intelligence Daily* (NID) he had been receiving. An Agency current intelligence specialist, David Peterson, was assigned to provide continuing intelligence support to the vice president.

---

[15] William Colby and Peter Forbath, *Honorable Men My Life in the CIA* (New York: Simon and Schuster, 1978), 373.

[16] The material that follows regarding the Agency's support of President Ford was in large part drafted by David A. Peterson.

[17] In the election campaign of 1972, there had been no special intelligence briefings. Nixon, as the incumbent president, continued to receive the PDB. His Democratic opponent, Senator George McGovern, at one point had agreed (against the counsel of his advisers) to receive an intelligence briefing from Kissinger. The CIA was to follow up with regular briefings. Unfortunately, the political crisis involving McGovern's running mate, Senator Thomas Eagleton, forced the cancellation of the Kissinger briefing, and it proved impossible to reschedule either that briefing or the others that were to follow.

Ford accepted a suggestion that the PDB be brought to him directly, acknowledging that this would be the most secure way to receive the sensitive document. He specified that he would like to see it early each morning, preferably as his first appointment. Beginning 1 July that became the regular routine, one that was altered only occasionally by such diversions as a vice-presidential breakfast with the president or a speaking engagement out of town. On a few occasions Ford was seen at his Alexandria home before he flew off to keep such an engagement. Always a gracious host, he brewed and served instant coffee.

Ford came to the vice-presidency an informed consumer of the products of the Intelligence Community. He notes that he "had become familiar with CIA first as a member of the Intelligence subcommittee on Appropriations; later in other roles, including Minority Leader. I knew Colby from my days in Congress." This familiarity, particularly with Colby personally, was to provide the Agency at least a temporary buffer in some difficult times to come.[18]

When Nixon resigned and Ford was sworn in as president on 9 August 1974, Agency officers were uncertain whether the briefings would continue. It seemed probable that Kissinger would intervene and terminate the sessions, substituting some other arrangement. (He was described later as "furious" when he learned of the CIA briefing routine, of which he had not been informed.) The uncertainty was short lived; that evening Ford passed the word that he wanted his usual briefing the next morning at the White House.

On Saturday morning, 10 August, Ford seemed as awed as Peterson when he entered the Oval Office to begin his first full day as chief executive. Gen. Alexander Haig, who was to carry on as chief of the White House staff, was also present. The walls and furniture in the Office were bare following the removal of Nixon's pictures and possessions. The famous desk had only a telephone console on it, prompting the new president to tell Haig that he would rely on him to help keep the desk uncluttered.

To Peterson's surprise, in view of Haig's presence, the president first asked for his intelligence briefing. He was given a status report on a sensitive operation that interested him, after which he read the PDB, punctuating his perusal with a couple of questions.

During that first session, Ford asked Haig for his views on how the intelligence briefing should fit into the daily presidential schedule. Haig replied that Nixon had received the PDB along with several other reports, cables, and overnight summaries to read as time permitted during the day. The general

---

[18] Gerald Ford, interview by the author in Beaver Creek, Colorado, 8 September 1993. Unless otherwise indicated, all observations by Ford come from this interview.

CHAPTER 3

went on to say, however, that an early daily intelligence briefing was a better idea. Ford agreed, expressing satisfaction with the routine that had been established and observing that such an arrangement would help prepare him for a subsequent daily meeting with Kissinger. The new president evidently felt at some disadvantage in discussing foreign affairs with his secretary of state and wanted as much advance support as he could get. Accordingly, the CIA briefer would continue to be the president's first appointment each morning.

Peterson's initial session in the Oval Office ended on a mildly embarrassing note. He exited the room through the nearest door—only to find himself at a dead end. A second door, which he later learned led to a smaller, more private office for the president, was locked, trapping him in the passageway. The presidential lavatory was on one side opposite a Pullman kitchen where stewards prepared refreshments. It was obvious that unless he was prepared to stay indefinitely, he would have to reenter the Oval Office, where the president and Haig were still conferring. Peterson knocked, opened the door with apologies and sheepishly explained his predicament. The president laughed and professed that he didn't yet know his way around the West Wing very well either. He directed Peterson out another door to the hallway. The observant briefer noticed that this door had no frame and was papered to blend with the wall.

For two days during the first week of the Ford presidency, Peterson met alone with the president each morning. On the third morning, Gen. Brent Scowcroft, then Kissinger's assistant as national security advisor, indicated that henceforth he would accompany Peterson. Although this arrangement probably was prompted, in part, by Kissinger's desire to know what CIA was telling the president, Scowcroft's presence undoubtedly enhanced the value of the session for Mr. Ford. The president would raise questions about the policy implications of the intelligence, and Scowcroft would either provide the answers or undertake to obtain an early assessment. It soon became evident that no previous president had derived such prompt benefit from the Agency's current intelligence reports.

The daily contact with Ford facilitated CIA's ability to respond to his intelligence needs. Immediately after each briefing session, Peterson would report via secure telephone to his immediate boss, the director of the Office of Current Intelligence, who would relay any presidential queries, messages, or comments to the DCI's daily staff meeting at 9:00 a.m. With that kind of communication, the director and his senior aides could get rapid feedback, and the president's needs could promptly be served.

A further advantage of the direct contact involved the security of the PDB. By carrying it away after the president read it, CIA was able to maintain complete control of his copy of the publication. Coupled with the more stringent controls that were applied to a second copy provided Scowcroft, which he later showed to Kissinger, CIA was able to terminate the wide exposure that the PDB had had among members of the White House and National Security Council staffs during the Nixon presidency.

Once it was clear that the Agency had established a secure and expeditious channel for providing sensitive material directly to the president, the Agency's director and the deputy director for operations granted permission to publish articles drawn from the Agency's most protected sources. Occasionally operational activities also were reported. Highly sensitive intercepted messages were included on a regular basis for the first time. To limit access to such compartmented material even within the Agency, it was typed on loose pages that were stapled into the copies for the president and Kissinger.

Discussing Operations and Intelligence

One tightly held operation was not covered in the PDB, but Ford was provided an oral account of its status each morning while it was in progress. That operation, the *Glomar Explorer* project, was an intricate undertaking to raise a Soviet ballistic missile submarine that had sunk in the Pacific. In his memoirs, Ford wrote of the deliberations that occurred "on the second morning of my Presidency, [when] Kissinger, Scowcroft, Schlesinger, and CIA Director William Colby came to the Oval Office to advise me that *Glomar Explorer* was on station and ready to drop the claws."[19]

Two decades after the event, the former president remembered well his apprehensions about the operation: "I did feel the *Glomar* action was a gamble. We didn't know what the Soviets would do. But I was convinced we had to take the risk, in terms of what we stood to gain."

Fortunately, Ford had been briefed on the *Glomar* project in detail during his visit to CIA as vice president two months earlier. Like Kennedy on the Bay of Pigs operation, Ford had less time than he would have liked to become familiar with the plans. Unlike the Cuban undertaking, however, the operation in the Pacific did not result in a challenge to a new president. The Soviets, unaware of their lost vessel's location, watched the "deep-sea mining" operation with interest, but did not attempt to thwart it.

There is no doubt that the drama associated with the *Glomar* endeavor and Ford's keen interest in it helped to certify for him the utility of the daily briefing sessions. Later, however, it was Peterson's unhappy lot to inform the pres-

---

[19] Gerald Ford, *A Time to Heal* (New York: Harper and Row, 1979), 135–36.

CHAPTER 3

ident that an accident during the lifting operation had caused the fragile hulk to break apart, resulting in the loss of a critical portion of the submarine.

An ancillary benefit from these daily meetings with Ford was the closer cooperation that developed between the PDB staff and the White House Situation Room, which provides round-the-clock support to the president on foreign developments and national security affairs. At Scowcroft's request, after each briefing session the Agency representative would give an account of the meeting to Situation Room personnel so they could get a better insight on the president's interests and concerns. In addition, CIA's PDB staff began to inform them each evening of the topics to be covered in the PDB the following morning so they would not duplicate coverage of any current development in their own morning summary for the president.[20]

The president soon became acutely conscious that CIA's reporting was problem oriented. Told on one occasion that the Agency did not have much to tell him that day, he replied that he wasn't disappointed: "When there is more to report, that usually means you have more bad news."

Sometimes the bad news was political and preceded the Agency's briefer into the Oval Office. One such occasion came in March 1975, the day after the DCI had testified before the Senate Foreign Relations Committee on the situation in Cambodia, where the Lon Nol regime was under heavy attack by Khmer Rouge forces. The president's first words that morning were that he was unhappy about "what your boss said on the Hill yesterday." He had read an account of the director's testimony in the *Washington Post*, which quoted Colby as saying the Lon Nol regime would have little chance to survive even with the supplemental US aid the president had requested from Congress. Scowcroft helpfully pointed out that the advance text of the director's statement did not include any such remark. It turned out the DCI's response to a question from the committee had been quoted out of context.

The eventual success of the Khmer Rouge and the forced US withdrawal from Vietnam soon led to the *Mayaguez* affair. The seizure of the US-owned container ship by the communist forces occurred in the early hours (Washington time) of 12 May 1975. Before the CIA briefer left for the White House, the Agency's Operations Center armed him with a map and the latest information on the incident, still in progress, including messages sent a short time earlier by the ship's radioman as Khmer Rouge troops were boarding the vessel.

---

[20] One morning Ford's dog, Liberty, was in the Oval Office. While the president read the PDB, the friendly and handsome golden retriever padded back and forth between Scowcroft and Peterson. All was well until her wagging tail struck the president's nearby pipe rack. The clatter of pipes and other smoking paraphernalia brought swift presidential retribution; Liberty was banished, never again to appear during a PDB meeting.

The president was distressed to receive this news, but by the time Kissinger got to him on the telephone during the PDB session Ford had absorbed the facts and had given some thought to the implications. Plans for the subsequent rescue operation began to formulate during that conversation with Kissinger. Ford recalls that, in the end, the *Mayaguez* incident "gave us a welcome opportunity to show that we were not going to be nibbled at by our enemies."

The morning briefing session was not confined solely to current intelligence. Selected national intelligence estimates and other memorandums occasionally were provided as well. The most timely and effective example of this occurred shortly before Ford's meeting with Soviet President Leonid Brezhnev at Vladivostok in November 1974. The day before the president's departure, the PDB carried the key judgments of the annual estimate of Soviet strategic forces, and the briefer emphasized the underlying rationale and principal conclusions of the study. A copy of the complete NIE with its voluminous annexes was given to him to take along on the trip. The Agency also had put together a 10-minute film with color footage of Brezhnev in an informal setting that was shown to Ford in the cabinet room before his departure.

Events had pressed Ford to decide very quickly in his presidency whether to follow through with Nixon's commitment to the Vladivostok meeting. As a result, he probably studied the intelligence reporting on this issue as closely as any. The president recalls, "[Although] I had only a few months, I felt fully prepared to discuss the substantive issues as a result of the briefings I had received in Congress, as Vice President, and then as President."

In 1993, Ford remembered clearly the distrust of Agency analysis he had felt during his early years in Congress, when Allen Dulles and others seemed to be exaggerating the Soviet threat. He claimed to have had no similar reaction to the Agency's work during his own brief presidency but offered the cautious assessment that "in part it may have been that by then I had a pretty good understanding of my own of what the situation in the USSR was all about."

Ford did not receive his intelligence material exclusively through the PDB. He used NSC meetings much more effectively than his predecessor; indeed, he probably used them more effectively than any president since Eisenhower. The NSC sessions almost always began with an intelligence update. Colby remembers that Ford, unlike Nixon, "always paid attention and was engaged. He was well informed."

Ford, too, remembers the formal NSC meetings as useful. In thinking back on those sessions, he remarked, "On substantive performance, I thought very highly of Bill Colby. I saw him primarily at the NSC. He always briefed, for example on Vietnam as we were forced to withdraw, on the *Mayaguez* seizure by the Cambodians, and on SALT."

CHAPTER 3

President Gerald Ford, flanked by Secretary of State Kissinger and Defense Secretary Schlesinger, presides over an NSC meeting. DCI Colby is seated at the far left.

Outside the formal NSC structure, however, Colby had few contacts with Ford and, thus, little direct personal knowledge of the issues the president was concentrating on at a given time and his intelligence needs. Colby described the situation this way: "My own reluctance to push into the Oval Office unless I was invited or had something that I thought demanded my personal presence, combined with a lively awareness of the probable reaction if I had tried to elbow past Henry Kissinger, kept me from pressing for personal access to either Nixon or Ford. In retrospect, I consider this one of the errors I made as Director, although I am not sure how I could have done any differently."[21]

Ford makes the same point: "The Sunday when Colby came to my office to resign was probably the first time I met with him one-on-one. I don't remember ever telephoning him directly for information."

Political Problems Undermine the Briefing Process

Regrettably, the domestic political problems the CIA created for Ford before long began to outweigh the good will built up by the Agency's substantive sup-

---

[21] Colby, *Honorable Men*, 373–74.

port. Within months of Ford's accession to the presidency, the Agency, and then the White House, were buffeted by public accounts of CIA's past involvement in domestic spying, feckless preparations for possible assassinations, and covert action undertakings in Chile. As the Rockefeller Commission and the Church and Pike Committees exposed more and more information about the Agency's real and imagined misdeeds, the director's standing with Ford weakened. Colby was not responsible for the sins of the past and, in fact, had ordered some controversial programs halted, but his handling of the issues—in particular, his failure to forewarn the White House of breaking embarrassments—caused Ford and Kissinger to lose confidence in him.

Ford recalls that in 1975 he "talked with Colby, although not regularly, about the difficulties the Agency was having with the Church and Pike Committees. In addition to the real problems, the committees were up to some political mischiefmaking. We went through a terrible time. We just needed a fresh start with the Congress."

Intended or not, the system of PDB briefings of the president became a casualty of the shakeup Ford instituted on 3 November 1975 among his senior national security officers. Colby and Secretary of Defense James Schlesinger were replaced, respectively, by Ambassador George Bush and Donald Rumsfeld, until then the president's White House chief of staff. Scowcroft was elevated to assistant to the president for national security affairs, the position Kissinger had retained with Scowcroft as his deputy, after assuming stewardship of the Department of State.

Concerning the change in procedures that accompanied the personnel shifts, Ford recalls:

The result was we set up a better system where I had an oral presentation [of information available from all agencies] *by Brent* [Scowcroft]. *Dave Peterson had been very helpful, but his separate sessions were no longer necessary. Scowcroft had more time for the daily briefs than Henry had. Kissinger had been wearing two hats and didn't have time to handle the morning meetings properly. I took away his second hat. Henry was not happy about that, but he understood.*

Ford maintains that under the new procedures he "continued to be very conscientious about reading the PDB [and] interested in the information." CIA, no longer present, lost the benefit of the president's immediate reaction to each PDB. Scowcroft saw the president often, but he was not normally present when the president read the PDB and, therefore, had little to pass on in the way of the president's views and questions relating to the intelligence he was receiving. As a consequence, the PDB could no longer be tailored as well to suit Ford's personal needs.

CHAPTER 3

Former Ambassador George H.W. Bush receives congratulations from out-going DCI Colby and President Ford after his swearing in at the CIA Headquarters Auditorium.

There was no indication that Ford felt deprived after the daily PDB sessions ended. At the CIA, however, the experience of 14 months of daily meetings with the president, contrasted with the succeeding months without those meetings, confirmed vividly the stark truth that there is no substitute for direct access to the president.

George Bush returned from China to become DCI in January 1976. He had been a colleague of Ford's in Congress and was untainted by the Agency's image problems. Even in these improved circumstances, however, he found it necessary to rely primarily on the written PDB and on briefing opportunities at NSC meetings to keep the president informed. Even he had relatively few one-on-one meetings with the president. For his part, Ford remembers that there was "no material change" in his relationship with Bush (compared with Colby) as far as the presentation of substantive intelligence was concerned.

Ironically, it would not be until Bush himself was in the Oval Office that CIA would again establish with a president a working relationship as fruitful as the one it had enjoyed during the first half of the Ford presidency.

⌘ ⌘ ⌘

CHAPTER 4

IN-DEPTH DISCUSSIONS WITH CARTER

In late June 1976, Georgia Governor Jimmy Carter distinguished himself in the eyes of CIA officials by becoming the first presidential hopeful to request intelligence briefings even before receiving his party's nomination. Carter's request, which was directed to President Ford, prompted discussions involving the president, CIA Director George Bush, and National Security Advisor Brent Scowcroft about who should provide such briefings and when they should be made available to the candidate. Bush recommended to Ford that as a first step he, Bush, should meet with Carter to discuss the ground rules and arrange for follow-on briefings, which would be delivered by intelligence professionals. The ever-cautious Scowcroft recommended instead that all briefings should be given by the DCI, accompanied and supported by the appropriate national intelligence officers (NIOs), who were the Intelligence Community's senior substantive experts.

These deliberations resulted in a decision by Ford that Bush should meet with Carter to discuss the parameters and arrangements for the provision of intelligence support. Such a session could be arranged before the nomination. Following the nomination, NIOs would provide Carter in-depth intelligence briefings. The president insisted that the DCI chair the sessions even though he would not necessarily be obliged to give the briefings himself.

Pursuant to the president's instructions, Bush contacted Carter to arrange a meeting. The two met on 5 July in Hershey, Pennsylvania, where Carter was attending a meeting of Democratic governors. In the course of the meeting, the director informed Carter that the president had asked him to preside over the briefings that would follow. Bush introduced to Carter one senior Agency officer, Deputy to the DCI for National Intelligence Richard Lehman, noting that he would be the action officer in charge of preparing the briefings that would follow in Plains, Georgia. They would begin after the Democratic convention the next week. Carter, in turn, indicated that he would welcome detailed discussions of selected subjects such as Soviet strategic programs. He designated his "issues man," Stuart Eizenstat, to be his contact and proposed to receive briefings every week to 10 days.

CHAPTER 4

Although the initial meeting was to have been limited to a discussion of the arrangements for future briefings, Lehman's account noted that the conversation "ranged over virtually the entire field of intelligence."[1] Carter was briefed on a number of current developments abroad and was shown a variety of intelligence materials and publications, including satellite photographs. Lehman reported that the governor asked a great many questions "ranging from the future of Rhodesia to morale in the Agency."

In thinking back to that pre-nomination meeting with the DCI in Pennsylvania, Carter remembered, "I was very honored to have President [then DCI] Bush come to brief me. President Ford offered every assistance. I hardly knew him and had never been in the Oval Office."[2]

In soliciting the CIA briefings, Carter was already displaying the interest in detail that was to be a mark of his presidency. The day following his meeting with Bush in Pennsylvania, Carter told newsmen that he would receive "a six-hour briefing" shortly after the Democratic nomination. On several subsequent occasions during the campaign, the governor expressed the hope that by being fully informed he could avoid committing himself to positions that might later embarrass him as a candidate or as president. Asked in 1993 about his motives in arranging what became a series of immensely time-consuming sessions, Carter replied, "I wanted the long briefings in Plains. I wanted particularly not to make any inadvertent mistake that would complicate things for President Ford on SALT or later for me." Just prior to the presidential debates, Carter remembers, "I wanted to know what was going on."

Extended Preelection Briefings

When the time came in late July to meet Carter in Plains, Agency officers discovered that the first challenge was to get there. CIA's director in 1976 normally used a Gulfstream aircraft for his travel within the United States. Plains had a 4,400-foot sod airstrip that was not suitable for Gulfstream operations. The manager of the airfield at Americus, Georgia, some 10 miles from Plains, informed the Agency aircrew that Gulfstream aircraft had occasionally used his 4,200-foot paved airstrip, but that they should be aware there was no kerosene fuel available at the facility. Moreover, the airfield at Americus had no control tower and, thus, was suitable for operation only in daylight hours. On discovering that the nearest all-weather facility with an instrument landing

---

[1] Richard Lehman, "Meeting with Governor Carter," memorandum for the record, 6 July 1976.
[2] Jimmy Carter, interview by the author in Atlanta, Georgia, 23 June 1993. Unless otherwise indicated, subsequent quotations from Carter come from this interview.

system was at Albany, some 45 miles from Plains, Agency officials sought help from the US military.

A few phone calls resulted in arrangements whereby Bush and his party would travel from Washington, DC, directly to Lawson Army Airfield at Fort Benning, Georgia. At Fort Benning, they were told, the director would be transferred to a US Army Bell helicopter for a 30-minute flight to Peterson Field at Plains. The Agency aircrew that normally flew the DCI was puzzled that the manuals made no mention of Peterson Field. Another call revealed that it was not exactly Peterson Field; rather, it was Peterson's field, Peterson being a farmer who owned land at the edge of Plains.

In the planning stages of the first visit, Lehman and Carter's press secretary, Jody Powell, agreed that they should minimize press attention to the director's visit. This was intended to reinforce the nonpolitical nature of the briefings, Powell having assured CIA that the governor wanted to avoid any appearance of taking political advantage of the Agency briefing. However, with the growing number of reporters in Plains desperate for news and with the expected helicopter arrival, it became obvious that the visit would not go unnoticed. The press was, therefore, informed of the time and place of the director's arrival. Bush talked briefly with reporters after disembarking from the helicopter, enabling the rest of the party to unload the briefing materials and travel the short distance to Carter's home. Despite the original intentions of the planners, Lehman remembers that the visit "could not possibly have been more conspicuous."[3]

The first CIA session was highly publicized for another reason as well—it was sandwiched into a week filled with other high-level briefings of the nominee. The Agency's presentation occurred on Wednesday, 28 July, preceded by a discussion of defense issues that lasted most of the day Monday, and a session with leading economists on Tuesday. Thursday was dedicated to a foreign policy presentation by Secretary of State Henry Kissinger. Commenting on this series of briefings in 1993, Carter remembered especially "the value of Secretary Kissinger's whole day of briefings."

Carter himself drew added press attention to the Agency briefing by discussing it at some length with reporters the day before. On Tuesday the governor informed newsmen that he had asked the CIA "to brief him on confidential information concerning Lebanon and the Middle East, Rhodesia, South Africa, and South Korea, plus the interrelationships between the United States, the Soviet Union, and China."[4] He piqued reporters' interest by volunteering that

---

[3] Richard Lehman, interview by the author in McLean, Virginia, 10 March 1993. Unless otherwise indicated, subsequent comments are also from this interview.

CHAPTER 4

he had not decided whether, if he were elected president, he would replace Bush as CIA director. The governor noted that Bush had previously been involved in Republican politics but added that he had "brought the CIA a good background as former UN ambassador and US representative to China." Carter added his choice for CIA head would be a person "with stature with the American people, whose integrity was beyond doubt and with some analytic ability."

CIA's session with Carter began about 1:00 p.m. and continued without interruption for a full six hours, adjourning about 7:00 p.m.[5] The session included a current intelligence review of world trouble spots: Lebanon, Iraqi-Syrian relations, strains between Egypt and Libya, the Taiwan Straits, Rhodesia, the Cuban presence in Angola, and developments in Uganda. These subjects were covered in approximately 30 minutes. The bulk of the afternoon was devoted to a discussion of Soviet strategic programs and the status of the SALT talks.

Bush made some brief introductory comments, but most of the briefing was delivered by two Agency experts in strategic systems, Howard Stoertz and Ray McCrory. The two provided a detailed description of Soviet forces for intercontinental nuclear attack and for nuclear attack on the Eurasian periphery. Their presentation focused also on Soviet strategic defense capabilities and US estimates of long-term prospects for the strategic balance. An ensuing discussion of SALT compliance issues was very detailed; it included a description of how monitoring was carried out and how the process worked within the US government for determining whether a violation had occurred. Participants from the Agency were surprised that the discussion of strategic issues went on so long that they were forced to jettison plans to discuss Soviet political developments, foreign policy, and the state of the Soviet economy.

Carter was a very careful and interested listener and an active participant. All who were present remember that he asked a great many questions, often in minute detail. He was especially interested in the nature of the Intelligence Community's evidence, including satellite photography of deployed Soviet weapons. The governor asked detailed questions about the obligations of the USSR and the United States under the interim agreement and about the truth of the charges being made in the press that the Soviets were violating SALT I understandings.

Carter's running mate, Senator Walter "Fritz" Mondale, also attended the briefing. He was especially interested in the role and knowledge of the Con-

---

[4] Associated Press, 28 July 1976.
[5] Richard Lehman, "First Briefing of Governor Carter," memorandum for the record, 29 July 1976.

gress in arms control issues. He wanted to understand precisely whether the Soviets were justified in any of their charges that the United States had violated the SALT I agreement. Mondale also was well informed about and sensitive to the specific issue of whether Minuteman missile shelters constituted a violation of the interim agreement.

A different set of questions from Mondale caused the CIA director some concern because they raised sensitive policy issues. In some cases his queries related to ongoing CIA relationships with foreign liaison services or the Agency's operations. Lehman noted in a memorandum for the record some days after the July briefing that he had informed Carter aide Eizenstat that the DCI had been uncomfortable with some of Mondale's questions, particularly those concerning covert action.[6] Lehman explained that the director felt that answering these questions would go beyond the guidelines set by President Ford. He underscored that the DCI hoped to avoid being put in the position of having to refuse to answer certain questions.

Carter, Mondale, and Eizenstat left with Agency officers a number of factual questions that there had not been time to discuss during the briefing. Lehman provided Eizenstat answers to some of these questions by telephone; others were simply lost in the press of business. One matter about which Carter asked showed he had carefully studied the foreign policy issues in which John Kennedy had become involved during his candidacy some 16 years earlier. That was Taiwan and the offshore islands. Lehman consulted in Washington before articulating precisely for the governor what the US commitment was to defending Quemoy, Matsu, and certain other territories. In fact, this issue, which had been so important in the 1960 campaign, did not play a significant role in 1976.

Agency officers were pleased when Eizenstat informed Lehman on 29 July, the day following the initial session, that Carter had been "extremely pleased with the briefings." In response to Lehman's question, Eizenstat indicated the governor had no suggestions for any changes in the format, the level of detail, or the length of the briefings, having described them as just right. Senior Agency officers had been anxious, unable to believe that Carter really wanted to sit through six hours of nonstop briefings. The participants had been impressed not only with the governor's endurance and interest but with the hospitality he and Mrs. Carter had shown them. They were particularly touched that Mrs. Carter brought in a bowl of peaches in the late afternoon, a welcome diversion after several hours of briefings.

---

[6] Richard Lehman, "Conversation with Stuart Eizenstat," memorandum for the record, 3 August 1976.

CHAPTER 4

The second major preelection briefing of Carter took place in Plains two weeks later on 12 August. At least in the memory of one working-level officer who took part, the most dramatic and memorable moment occurred not during the session with Carter himself but during the helicopter flight from Fort Benning to Plains. Asked if he had had a difficult flight, he remembered, "Not at all. It was fine. The problem was that during the short flight I realized I had left my briefing materials back in the Operations Center at Headquarters. It was your worst nightmare, going with the director to brief the man who may be the next president and forgetting your materials."

The rattled briefers were further shaken when they arrived. With some time to spare before they were due at Carter's home, they visited the Carter campaign headquarters where they were introduced to the governor's mother, Lillian Carter. Upon meeting the CIA officers, Mrs. Carter volunteered that she understood that "Jimmy was going to clear the government of all vestiges of Republicans, including CIA Director Bush." Her plainspoken prediction reflected progressively more pointed comments the candidate had been making to the press about the possibility of replacing key government officials, including Bush.

Bush himself was realistic and outwardly relaxed about the likelihood that he would be replaced, joking about it with his CIA colleagues. The latter were more apprehensive about the prospect that, if their boss were replaced, the job would be "politicized." They were acutely aware that the four previous presidents had not appointed a new DCI when they came into office. The last such occasion had been Eisenhower's appointment of Allen Dulles 24 years earlier.

Having learned in the first session that Carter was likely to ask numerous and detailed questions, Bush brought eight CIA officers with him to the second briefing to ensure that the team could handle any subject the governor might raise. Carter again asked that Mondale be present and this time also included Eizenstat and Mondale's foreign policy aide, David Aaron. Aaron's inclusion, at Carter's request, helped relieve an awkward situation. Aaron had shown up at the first session but had not been permitted to attend, as his role was unclear. In time, he was to become the deputy national security advisor. Zbigniew Brzezinski had not yet been named national security advisor and did not attend any of the briefing sessions.

The substantive issues discussed during the second session related primarily to the status of Soviet conventional forces and to developments in China. In addition, an overview of current developments was provided that focused on Greek-Turkish tensions, strains between Egypt and Libya, a recent Rhodesian raid into Mozambique, the problems of Somalia and Djibouti, a recent exchange of fire across the Demilitarized Zone in Korea, and civil strife in Lebanon. There was also considerable discussion, as at the first briefing, of Soviet strategic programs and arms control negotiating issues. The status of Soviet Backfire bomber and SS-X-20 missile programs was carefully reviewed.[7]

Obviously feeling more relaxed than he had in the earlier session, Bush led off this second exchange with some more expansive general comments and introductions of the other participants. Throughout the discussions he made occasional comments, using to advantage his experience as US representative in Beijing. Carter was again a very active participant with so many questions and comments that the briefers were unable to cover the requested topics, even though the session lasted from 11:00 a m. until almost 5:00 p m.

One of the participants remembers, "I was impressed with Carter. He was a very, very quick study, able to digest immediately everything we gave him—fact after fact. He seemed to have a photographic memory and would often repeat back to us the points we had made to be absolutely sure that he understood. He used his very detailed questions to be certain he understood the nuances, which he described with precision when he rephrased the points we had made."[8] The CIA participants, arrayed in a circle in Carter's family room, watched with fascination as the governor, from his corner of the room, would spin the globe next to his chair as if to allow it to determine the country about which he would ask next. By the time the afternoon was over they felt they had covered the world.

In addition to pleasing his visitors with his obvious interest in the substance of their business, Carter was a more relaxed host during the second session. He adjourned the proceedings for an hour or so while Mrs. Carter served lunch. The participants, during the break, spelled one another playing with Amy Carter and her cat on the couch.

Toward the end of the briefing, Mondale made an unsolicited contribution that greatly pleased the Agency officers in attendance. In remarks seemingly directed both to Carter and Bush, Mondale expressed his respect for the Agency. He said CIA had reformed itself completely over the last two years, underscoring that this was a remarkable achievement for any government organization. Mondale was referring, of course, to the efforts CIA Directors Colby and Bush had undertaken in the wake of the revelations of CIA misdeeds that had been so widely publicized in the early 1970s. The senator's background enabled him also to make some perceptive and useful comments about the nature of congressional review of the Intelligence Community and its budget.

---

[7] Richard Lehman, "Briefing of Governor Carter, 12 August 1976," memorandum for the record, 16 August 1976.
[8] Wayne Wolfe, interview by the author in McLean, Virginia, 13 December 1993.

CHAPTER 4

Like candidates before and after them, Carter and Mondale were shown and took an interest in certain unique CIA products. They were each given copies of an Agency compilation of foreign, particularly Soviet, press commentary on their candidacies. Carter was interested in studying some sample satellite photography showing much of southwest Georgia. The governor seemed to find tracking the geography of his home region a useful technique for understanding the capabilities of the imaging system.

Reflecting the governor's insatiable interests, the Carter team had provided CIA in advance of the briefing a list of 44 specific questions that they hoped could be answered. A few of the questions raised delicate policy and operational issues, just as Mondale's questions had done two weeks earlier. Because the president had not approved the Agency's discussion of these matters before the election, the director reiterated the ground rules at the outset of the briefing.

In fact, by the time the group turned to the list of 44 questions late in the afternoon, time was running out and the awkward issue of political delicacy did not have to be faced directly. In his memorandum for the record, Lehman recorded that he was "able to give very brief, often one-sentence answers…this moved so fast that our listeners were unable to check our replies against their list of questions, probably a highly desirable thing." As Lehman's comment implied, at the time it seemed sensible simply to stick to the essential facts and avoid addressing the complicated policy issues, but the matter was not that simple and did not go away.

Not only did the problem persist, it returned within a week, precipitated by events in Korea. On 18 August a donnybrook over the removal of a tree from the Demilitarized Zone dramatically raised tensions on the Peninsula. In the days following that incident, Carter received a number of questions from the press regarding his position on Korea and asked Eizenstat to call Lehman and request a briefing on the situation. The available facts were fairly straightforward, and it was decided that a formal briefing was unnecessary. A senior Agency analyst, John Whitman, briefed Eizenstat by telephone regarding developments in North Korea and the Chinese and Soviet reactions.

Understandably in the circumstances, Eizenstat was interested also in the status of US forces and in the US reaction to the heightened tensions but was reminded that the president's guidelines provided that the Agency should brief only on foreign developments and not on US policy or actions. Eizenstat was asked if he had channels to the Departments of State and Defense that he could use to acquire the information that Carter needed. On hearing that such channels did not exist, Whitman suggested that he or Carter might wish to contact Scowcroft. Eizenstat responded that the governor did not want to approach Scowcroft "lest he [Carter] become enmeshed."

Whitman recorded in a memorandum for the record that Eizenstat appreciated the prompt telephone update on Korea and that their exchange on the ground rules of CIA's liaison with the Carter team was an amiable one.[9] Whitman also recorded: "It is nevertheless clear that, since we are their only official channel to the Executive Branch, dicey moments may occur in the future." In many similar circumstances over the years, CIA was to be the only authorized ongoing link between a sitting administration and a presidential candidate or president-elect of the other party. Agency officers have cherished such opportunities, in part, for their implicit acknowledgment that CIA can be trusted to provide information in a nonpolitical manner. At the same time, however, they have often had concerns about whether this exclusive system might not unduly limit an incoming administration.

Before the end of August 1976, separate briefings were also given the two vice-presidential candidates. On 23 August, Bush and seven senior Agency experts briefed Ford's running mate, Senator Robert Dole, in a comprehensive session that covered Soviet strategic programs and conventional forces. The group also informed Dole of current intelligence related to the Korea crisis, tensions between Egypt and Libya, and developments in South Africa and Rhodesia. The senator's questions related primarily to the military strengths of the two sides in Korea.[10]

On 24 August, Whitman provided a briefing to Mondale and Aaron that focused primarily on Soviet ICBM dismantling and destruction. He also covered developments in Korea and answered a number of questions from the senator related to US satellite reconnaissance capabilities. On this occasion, Aaron raised with Whitman the possibility of the Agency providing another briefing along the lines of those given in Plains, this time focusing on the Middle East and southern Africa. Given Carter's heavy schedule, the two discussed the possibility of providing such a briefing in Washington to Mondale, Aaron, and Eizenstat,[11] but there was no time available in the campaign schedule and the Carter-Mondale team received no further intelligence briefings until after the election on 3 November.

In the 1976 campaign there were three 90-minute debates between candidates Ford and Carter. The resumption of debates during a presidential cam-

---

[9] John Whitman, "Inquiry from Governor Carter on Korea," memorandum for the record, 20 August 1976.
[10] John Whitman, "Briefing of Senator Dole," memorandum for the record, 24 August 1976.
[11] John Whitman, "Conversation with Senator Mondale," memorandum for the record, 24 August 1976.

CHAPTER 4

paign after a 16-year hiatus raised concerns in the minds of senior Agency executives, who had an all-too-clear memory of how CIA had been caught up in the controversial issues raised in the Kennedy-Nixon encounters in 1960. In July and August 1976, Agency officers were heartened by Carter's repeated reassurances that he did not want to take political advantage of intelligence briefings and statements and that he wanted only to understand the facts to avoid making mistakes.

In fact, two of the three presidential debates included virtually no discussion of foreign policy issues. The debate on 23 September in Philadelphia focused on domestic and economic policy matters. The debate on 22 October in Williamsburg, Virginia, contained only a very brief exchange on Yugoslavia, including specifically the question of the appropriate US response to a possible post-Tito Soviet invasion of that country. The remainder of that debate addressed domestic issues.

The one debate dedicated to foreign and defense issues was held on 6 October in San Francisco. Agency officers were relieved that the CIA and its programs did not become a big part of any of the key subjects discussed. These included US leadership abroad, the proper level for the US defense budget, the US position for future SALT talks, cooperation with authoritarian regimes, grain sales to the Soviet Union, arms sales and peace negotiations in the Middle East, energy policy, proliferation, and the future of the Panama Canal.

CIA was mentioned only twice during the debate, both times by Carter as part of his comments on integrity and leadership in foreign affairs. Early in the debate the governor said, "I've traveled the last 21 months among the people of this country. I've talked to them and I've listened. And I've seen at first hand in a very vivid way the deep hurt that has come to this country in the aftermath of Vietnam and Cambodia, Chile and Pakistan, and Angola and Watergate, the CIA revelations." There could be no doubt that he had carefully planned this formulation: he used almost exactly the same words more than an hour later in his closing statement, saying, "And we've been hurt in recent years in this country in the aftermath of Vietnam, Cambodia, Chile, Pakistan, Angola, Watergate, CIA."[12]

From the Agency's point of view, Carter's formulation was unfortunate. At the same time, there was relief that he had made only passing references, that the Intelligence Community's activities had not become a bigger issue in the campaign, and that the Agency's operations and analyses had not become entwined in discussion of the substantive issues. Thinking back on this spe-

---

[12] *New York Times*, 7 October 1976, 36.

cific issue in 1993, Carter commented that, in his mind, "Politicization of intelligence was not a problem in the debates or otherwise."

Operational and Political Issues Arise

Three days following the election on 2 November, Bush telephoned Carter to offer his congratulations and tender his resignation as CIA director. He told Carter frankly that he was unclear about the protocol in such a situation and asked if the president-elect would like a letter of resignation. Carter graciously said that was not necessary and thanked Bush for his call.[13]

In the telephone conversation, Bush proposed they get together soon so he could inform Carter about certain "exotic and very closely held items relating to sources and methods." Bush informed Carter of the kinds of support CIA had offered past presidents-elect during periods of transition, describing specifically the office that had been set up for Nixon in New York in 1968. In reply, the new president-elect said that he would be very interested in having such a session. The two resolved to leave the arrangements to Lehman and Eizenstat, as they had done for the preelection briefings.

The one postelection session with Carter that Bush chaired took place on 19 November. This meeting was another multihour session in which Bush was assisted by a half-dozen senior officers. The most significant discussions of the day, however, were in the first 45 minutes, during which Bush met privately with Carter and Mondale, accompanied only by his personal assistant, Jennifer Fitzgerald. This group of four assembled in the little-used small living room in the Carter home while the larger group of aides from both sides waited in the larger and more informal study.

Bush informed Carter that he wanted to discuss a personal matter and reopened the question of the CIA directorship. The DCI reminded Carter that there had been charges of politics when Bush was nominated to head CIA and that he, Bush, felt that if he were to leave at the end of the Ford presidency there might well be another political outcry. He elaborated, stating that, if he were seen to have done a reasonable job, the charge could be made that replacing him had politicized the Agency. Bush volunteered that he could be helpful in muting such criticism. He added that any CIA director needed to have direct access to the president and cited occasions when he had used such access to President Ford. Later Bush recorded that, after "weighing both the political problem and the confidence/direct access problem that I felt clearly

---

[13] George [H. W.] Bush, "President-Elect Jimmy Carter," memorandum of conversation, 6 November 1976.

that I should leave and the President-elect should put his own man in the organization in whom he had confidence."[14]

Whatever Bush's intent may have been, his reopening the question of his own tenure clearly surprised Carter, who had thought the matter settled when Bush had telephoned him two weeks earlier. In 1993, Carter volunteered that his impression from that exchange in 1976 was that "Bush wanted to be kept on as DCI." Parenthetically and laughingly, he added, "If I had agreed to that [Bush] never would have become president. His career would have gone off on a whole different track!"

Carter explained, "It would be good in general to have some overlap [of a DCI serving from one president to the next]. But the job of DCI must be depoliticized. Bush was too political. That is why I selected Stan Turner. He didn't want the job, he wanted to be CNO [Chief of Naval Operations]."

Carter was unambiguous in his response after Bush finished his discussion of the pros and cons of staying on as director. The DCI had finished with an observation that—all things considered—he probably should be replaced. The president-elect, according to Bush, "simply said 'Okay,' or something like this, with no discussion, no questions about any of the points I had made…. As in the rest of the briefing, Carter was very cold or cool, no editorializing, no niceties, very business-like." Bush also noted that Mondale at this point "spoke up and rather generously said that things had gotten better since I'd been there." The three concluded with a discussion of the timing of the announcement of a new CIA director-designate.

Given Carter's expressed views on the politicization issue, senior Agency officers later found it ironic that his first choice for CIA Director was Theodore Sorensen, the former Kennedy political adviser and speechwriter. Sorensen was nominated on 24 December but in mid-January withdrew his name because of mounting criticism that he had played a very political role in the Kennedy administration.

His private session with Carter gave Bush the opportunity to inform the president-elect of a variety of sensitive human-source and technical collection programs. In the first such session since Kennedy was briefed by Allen Dulles on covert action activities in Cuba, the DCI took 30 minutes or more to inform Carter of specific operational undertakings he needed to be aware of early in his presidency. He also showed Carter and Mondale samples of reporting from sensitive sources, underscoring that the lives of CIA assets were literally at stake. Bush underscored that if the president-elect felt he needed additional information he could, of course, contact CIA.

---

[14] George [H. W.] Bush, memorandum of conversation, 22 November 1976.

President Jimmy Carter welcomes DCI-designate VAdm. Stansfield Turner.

The DCI also used the occasion of the small group meeting to show the president-elect a copy of the *President's Daily Brief*. He described the distribution of the publication and informed Carter that President Ford had approved providing it to him on a daily basis starting immediately. This subject was to be discussed further in the larger briefing session.

In all, Bush described to the president-elect more than a dozen sensitive CIA programs and issues. At the time of the briefing, and when discussing it

CHAPTER 4

some 17 years after the fact, Bush was puzzled that Carter had virtually no comment and asked no questions during the whole session. He had not indicated whether he thought the operations were good or bad, or that he was surprised or not surprised. He asked for no follow-up action or information. Bush commented that Carter "seemed a little impatient; he didn't say much but seemed to be a little turned off. He tended to moralize."[15]

In fact, Carter was "turned off" and uncomfortable with many of the Agency's sensitive collection programs. He ordered some discontinued during the brief period when Henry Knoche served as acting director from late January to early March 1977. There was only one item raised in the discussion of sensitive matters between Bush and Carter to which the president-elect reacted positively. Somewhat incongruously, Bush had taken with him to Plains a letter to the president-elect from John Harper, rector of St. John's Episcopal Church in Washington, DC, inviting President Carter to worship there. Without a moment's thought, the president-elect said that he felt sure he would be able to do this.

Bush was obviously relieved when the smaller session was finished and he and Carter joined the larger group for the substantive briefings. The DCI recorded that Carter, in the larger session that followed, "was very attentive, listening intently and showing much more warmth in the bigger meeting than in the smaller.... He called the briefers by their first names. Actually, he referred to me a little more in this briefing than he did in the earlier ones where I had the distinct feeling he was somewhat uncomfortable with my being there."

During the larger group session on the afternoon of 19 November, Carter and Mondale were briefed on the US Intelligence Community in more detail than had been given any other president-elect before or since. Recalling the session in 1993, Bush said, "I felt that a president-elect should get a formal briefing early on how intelligence works—what the assets are, what's available real time, methodology, sources and methods protection, etc." If Bush was the inspiration for the session, the bulk of the actual briefing was by Knoche, then deputy director of central intelligence, and Adm. Daniel Murphy, director of the Intelligence Community Staff.

The two primary briefers discussed the priorities and budget of the Intelligence Community and the array of satellites and aircraft that comprised its technical intelligence reconnaissance program. There was considerable discussion of the CIA's management of its covert action programs. Knoche ensured that the governor was aware of the procedures involved with authoriz-

---

[15] George H. W. Bush, interview by the author in Kennebunkport, Maine, 6 May 1993.

ing such programs, including the director's authorities, the role of the Operations Advisory Group and the oversight responsibilities of the Congress. He discussed CIA's clandestine intelligence collection efforts and showed the governor examples of some of the technical collection gear used by CIA assets abroad. Knoche also spent some time discussing the Agency's unique contacts with foreign leaders and how CIA activities abroad are coordinated with the US ambassador in the country concerned.

The group reviewed the history of the CIA from the time of the Office of Strategic Services, emphasizing how intelligence priorities, programs, and resource levels had evolved through the decades of the 1950s and 1960s and until 1976. As a result of this extended discussion, Carter came to the presidency with a more detailed understanding of the capabilities and activities of the US Intelligence Community than any previous president had possessed at that early stage.

During the afternoon session there was also a discussion of selected substantive issues in which Carter had specifically indicated an interest. These included the politics of OPEC and the international petroleum situation. As in the preelection sessions, the Agency's director of current intelligence provided an update on crisis areas: Lebanon, the Arab-Israeli situation, the Horn of Africa, Rhodesia, and Soviet-Polish tensions. The governor was also provided an oral briefing and written information regarding Soviet views and statements on the incoming administration, specifically related to the politics of arms control.[16]

Throughout the day, Carter continued to be an active participant in the discussions; he and Mondale both had numerous comments and questions about the Soviet topics. They had received communications from Soviet General Secretary Brezhnev and Ambassador Dobrynin and were interested in discussing the meaning and implications of those messages. The president- and vice president-elect repeatedly sought to clarify whether one dared rely on Soviet statements. Bush and Lehman, a long-time CIA Soviet expert, came away from the session pleased at the depth of Carter's interest in Soviet matters. They appreciated the perceptive questions he asked but also thought he had some decidedly naive and unrealistic ideas about the Soviet Union. Lehman recalled in 1993 that, while Carter clearly understood the issues in an abstract way, he "obviously had no comprehension of the Soviet system as it actually worked. Later, when the Soviets invaded Afghanistan, it was as if the scales had dropped from his eyes."

---

[16] Richard Lehman, "Briefing of the President-elect," memorandum for the record, 19 November 1976.

CHAPTER 4

Lehman at one point offered to have Agency specialists prepare a paper for Carter on the subject of how the Soviet system worked. Back in Washington, with the paper in preparation, Lehman was discouraged when Mondale adviser Aaron called "with glee" to report that the president-elect had declined to have the paper prepared after all. Unintentionally, perhaps, senior Agency officers had got themselves in the middle of some delicate maneuvering among Carter's advisers regarding who would have the new president's ear regarding how he should look at the Soviet Union and its leaders.

The last item of the day was to clarify with the governor whether he wished to receive the PDB on a daily basis in Plains. Bush had extended President Ford's offer during their private session several hours earlier, and Carter apparently had been pondering it throughout the afternoon briefings. When Lehman raised the question again before their departure, Carter accepted Ford's offer and said the sample copy that had been shown him looked useful. Lehman noted that, although Aaron objected—presumably because he would not be present—the decision was made to station a CIA officer in Plains to provide the PDB. This daily support began on 29 November.

Knoche, the most active player on the Agency's side, came away from the 19 November session predicting that CIA would find "a good customer and champion of intelligence during Carter's incumbency in the White House." Lehman recorded that "the general tone of the entire session was extremely friendly and as intense as the previous ones." For his part, the president-elect, during an unusual public session with the Senate Foreign Relations Committee, said on 23 November: "President Ford has been very gracious to me in letting me meet with his key leaders.... I have had a complete briefing from the CIA which will be set up on a daily basis from now on."[17]

With Carter having clarified his intention to replace Bush as DCI during the 19 November meeting, the director on 24 November publicly announced his resignation. To no one's surprise, the novelty of a newly elected president promptly replacing the CIA director led the press to read the most ominous possible interpretation into the announcement. Evans and Novak, for example, opined that "the departure of George Bush from the CIA sooner than anybody expected...stems from the nature of his encounter with President-elect Carter during the transition." The journalist team wrote that "Bush's six-hour intelligence briefing of Carter at Plains on November 19 was called a 'disaster' by one Carter insider." They cited a "key Carterite" as telling them that "Jimmy just wasn't impressed with Bush."[18]

---

[17] Jimmy Carter, "President-elect Jimmy Carter's Views Concerning Foreign Policy," Briefing Before the Committee on Foreign Relations, US Senate, 23 November 1976.
[18] Rowland Evans and Robert Novak, *Washington Post*, 27 November 1976.

The Evans-Novak article appeared on a Saturday morning. By midafternoon, Jody Powell telephoned Bush to report that Carter had asked him to pass along his feeling that the article was all nonsense (in fact using a more graphic term to characterize the nonsense). Powell expressed Carter's very high regard for Bush and indicated the president-elect would be making a statement personally to set the record straight. At the same time, Aaron telephoned Knoche to pass along much the same message and to underscore that Carter was very high on CIA. Agency personnel were heartened on 29 November when Carter released a statement describing as "completely untrue" reports that he was displeased with the caliber of the briefings he had received from the outgoing CIA director. Powell added on that date that Carter had found the briefings "professional, competent, and most helpful."[19]

In discussing the sessions during an interview in 1994, Ambassador Mondale recalled that Carter had been particularly fond of the briefings and focused on the material "with extraordinary intensity." He remembered with a smile that "a fellow named George Bush came down" to Plains to guide them through "stacks of maps and graphs and other data." Mondale observed that he and Carter found the sessions "extremely useful in helping to understand the realities of foreign events at the time."[20]

A final briefing session was held in Plains on 3 December, without the DCI and the large contingent of experts. Lehman recalls, "I traveled to Plains alone. It was pouring rain, there was a cordon of Secret Service at the governor's home and he was in the house alone; no servants, no staff, nobody. For two and a half hours we roamed over a wide range of intelligence business and certain substantive issues." Two additional sessions were held on 9 and 10 December at Blair House in Washington, DC. Lehman was also the briefer at these sessions, which were abbreviated but included the usual mix of agenda items touching on intelligence operations and developments abroad. Bush stopped by the session on 9 December to give Carter a 20-minute update on a half-dozen sensitive operational developments and to inquire how the briefings were going. Carter expressed his satisfaction with the support he was receiving, including in Plains. He good-naturedly refused to be drawn out on who would be appointed DCI.

---

[19] United Press International, 29 November 1976.
[20] Walter Mondale, interview by an Agency officer in Tokyo, Japan, 15 April 1994.

CHAPTER 4

Carter's Use of the *President's Daily Brief*

Immediately after the Thanksgiving holiday, the Agency began to send the PDB to Carter in Plains on a daily basis. This established another precedent in terms of the level of support provided a president-elect during the transition period. Each morning at 6:30, a copy of exactly the same document that was about to be shown President Ford was faxed to Plains by the White House Communications Agency. At the Georgia end, CIA had stationed a midlevel officer who was responsible for receiving the document and delivering it to Carter personally at 8:00.

The CIA officer who met with Carter was John Biddiscomb, an imagery specialist from the Directorate of Science and Technology. Biddiscomb was selected because he would be adept at answering any questions Carter had on the satellite photography that was sent to Plains along with the text of the daily current intelligence items. It was not thought that the Agency should station a more senior substantive expert in Plains, in part, because Carter's foreign affairs advisers were in Atlanta or Washington and were uneasy at the prospect that the daily sessions might turn into extended substantive discussions in which they were not involved. Carter was a punctual and interested reader. He would arrive at his office each morning at 8:00 to meet Biddiscomb and would typically spend 30 to 45 minutes reading through the day's current intelligence. Biddiscomb recalls that Carter always extended a warm welcome and was appreciative of the material made available to him. He showed particular interest in items on the Soviet Union and international petroleum matters.[21]

As the weeks went along, Carter was sent a considerable volume of supplementary material in addition to the PDB. This material included biographies of key world leaders, more detailed information on crises abroad, and the reactions of foreign governments to the new US administration. When Carter had finished reading the PDB or other material, he would initial it with a "JC." At the conclusion of each day's session, Biddiscomb would telephone Lehman at CIA with feedback on Carter's interests and to pass along any questions that the governor may have had.

The Agency's continuous presence in Plains gave it an unusual degree of access to the president-elect. The ground rules in Plains were that only Biddiscomb and Carter's own appointments secretary had the authority to call him directly at any time. In fact, CIA did not exercise this prerogative of special access with the exception of one occasion on which Biddiscomb contacted Carter late one evening to pass along a message from Aaron in Washington. While Biddiscomb appreciated Carter's graciousness and the access he was

---

[21] John Biddiscomb, telephone interview by the author, 28 April 1993.

granted, there was throughout the period a continuing formality to the early-morning sessions that did not really permit the establishment of a familiar relationship with the president-elect.

The occasional light moments that occurred arose typically when Carter's brother, Billy, would put in an appearance at the president-elect's office. On one occasion Billy inquired of his brother whether he had permission to ask the CIA to "take care of some of these reporters" who were becoming a bit oppressive. Ever cautious, the president-elect said, "You'll have to ask Mr. Biddiscomb about that." Biddiscomb wisely replied that the Agency had its hands full dealing with reporters itself and probably could not be much help. In reality, Biddiscomb was relieved that the press contingent in Georgia showed very little interest in the CIA presence, once it had become clear that it was a routine daily operation that would result in no announcements to the press. He had made no particular efforts to avoid the press, which in any case would have been impossible in the setting. Not infrequently, for example, he found himself in a local restaurant surrounded by reporters and Secret Service officers. On one occasion, the president-elect and his family were there as well.

When Lehman briefed Carter in Plains on 3 December and during his visit to Washington on 9 December, the first item on his agenda was to elicit Carter's reaction to the PDB and the supplementary material he had been receiving since Thanksgiving.[22] Lehman's memorandums for the record make clear that Carter did not find the PDB satisfactory. The governor was aware that no changes would be made until after his inauguration on 21 January, but he underscored that he would expect changes, once that date arrived. Carter stressed that he was "a voracious reader of the press" and would prefer a publication that contained only items not covered in the newspapers.

During their first discussion of the PDB format, Lehman left with Carter samples of PDBs that had been prepared for the last four presidents to illustrate some of the different options available. As a first step, Carter asked Lehman to experiment with the supplemental material, adding longer pieces with more background material. These were to include "insights into proposals that might be coming from other countries," for example those relating to Middle East peace negotiations. Carter also asked on that date for additional biographical material on foreign leaders. Lehman left with him a collection of biographies on key Chinese officials.

By the time Carter and Lehman met at Blair House on 10 December, it was obvious the president-elect was a little impatient that he would have to wait

---

[22] Richard Lehman, "Briefing of the President-elect," memorandum for the record, 13 December 1976.

until January to receive the publications in the form he preferred. A big part of the problem seemed to be that the PDB being prepared for the outgoing president appeared in a different format than the material prepared for the president-elect in the separate supplement. The governor was reading both but was unhappy. Lehman's reaction was to direct that for the next few weeks CIA should print the supplement in the same format as the PDB and transmit both to Plains at the same time and as one package so that they would look alike to the governor. Following the inauguration, the supplement could be dropped and all appropriate material published in the PDB in whatever format the governor preferred.

On 10 December, Lehman also took the opportunity to introduce David Peterson, the CIA officer responsible for the production of the PDB. Lehman indicated that Peterson would deliver the PDB to Governor Carter the next time he came to Washington. In his memorandum for the record, Lehman, obviously mindful of the Agency's practice earlier in the Ford administration, noted that he hoped to develop a situation in which Peterson would be briefing the president every morning after the inauguration, adding that he had not yet suggested this to the Carter entourage. During their first meeting, Carter remarked to Peterson that he liked the PDB but would want to talk with him further about its contents at a later time, probably after the inauguration.[23]

Carter seemed to enjoy and benefit from the substantive discussions held at Blair House during his visits to Washington in the transition period. In the presence of more senior Agency officers in Washington, he was considerably more expansive in his comments than he was during the daily current intelligence sessions in Plains. In these relatively informal and relaxed sessions, the president-elect was even able occasionally to find some humor in the intelligence he was provided, joking among other things about the positive statements Libyan leader Qadhafi was making about the upcoming Democratic administration in Washington. Carter commented in 1993 that he remembered the Blair House sessions as being very useful to him—not only the briefings provided by CIA but also one given him by representatives of the Joint Chiefs of Staff.

The JCS briefers had met with Carter at Blair House to go over with him his responsibilities in the event of nuclear attack. Carter recalls taking particular pride in insisting that the vice president-elect also receive this briefing in order to prepare for the eventuality that he might need to discharge those weighty responsibilities. To Carter's knowledge, vice presidents had not previously been briefed in such a way.

---

[23] David Peterson, interview by the author in McLean, Virginia, 4 March 1993.

During the last of the Blair House sessions, Carter settled on a version of the PDB that he liked. The format he selected was notable primarily for the large amount of white space on the page—space in which he could write notes. On Inauguration Day, 20 January, Peterson met with Carter and presented him the first issue of the PDB printed in the new format.

With Bush having resigned effective 20 January, it fell to Acting DCI Knoche to meet with the new president and his national security advisor, Zbigniew Brzezinski, the next day to brief them on a sensitive satellite collection capability that had not previously been discussed. On that occasion Carter affirmed to Knoche personally that he wanted him to act as DCI until a successor was confirmed (Sorensen by that time had withdrawn his name). Carter expressed his pride in CIA and indicated that Knoche had his full confidence. A bit more than two weeks later, on 5 February, Carter telephoned Knoche to inform him that Adm. Stansfield Turner would be nominated to be the next director.

Carter used the occasion of the first meeting of the National Security Council on 22 January to underscore to all attendees the importance of the PDB, which he thought had "sharpened in focus in recent days."[24] Confirming again that he had been disappointed by earlier versions that he found wordy and "no different from the *New York Times*," he asked Knoche to ensure that the publication continued to be "sharp and focused, brief and clear as to what the intelligence is." Carter directed that Knoche should disseminate the PDB only to him, the vice president, the secretaries of state and defense, and the national security advisor, at the same time informing both secretaries that their deputies would not receive it.

Brzezinski and Aaron had not been seeing the PDB during the transition period, so it fell to Peterson to talk with them following the inauguration to familiarize them with the publication and procedures for distributing it. Carter had obviously been discussing his preferences with Brzezinski, because the latter reiterated Carter's guidelines for the publication, underscoring that it should not repeat material available in the newspapers.

The new president quickly put into place a system for keeping himself informed of developments abroad on a day-to-day basis that was very similar to the process Ford used. That is, he preferred to start each morning with a one-on-one meeting with his national security advisor. Carter later wrote in his memoirs:

> *The PDB Zbig brought to me each morning was a highly secret document, distributed to only five people...Zbig and I would discuss the report and other developments relating to defense and foreign*

---

[24] Henry Knoche, Memorandum for the Record, "PDB," 24 January 1977.

CHAPTER 4

National Security Advisor Zbignew Brzezinski and President Carter confer over the day's edition of the President's Daily Brief.

affairs. Often, while he was still present, I would call the Secretary of State or the Secretary of Defense on a secure telephone to obtain additional information or get their opinions. They, too, were early risers, always at their desks by seven o'clock.[25]

The downside of this system from the CIA perspective was that the Agency's briefing officer was not present when the president read through the day's current intelligence. In discussing this set of procedures in 1993, Carter evinced awareness that the system he adopted had the effect of denying CIA immediate feedback on his reactions and questions, but made clear he thought good management demanded that he work through the national security advisor. Carter remembered, "Zbig was enough day-to-day. I read the PDB and the Secretary of State's Morning Report. I wanted Brzezinski to draw to my attention things I needed to do something about. If [Secretary of Defense] Harold Brown could handle a matter and I didn't need to be aware of it that was fine."

In fact, the CIA received considerably more feedback from Carter than it had from Ford. Heartening evidence that this would be the case appeared within days of the inauguration, because the president frequently wrote com-

---

[25] Jimmy Carter, *Keeping Faith Memoirs of a President* (New York: Bantam Books, 1982), 55.

ments on his copy of the PDB. But this practice was to create another minor problem.

Peterson would deliver the PDB to Brzezinski each morning, retrieve the previous day's edition, and note down any reactions Carter may have expressed to Brzezinski. On 31 January, Brzezinski informed Peterson that he would no longer be able to return to the Agency the president's copy of the PDB.[26] Brzezinski showed Peterson the issue for Saturday, 29 January, on which the president had written several action directives and questions addressed to Brzezinski and Secretary of State Cyrus Vance. Brzezinski decreed that these presidential notations demanded that the original copies of the PDBs should be securely stored at the White House. CIA had no problem with this procedure because Brzezinski offered assurances that the Agency would be informed of the president's annotations whenever his comments related to the substance of the intelligence.

Peterson recalls that the president often wrote on the PDB and that the copies were shown to him as promised. Carter's notations usually were instructions to his senior policymakers. Such directives obviously were properly the property of the president, the National Security Council staff, and the Departments of State and Defense. For planning purposes, however, it proved very useful to the Agency to be informed of these directives in order that timely and relevant intelligence could be provided to the president.

In the months that followed, Carter initiated one other practice that was immensely valuable in keeping the CIA informed of his policy and intelligence interests and opened opportunities for the Intelligence Community to provide useful service to the new president. When Turner took up the post of DCI in mid-March, he began—at the president's invitation—a practice of personally providing Carter in-depth weekly briefings on a subject of particular interest. The Agency had not had such an opportunity since the period when DCI "Beedle" Smith regularly briefed President Harry Truman. The five intervening presidents had been briefed in varying ways, sometimes frequently and in depth, but never in the systematic way that the Agency was able to establish with Carter.

In thinking back over the intelligence support he received, Carter in 1993 recalled that he valued Turner's briefings highly, even though they were later to slip from their regular weekly schedule. He noted, "From the daily material—the PDB—I selected the items I wanted discussed in more detail the next week by the DCI. I particularly remember the briefings I received on confes-

---

[26] David Peterson, "White House Copy of the PDB," memorandum for the record, 31 January 1977.

CHAPTER 4

sional and political groups in Lebanon, on a new imaging system, and on the South African nuclear program."

Carter began his presidency with a deep understanding of intelligence. He had received in-depth briefings on developments abroad and on the most sensitive operations of the US Intelligence Community. He had received daily current intelligence support—the PDB—during the transition period that continued once he was in office. Throughout his presidency he received weekly substantive briefings. In the course of four years, Carter was to enjoy great foreign policy successes, like the Camp David Accords, and to suffer great disappointments, as with the Iranian seizure of US hostages. Throughout it all, he received an unprecedented level of detailed intelligence information.

⌘ ⌘ ⌘

CHAPTER 5

REAGAN AND BUSH - A STUDY IN CONTRASTS

The 12-year period from 1980 to 1992 presented CIA with two presidents who were virtual polar opposites in terms of their familiarity with and use of intelligence. Governor Ronald Reagan of California had the least experience as a regular consumer of national-level intelligence of any president elected since CIA was founded; Ambassador George H. W. Bush, on the other hand, was completely familiar and comfortable with intelligence in a way that only a former DCI could be. Reagan brought to the presidency deep convictions about key national security issues and felt the need for only limited, very general intelligence information. Bush approached developments abroad as a pragmatic activist and expected from the Intelligence Community an unprecedented level of day-to-day support and detail. Both, however, received Agency officers warmly and were openly appreciative of their support.

Before the election, candidate Reagan received only one intelligence briefing. It was held on 4 October 1980 at Wexford, a borrowed country estate near Middleburg, Virginia, where the governor was staying for a period during the campaign. The DCI, Adm. Stansfield Turner, accompanied by three senior Agency officers, represented CIA. Reagan was accompanied by vice-presidential candidate George Bush; his transition chief of staff Ed Meese; campaign director William Casey; and Richard Allen, his adviser on national security matters.

Participants in that first briefing remember it as a "circus." The living room of the Middleburg home where the session was held was like a chaotic movie set with chairs scattered more or less randomly about the room and people constantly coming and going. The governor was an engaging host, but in the impossible setting it was extraordinarily difficult to make effective use of the briefing aids and other materials that Turner had brought with him. Throughout the meeting, which went on for approximately one hour, the CIA participants had the feeling that the Reagan camp had accepted the briefing simply because it had been offered and they had to do it. There was no evidence that anyone had the expectation that the governor would engage in an in-depth review of the substantive issues.

111

CHAPTER 5

Even in these awkward circumstances there was some serious discussion of developments in the Middle East, the agreed focus of the session. Turner discussed the petroleum aspects of the issue and the conflicts between Iran and Iraq and in Afghanistan. National Intelligence Officer for the Middle East Robert Ames briefed on the internal politics of Saudi Arabia and Iran. Richard Lehman, from the National Intelligence Council, elaborated on the impact of the Iran-Iraq war on the region and on the Soviet role.

Reagan posed a few questions to be sure that he understood the essential points the Agency was trying to make. He asked straightforward, common sense questions, primarily related to the oil situation. Agency participants were interested to observe that there was absolutely nothing ideological in the governor's approach and that no policy issues arose.

Richard Allen asked the most questions, including some related to Afghanistan that put the DCI on the spot. In replying to a direct question from Allen about whether the US government was engaged in supplying arms to the insurgents in Afghanistan, Turner felt obliged to be more elliptical than he would have preferred. The DCI left no doubt in the listeners' minds that the United States was supporting the insurgents through Pakistan, but he also tried to make clear that this was a very sensitive covert action program that he was not in a position to describe in detail, inasmuch as the governor was still a candidate for the presidency rather than president-elect.

In recalling his exchange with Reagan in 1993, Turner commented that his reticence on the Afghan program had a serious substantive aspect as well. In early October 1980, the "Afghan story had not yet leaked and we were scared about Pakistan's position."[1] Turner's concerns reflected the fact that, particularly during the early years of the Afghan conflict, the US government was concerned lest Pakistan become the ultimate casualty of a US program, undertaken with vital Pakistani cooperation, to expel Soviet forces from Afghanistan. This concern for security had to be weighed against Turner's larger motive in providing as much information as possible to Reagan "because we didn't want him saying something he would regret if he became president."

The press had been informed in advance that Reagan would receive an intelligence briefing on the Middle East on 4 October. Reporters were eagerly awaiting the candidate's reaction, knowing the briefing was potentially politically significant inasmuch as Reagan had previously criticized the Carter administration for its failure to have done more to support the late shah of Iran. In fact, after the briefing, Reagan left it to Bush to discuss the session with the

---

[1] Stansfield Turner, interview by the author in McLean, Virginia, 20 April 1993. Subsequent quotations from Turner also come from this interview.

press. The latter called the discussion "pure intelligence and said that neither he nor Mr. Reagan intended to use the information as ammunition to criticize President Carter."[2] Bush added that he was "impressed" with the information. "I feel better informed about the world," he told reporters, "I can't tell you I feel more optimistic about it." For his part, Reagan declined to discuss the briefing with newsmen, although he did characterize it as "most interesting."

The one presidential debate held during the 1980 campaign that involved the candidates of the major parties was held in Cleveland, Ohio, on 28 October, some three weeks after Reagan's intelligence briefing. At least half of the 90-minute debate was devoted to developments abroad and US national security policy. The international portion of the debate was largely a discussion of Middle East issues: Arab-Israeli peace negotiations; Persian Gulf oil; the terrorist threat, specifically that from Iran related to the ongoing hostage crisis; the Iran-Iraq war; and weapons proliferation. Agency officers were relieved that during this extended discussion there was, unlike the situation four years earlier in 1976, no mention whatever of CIA.

In response to a question from the moderator of the debate on what he might do to deal with terrorism, Reagan made clear that he did not want to "say anything that would inadvertently delay in any way the return of those hostages" and that he was fearful he might "say something that was presently under way or in negotiation and thus expose it and endanger the hostages." He also made clear that he did not have "access to the information in which I would know all the options that are open."[3] Senior Agency officers were not surprised that the governor would handle the hostage issue this way during the debate; they had been struck—and remembered their reaction clearly in 1993—that there had been no discussion whatever of the hostage issue during their briefing of the candidate two weeks earlier.

Ironically, in light of the highly charged politics of the hostage issue that would ensue in succeeding years, the only discussion of the issue that occurred during CIA's formal briefings in the preelection period in 1980 occurred not with Reagan but with third-party candidate John Anderson. On Sunday afternoon, 5 October, Turner and three senior Agency officers spent two hours providing Anderson the same briefing on the Middle East that had been given to Reagan the previous day. In 1993, Turner recounted that on that occasion Anderson reported to him that he had been approached by an Iranian intermediary who raised the possibility of an arms-for-hostages exchange with Iran. The DCI promptly reported this approach to the State Department and took no further action himself.

---

[2] *New York Times*, 5 October 1980, 34.
[3] Ibid., 29 October 1980, A27.

CHAPTER 5

Those involved in the briefing of Anderson recall it as a deeply substantive and intellectual discussion that went on without interruption for more than two hours. Anderson impressed the Agency officers with a number of perceptive and informed questions. Turner recalled vividly the contrast between the Reagan and Anderson briefings, saying that he received "more sensible questions from Anderson than we got from the Reagan people."

Postelection Briefings

In response to the Agency's standing invitation, Reagan aide Ed Meese telephoned Turner some two weeks following the November election to arrange for intelligence support for the new president-elect. Although Reagan himself was to divide his time between Washington and California, his transition staff had set up offices in Washington, and it was decided that the director's follow-on briefings should be given in the capital. As the scheduling worked out, these sessions occurred on 19 and 20 November at the townhouse Reagan used as his headquarters on Jackson Place, near the White House. Briefings were also provided on 11 December and 15 January at Blair House, the much larger and more elaborate presidential guest house across Pennsylvania Avenue from the White House.

It was decided to devote the first of the postelection briefings to an update on the Middle East, inasmuch as it had been more than six weeks since the last meeting with Reagan in early October. In his opening remarks Turner described the structure and functions of the various elements of the US Intelligence Community. He then turned the floor over to the Agency's assistant NIO for the Middle East, Martha Neff Kessler, who did the bulk of the substantive briefing.

Thinking back on the session in 1993, Kessler remembered primarily how Turner, Lehman, and she were invited to join the president-elect and his staff around the dining room table of the Jackson Place townhouse but that the room was already so crowded with Reagan aides that it was all but impossible to even sit down. The result was that while Kessler was able literally to rub elbows with Reagan and Bush simultaneously, she was unable to open the briefing book. She gave a more spontaneous and informal briefing than might otherwise have been the case.

In contrast to the briefing provided six weeks earlier, Kessler recalled that, in late November, Reagan was an active participant who posed a number of questions regarding Middle East peace issues. He focused on the Golan Heights, Syrian and Palestinian politics, and relations among the various Middle East countries. According to Kessler, Reagan's questions "reflected considerable

President Ronald Reagan talks with veteran CIA analyst Peter Dixon Davis.

knowledge. He was by no means a rightwing ideologue as the press charged. He was very current and extremely alert."[4] Allen also asked a number of questions, and his often had an edge. Bush, who had been instrumental in setting up these sessions, made a number of comments elaborating on CIA activities.

Participants in the briefing on 19 November remember it as one of the more notable cases when an analytic prediction provided to a president came true. In the course of her discussion of the high stakes of the ongoing Middle East negotiations, Kessler remarked, "We could lose Sadat." Reagan interrupted, "What do you mean, lose Sadat?" to which Kessler replied that he could be overthrown or killed. Her concerns were based on her assessment of the tensions in the region rather than on any specific intelligence reporting. Tragically, this premonition was to come to pass less than a year later, in October 1981.

The session held the following day, 20 November, also took place in the crowded Jackson Place townhouse. It was to have been a review of the US-Soviet strategic force balance, the NATO–Warsaw Pact conventional force

---

[4] Martha Neff Kessler, interview by the author in McLean, Virginia, 30 March 1993.

CHAPTER 5

balance, the Soviet threat to Poland, and developments in Central America. In fact, no systematic briefing occurred at all. Instead, there was a general and relatively brief discussion of the Soviet threat to Poland and the situation in Central America.

Reagan's expressed interests during the session on 20 November included the relationship between the Soviets' involvement in Eastern Europe and their ability to pursue their interests in other parts of the world. He was well informed on Mexico's role in Central America, Cuba, and the region, attributing this to his California background. Concerning both Central America and Eastern Europe, the president-elect's comments often addressed the policy aspects of what the United States was doing and should do. Obliged to demur on the policy questions, the CIA briefers came away concerned about whether they had been very helpful.

By the time of the briefing on 11 December, the Reagan team had relocated its operation to Blair House, which provided a much better setting for an organized presentation. The Agency's primary briefer on that occasion was Douglas Diamond, a specialist on the Soviet economy who had been one of the briefers of President Jimmy Carter in Plains four years earlier. Diamond later recalled that the briefing covered not only the Soviet economy, but also the implications of the economic situation for the USSR's military programs, the US-Soviet strategic balance, and the Sino-Soviet situation. He found Reagan a friendly and interested recipient who raised a number of factual questions. On the other hand, Diamond also remembered in 1993 that "the sun certainly didn't go down on this briefing like it had in Plains."[5] It was brief, reflecting the dramatically contrasting styles of Reagan and Carter. Participants recall that Turner was careful to provide "a Ronald Reagan-type briefing, not a Carter briefing" in terms of the length and level of generality as well as its emphasis.

The CIA director's briefings of the president-elect during November and December were made somewhat awkward by the running speculation in the media about whether Turner would be replaced and by whom. As the weeks passed, the press more and more frequently suggested that campaign director Casey would be appointed DCI. One attendee at the November briefings recalled that, in these ambiguous circumstances, Turner simply "talked as though he expected to be kept on as DCI."[6] Another remembered Casey saying to Turner, following one of the November briefings, "You are doing exactly the right thing" in proceeding as if he would stay on as DCI.[7]

---

[5] Douglas Diamond, interview by the author in McLean, Virginia, 28 April 1993.
[6] Lehman interview, 10 March 1993.
[7] Kessler interview, 30 March 1993.

From the CIA perspective, it was never clear exactly when Reagan and Casey finally decided on the CIA directorship. Within a three-week period in November and December, Casey at first denied to Turner the press stories that he would become DCI; later, before the briefing of 11 December, he telephoned Turner to confirm that indeed the press stories were true. At the conclusion of the session on 11 December, Reagan informed Turner that the Casey nomination would be announced in a matter of hours.

Thinking back on the politics of the briefings and the CIA directorship in 1993, Reagan recalled, "My memory is of being completely satisfied with the briefings I received during the transition." But he also made clear that his satisfaction with the briefings had not for a moment led him to consider leaving the incumbent CIA director in place. Reagan recalled emphatically, "I disagreed so completely with everything that President Carter was doing that we thought a change was needed."[8]

In discussing the more general question of how CIA had kept him aware of Agency programs, Reagan noted that he had always thought he received sufficiently detailed information on CIA's activities. Specifically, he expressed appreciation for a briefing Turner provided the week before the inauguration on the Agency's sensitive technical and human-source collection efforts and on some covert action programs. That briefing, conducted on 15 January, was a particularly important one because it came at a time when the Reagan team had been criticizing the outgoing Carter administration for its inaction in countering the Soviet threat worldwide. Inevitably, much of this criticism was born of ignorance, because Reagan and his advisers, before the DCI's briefing, were unaware of the array of covert action and sensitive collection programs in place.

Turner's final briefing was provided only to Reagan, Bush, and Casey—by then DCI-designate—unlike the previous sessions that were attended by a large number of aides. The director described seven different covert action programs and a dozen sensitive collection undertakings. One of Turner's assistants later recalled hearing at the time that the recipients on that occasion had no idea of the number of programs that were in place and were extremely interested, especially in the Afghan program. Interestingly, in light of subsequent events, none of the participants in any of the formal, high-level briefings of Reagan during the transition remembers any discussion of the US hostages in Iran, nor do the classified records of those briefings indicate the issue was raised.

As a result of the briefing on 15 January, Reagan—like Carter, but unlike all other postwar presidents to that time—had a thorough understanding of CIA's

---

[8] Ronald Reagan, interview by the author in Los Angeles, California, 26 July 1993. Subsequent quotations from Reagan also come from this interview.

CHAPTER 5

DCI William Casey's close campaign relationship with Ronald Reagan won him close and frequent access to the president.

most sensitive activities at the time he became president. Ironically, Bush was responsible in both cases: he had briefed Carter personally in 1976 and had ensured that he and Reagan received such a briefing in 1981. Bush, with his unique perspective, was struck by the differing reactions of the two presidents. Bush had noticed in 1976 that Carter showed no reaction when he was informed of the Agency's sensitive programs; Reagan, on the other hand, supported them all enthusiastically.[9]

A Higher Level of Daily Support

Initially, it appeared doubtful that during the transition Reagan would accept the Agency's offer of daily intelligence briefings on current developments, as distinct from the more informal and occasional background briefings. The president-elect was known to be apprehensive that the outgoing president and his national security advisor, Zbigniew Brzezinski, would use such briefings to "put one over on him" and influence his future policies. In addition, several of

---

[9] George H. W. Bush, interview by the author in Kennebunkport, Maine, 6 May 1993. Subsequent quotes from Bush also come from this interview.

Reagan's key advisers doubted that he would learn anything from the briefings that he could not learn just as easily from the newspapers. Fortunately, from CIA's point of view, the vice president-elect was aware of these feelings within the Reagan camp and was determined to counter them. His view was that the president-elect—indeed, any president-elect—badly needed the experience of reading a daily intelligence report with an Agency officer in attendance to supplement and explain the material.

On Friday, 21 November, Reagan finished a week of briefings and meetings in Washington and departed for his home in Pacific Palisades, California. Bush rode with Reagan to the airport sendoff and used the occasion to urge the president-elect to accept daily intelligence briefings during the several weeks he would be in California. His appeal worked. A member of the Reagan staff telephoned from the governor's aircraft to ask that the Agency provide the PDB, beginning the next morning in California. Richard Kerr, who was taking over the transition team from CIA's longtime current intelligence chief, Richard Lehman, boarded a commercial flight to Los Angeles that evening.

Kerr recalls a very warm welcome from Reagan when he appeared at midday on the 22nd to present the PDB and a short briefing. Kerr and a colleague, Dixon Davis, shared the duty of providing such briefings from 22 November through 14 January 1981. They were interested that Reagan was almost always alone, or accompanied by a single staff assistant, during the period he was in California. The Reagan transition team was at work in Washington, and the candidate himself had a relatively relaxed and detached schedule. This was in marked contrast to most other transitions before and since.

Reagan proved to be a thorough and very intent reader during the typically 20-minute sessions that he held with the CIA visitors. Always friendly and respectful, he nevertheless displayed a certain wariness regarding the intelligence material that the briefers interpreted as reflecting his lack of familiarity with it. Mrs. Reagan was almost always present in the home but normally did not join the governor for the daily intelligence briefings. The first day was an exception; on that occasion she hosted a lunch for Kerr. In the weeks that followed, she frequently would pass through the room during the briefing. Mrs. Reagan seemed to have mixed feelings about the process, displaying some uneasiness that she was not privy to what her husband was hearing. The staffers who sometimes sat in on the briefings took no interest in the substance; their only interest was to ensure that the process did not take too much time.

During the last half of November 1980, the international situations that received the most prominent coverage in the press included the hostage crisis with Iran, the future of strategic arms talks with the Soviet Union, and domestic political developments in Israel and Poland—the latter including the question of possible Soviet meddling or intervention. The same issues were treated at length in the PDB, and the president-elect was an avid reader on all subjects. He also read very carefully the background pieces the briefers provided him. These supplementary papers, normally two pages long, were published on a regular basis to bring him up to date on trouble spots around the world. Within the first two weeks Reagan read backgrounders on the situations in Pakistan, Lebanon, Kampuchea, Morocco, the Philippines, and Somalia.

Taking into account the PDB, the accompanying oral briefings and the supplementary material, the intelligence Reagan received each day was significantly greater in volume and detail than that received by Carter during his transition four years earlier. At that time the practice had been simply to make the written PDB available for his perusal.

From late November 1980 until early January 1981, Reagan read a number of current intelligence items relating to the hostage crisis in Iran. These pieces contained no sensitive US operational material. Rather, they kept the president-elect informed of the activities of various Iranian and third-country figures and provided such information as was available on the condition of the hostages and on developments in Iran. Reagan asked many questions about the hostage situation as well as about developments in the Soviet Union, Mexico, and Cuba—countries in which he clearly took a special interest.

In the course of their daily meetings with the president-elect, Kerr and Davis provided considerable information about the US Intelligence Community and its collection programs. This practice, encouraged by Bush, was designed in part simply for the new president's general background knowledge but also to heighten his consciousness about what information should not be discussed publicly lest it jeopardize intelligence sources and methods. In these sessions there was no discussion whatever of CIA's covert action programs. In contrast with the daily briefings provided President-elect Clinton 12 years later, no support was provided directly to Reagan for use in telephone calls with foreign leaders, meetings with his own staff or visitors, or press conferences.

Throughout the briefing process, Reagan displayed some of the understandable impatience that Agency briefers have seen with other presidents-elect over the years. He commented on a number of occasions, for example, on the awkwardness of reading the daily intelligence material, "even though I am not in a position to affect US policy." He clearly was most interested in the items provided him on how foreign leaders and governments were reacting to his election, including their analyses and speculation about policies he would follow. Reagan was entertained by accounts of foreign judgments on his probable behavior and worried by misrepresentations of his positions.[10]

There was another side to the president-elect that the Agency briefers found challenging and frustrating. According to Davis, "The problem with Ronald Reagan was that his ideas were all fixed. He knew what he thought about everything—he was an old dog."[11] This was particularly apparent regarding issues involving the Palestinians. Reagan, by his own account, carried a decidedly pro-Israel attitude from his Hollywood associations over the years.

In response to comments and questions from Reagan, Agency analysts produced a three- or four-page memorandum on the subtleties of the Palestinian movement. The memorandum discussed the complex array of backgrounds, personalities, ideologies, tactics, and strategies that divided the Palestinian people and characterized the many groups inside and outside the Palestine Liberation Organization. Davis recalled that the president-elect read the memorandum "very slowly and thoughtfully—he must have taken 10 minutes. At the end he said, 'But they are all terrorists, aren't they?'—My heart just sank."[12]

During the 1980 transition, Bush and Allen, who was to become national security advisor, were also provided intelligence support on virtually a daily basis. In addition to playing an immensely important role in establishing the Agency's relationship with Reagan, Bush was a key consumer in his own right. He read the current intelligence publications every day and requested a great deal of additional support for his meetings with foreign leaders. Reagan had delegated to him the task of meeting with or taking most calls from numerous heads of government and foreign ambassadors. In many cases the Agency's supporting material was provided to Bush in person in Washington or in California. In other instances it was provided in Houston, particularly over the Christmas holiday. Bush's substantive interests paralleled Reagan's, with the exception that the vice president-elect had an even deeper interest in the details of any information relating to the hostages in Iran. His questions related primarily to information the Intelligence Community had on their health.

Beginning on 18 November, Allen was briefed daily through the remainder of the transition. He initially attempted to interpose himself between the Agency briefers and the president-elect, on the first occasion insisting that he receive the PDB and take it to Reagan for his reading. Bush's intervention with Reagan ensured that Agency briefers subsequently saw him directly. Allen then received the PDB separately. He also solicited significant additional support from the Agency for his own use and in support of Reagan. It was Allen, for example, who determined the subjects to be addressed in the

---

[10] Richard Kerr, interview by the author in McLean, Virginia, 9 March 1993.
[11] Dixon Davis, interview by the author in Washington, DC, 26 April 1993.
[12] Ibid.

first 10 "backgrounders" that were provided to Reagan, and it was he who requested information from the Agency to prepare the president-elect for a meeting with Mexican President José Lopez-Portillo.

The other two key players who were to be on the Reagan national security team, Secretary of State-designate Alexander Haig and Secretary of Defense-designate Caspar Weinberger, did not receive the PDB during the transition. Weinberger had requested PDB delivery as early as mid-December, but it was determined instead that he should receive the less sensitive *National Intelligence Daily* until he was sworn in. In fact, his first briefing with the PDB occurred within minutes of his swearing in as secretary of defense. Haig, too, began receiving PDB briefings on inauguration day.

After the Inauguration

The inauguration of Reagan marked a watershed in the CIA's relationship with him just as the inauguration of Carter had done four years before. In fact, it was even more decisive. During the transition, intelligence professionals had seen Reagan on a daily basis and had a relatively full discussion of international developments from which they could learn firsthand what his interests and needs were. Following the inauguration, with his staff trying to guard his time, this daily contact was cut off. Intelligence support was provided to the president only indirectly through the national security advisor, except in those cases where the CIA director himself had occasion to meet with the president.

In a meeting with Kerr on 2 January, shortly before inauguration, Allen had reviewed a variety of styles in which the PDB had been published over the years; he was not particularly taken with any of the previous formats. Agency officers had learned by this time to expect such a reaction. With virtually every administration, if the format had not been designed specifically for that president, either the president or his national security advisor would ask that the publication be altered substantially to make it their own.

In this case, change was minimized because Kerr had discussed on several occasions during December and early January the format and composition of the PDB directly with Reagan. On each occasion, he had expressed his complete satisfaction with the length of the PDB, the format in which it was presented, and the level of generality of the pieces included. He claimed to want no changes at all. On 13 January it was agreed by all parties that the PDB would be provided daily to Allen, who would forward it to the president. Additional copies were provided by individual CIA briefers to the vice president, the national security advisor, and the secretaries of defense and state.

Agency officers who provided daily intelligence support to the White House during the Reagan administration remember that his several national security advisors varied markedly in the time and attention they devoted to the PDB. In all cases, however, they received the Agency's briefer every day, read the PDB, and ensured that it was forwarded to the president. Of the group, Adm. John Poindexter was perhaps the least interested in reading the intelligence product.

Thinking back over the eight years of the Reagan administration, the Agency's briefing officer remembered only one or two occasions when the national security advisor took him into the Oval Office to brief the president directly. Unlike Carter, Reagan almost never wrote comments or questions on the PDB. On a day-to-day basis, therefore, the Agency's knowledge of the president's intelligence needs was limited. Such knowledge came only indirectly when Reagan's interests were passed on by the national security advisor or conveyed by the president directly to the CIA director.

Although distribution of the PDB theoretically was strictly controlled, as a practical matter the security of the document eroded during the Reagan years. At various points, several presidential advisers were receiving copies of the PDB. This situation unfortunately led the Agency to be circumspect in the items it included in the publication. This turn of events distressed Reagan's second CIA director, Judge William Webster, and Vice President Bush. Ultimately, the latter would be in a position to solve this problem and did.

The fact that Reagan did not receive daily oral briefings from CIA officers did not mean that he did not receive intelligence information. Indeed, throughout the first few years of his administration, Reagan talked often with CIA Director Casey as well as with his other key national security aides. The president valued receiving information directly from individuals he knew personally and with whom he was comfortable; he preferred informal sessions to the more formal NSC system, which was used only infrequently.

This practice created concern among senior intelligence professionals, who worried that the president was receiving, at best, information that was anecdotal and not necessarily as complete, relevant, or objective as it might have been. But it was a practice that clearly was in keeping with the president's management style and personal preferences. In discussing the way he handled intelligence in 1993, Reagan summed it up by saying that throughout his presidency he thought that "we received all the intelligence we needed to make decisions."

Looking back on his presidency, Reagan acknowledged that he had been aware of the widely publicized strains between Secretary of State George Shultz and Casey but claimed to have had no feeling that whatever tensions existed between the two men had affected the intelligence he received. He said he had not felt that the intelligence provided by the CIA was in any way politicized, volunteering that the Agency had given him the information he needed and did not tell him what to think.

In discussing Reagan's use of intelligence reporting, Bush noted that the president did indeed receive and read the key analytic pieces, especially the PDB. In Bush's judgment, Reagan was seeing information that was timely and relevant, but it had less impact because it was provided indirectly. Bush observed, "It was too bad that Ronald Reagan only read the intelligence at his leisure after he became president. The real benefit is having the briefer sit there with you."

The Transition to President Bush[13]

From the point of view of the US Intelligence Community, the transition to the Bush presidency in 1988 was undoubtedly the easiest of the eight transitions in which the CIA had been involved. In only two previous cases during the postwar period—Johnson in 1964 and Ford in 1974—had an incumbent vice president moved up to the presidency. Each of those accessions occurred amid unique and extraordinarily trying circumstances that made the intelligence transition difficult. The 1988 turnover, by comparison, was the smoothest in postwar history. It also happened to bring into office the only US president to have served as CIA director.

CIA officers had been pleased when Vice President Bush, even before the Republican convention in August 1988, reassured them that he wanted to continue receiving daily intelligence briefings throughout the campaign and after the election. Bush acknowledged that he would be forced to miss some of the daily briefings but asked that they be provided without fail when he was in Washington. An increased proportion of the meetings would have to be held at his residence rather than at his office, which Bush often bypassed as he traveled in and out of Washington during the campaign. The vice president also made clear to Agency officers that, if he won, he planned to alter the arrange-

---

[13] In 1984, presidential candidate Walter Mondale did not receive briefings from the CIA. National Security Advisor Bud McFarlane provided him one overview of developments abroad in Minneapolis during the summer, but Mondale did not seek follow-up sessions with the Agency. Remembering the events of a decade earlier during a discussion in Tokyo in April 1994, Ambassador Mondale joked that he might have come off better in campaign debates and sound bites had he had "more ammunition to work with." He observed that he should have asked for a series of CIA briefings but laughingly conceded that he "never really thought [he] stood much of a chance against Reagan, which probably kept [him] from even thinking about preparing seriously for the presidency!"

ments then in place to provide intelligence support to Reagan. Bush stressed that he wanted to continue his daily sessions with CIA briefers not only during the transition period but also after his inauguration because he considered the personal dialogue was useful. The CIA briefer with whom Bush spoke recalled in 1994 that he had suggested that, after the inauguration, the DCI, as the president's chief intelligence adviser, might wish to take over the daily briefings. Bush killed the idea on the spot; he "wanted working-level officers" to do the briefings.[14]

The Democratic candidate for president in 1988, Massachusetts Governor Michael Dukakis, was offered intelligence support and agreed to receive one briefing on worldwide developments at his home in Brookline, Massachusetts. The briefing was delivered on 22 August by CIA Director William Webster and his deputy, Robert Gates, whose most vivid memory of the occasion involved the difficulty the two had in reaching the Dukakis home. Agency security officers were apparently unaware that the route from the hotel where the CIA officials were staying to the Dukakis residence passed through an area near Fenway Park that was completely congested with vehicles and pedestrians trying to force their way to a makeup baseball game. Gates later remembered with some amusement one moment during which the two were stranded in their car surrounded by the crowd. One irate woman peered into their automobile and, on seeing the distinguished Judge Webster, called out to her accompanying friend, "It's that damn Lloyd Bentsen."[15]

Senator Bentsen was not in the car but, as Dukakis's running mate, did attend the briefing. Dukakis had also invited Congressmen Louis Stokes and Lee Hamilton, successive chairmen of the House Intelligence Committee, and his adviser on security matters, Madeleine Albright. When the whole group assembled, there was a peculiar feeling; all of them save one knew each other well from their experience in working together on intelligence matters in the Congress or on the NSC staff. Dukakis was the odd man out.

The governor was attentive as Webster and Gates talked, but he listened with the detached air of someone who was doing it out of a sense of obligation rather than out of any real interest in the substance. After Webster finished an extended one-and-a-quarter-hour presentation on worldwide developments and Gates followed with a 15-minute review of developments in the Soviet Union, Dukakis thanked them but raised no questions. Hamilton and Bentsen posed a few questions that were designed to illuminate matters for the governor but failed to spark his interest. Like the briefings given other presidential candidates in preelection periods, the one for Dukakis was devoted entirely to

---

[14] Charles Peters, telephone interview by the author, McLean, Virginia, 31 January 1994.
[15] Robert Gates, interview by the author in McLean, Virginia, 12 April 1993.

CHAPTER 5

developments abroad. It did not include a discussion of CIA covert action or sensitive collection programs.

In the presidential debates of 1988, CIA officials were expecting the worst from the time the first question was answered. That question, raised during the debate in Winston-Salem, North Carolina, on 25 September, related to narcotics use in the United States. In his answer, Dukakis charged that the administration of Reagan and Bush had been "dealing with a drug-running Panamanian dictator," Manuel Noriega. The governor did not specifically mention CIA, one of several US government agencies that had dealt with Noriega, but Bush did.

The vice president replied to Dukakis's charges by saying, "The other day my opponent was given a briefing by the CIA. I asked for and received the same briefing. I am very careful in public life about dealing with classified information, and what I'm about to say is unclassified." Bush then went on to explain that seven administrations had dealt with Noriega and it was the Reagan-Bush administration that had "brought this man to justice." CIA officers worried not about the facts of their activities in Panama, which they believed perfectly defensible, but were concerned that the Agency's briefings and programs were about to become a political football once again.[16]

The Agency was still the focus of much media attention generated by the activist policies of its late director, William Casey. Moreover, in the course of the first debate, the candidates addressed such politically charged issues as arms sales to Iran, policy toward Central America, US-Soviet arms control negotiations, and the future of the Strategic Defense Initiative, "Star Wars." Bush attacked Dukakis for his alleged failure to support the US military strike on Libya in 1986; Dukakis, in turn, criticized Bush for US policies on Angola. Yet, despite these heated and potentially explosive exchanges, CIA did not become a political issue in that debate or later in the campaign. The second and only other debate between the presidential candidates was held on 13 October in Los Angeles. On that occasion little attention was paid to foreign policy issues, and there was no mention whatever of the Central Intelligence Agency.

In the postelection period, Bush quickly directed the Agency to provide daily briefings to those who would make up his key national security team: Vice President Dan Quayle, Chief of Staff John Sununu, and National Security Advisor Brent Scowcroft. The president-elect also checked to make sure that the Agency was making the PDB available to the chairman of the Joint Chiefs of Staff, Adm. William Crowe. Bush wanted all these recipients to be reminded of what information came from sensitive sources and methods so

---

[16] "Bush and Dukakis, Face to Face on Key Issues," *Congressional Quarterly*, 1 October 1988, 2743.

President George H.W. Bush meets with CIA briefer Charles Peters (standing) and members of the president's national security team. DCI William Webster is seated on Peters's left.

that they would not inadvertently disclose what was classified. He further directed that he did not want the PDB "floating around"; CIA was to show the PDB to authorized recipients and then take it back—it was to be left with no one. His intent was to tighten control of the document "to ensure that the Agency felt free to include more sensitive material." Speaking for himself, Bush underscored that he did not want to "get lazy." The Agency briefer was to appear at 8:15 on his first day in office.[17]

During his four years in office, Bush routinely received the Agency briefer every working day, almost always as the first item of business in the morning. Webster attended these sessions regularly while he was DCI; Gates did so less frequently. The president read the PDB carefully and quite often examined some of the raw intelligence reports that elaborated on an article he found interesting in the PDB. Occasionally there would be an extended exchange between the president and the Agency's briefer; more often, the president or the national security advisor would pose a few specific questions. The briefer would answer these on the spot or take them back to the Agency to prepare a more satisfactory oral or written answer the following morning.

---

[17] Peters interview, 31 January 1994.

CHAPTER 5

This system provided the president direct and timely intelligence support and the CIA intimate knowledge of his interests and needs. The fact that the briefings were held in the early morning was especially helpful because that was when he was most likely to be making and receiving telephone calls to heads of state in Europe. Agency briefers were immediately at hand to respond to any information needed to deal with these calls. Bush was much quicker in his daily routine to use the telephone than his predecessors, not only to contact foreign leaders but also to contact the CIA director for an update on the latest developments.

In discussing the system of daily briefings, Bush observed, after his retirement in 1993, "The real payoff is having the Agency briefer there to follow up. But having too many people around creates a problem—I held it to the national security advisor and sometimes the chief of staff. If the group grows, pretty soon word gets out that 'He's considering bombing Bosnia' or whatever."

Thinking back on the transition from his eight years as vice president to the four years as president, Bush volunteered that there had been no real changes in his intelligence requirements after he moved up to be chief executive: "The big difference is that you have to make the decisions—that makes you read a lot more carefully."

On becoming president, Bush had sought no significant alterations in the format or composition of the PDB. He had become comfortable with it over the previous eight years. Looking retrospectively, he judged that the mix of items addressed had been well suited to his needs. He attributed that suitability to the presence of the briefer while he read the material, making the Agency aware that he needed more or less on a given subject. Bush was sensitive to the fact that his national security advisor and chief of staff would occasionally discuss with senior Agency officers the purported need to include more items on a specific subject in the PDB. Referring to the efforts of his aides to determine what was provided in the PDB, Bush offered this decisive judgment: "I felt well supported on the full range of issues. Don't let anybody else tell you what the president wants or needs in the PDB—ask him."

CIA's relationship with Bush was undoubtedly the most productive it had enjoyed with any of the nine presidents it served since the Agency's founding in 1947. Alone among postwar presidents, he had served as CIA director. Also uniquely, he succeeded to the presidency by election after receiving full intelligence support as vice president. These circumstances were obviously not of the CIA's making and may never be repeated, but they made the Agency's job immeasurably easier at the time.

The good relationship was also a result of Bush's deep personal interest in developments abroad and his experience as a diplomat representing the United

States in Beijing and at the United Nations. More than any other president, he was an experienced consumer of national-level intelligence. Also of critical importance was the fact that he had a highly capable and experienced national security advisor in Brent Scowcroft, who was determined to see that he received good intelligence support.

Bush was candid in telling CIA officers when he thought their analysis might be flawed and equally quick to commend them when they were helpful or identified an approaching key development before he did. There were many such developments because his presidency witnessed the most far-reaching international changes of the postwar period: the collapse of European communism, the reunification of Germany, the disintegration of the USSR and the rollback of Russian imperialism, and the full-scale involvement of the United States in a ground war in the Middle East. On these, and on the lesser issues of Tiananmen Square, Haiti, Bosnia, or Somalia, President Bush was uniquely and extraordinarily well informed.

⌘ ⌘ ⌘

CHAPTER 6

BRIEFING GOVERNOR CLINTON IN LITTLE ROCK

During the presidential campaign of 1992, President Bush continued to receive intelligence briefings on a regular basis just as he had for the previous 12 years. When he was on the road campaigning he was sent the PDB, which informed him each morning of new developments warranting his attention and provided him in-depth analysis of sensitive international situations. When he was in Washington, he would read the PDB with the Agency's briefing officer present so that he could hear of any late updates, review and discuss supplementary materials, and ask for new or follow-up information.

Fortunately, in light of the election outcome, President Bush's background had made him uniquely mindful of the value of providing intelligence briefings to the challenger as well. He had been director of central intelligence in 1976, and in that capacity had personally provided briefings to Governor Jimmy Carter at his home in Georgia. Bush played a major role in arranging briefings for Governor Ronald Reagan in 1980, and as vice president he received briefings during the transition to his own presidency in 1988. There was no doubt that as president he would approve briefings for Governor Bill Clinton, continuing uninterrupted the practice President Truman set in motion 40 years before.

The DCI Visits Little Rock

Soon after the Democratic convention in 1992, National Security Advisor Brent Scowcroft contacted Washington attorney Samuel Berger to offer intelligence briefings to Governor Clinton. At that time, Berger, who subsequently became deputy national security advisor, was serving as a primary adviser to Governor Clinton on foreign policy matters. Scowcroft and Berger agreed that, as a first step, DCI Robert Gates would travel to Little Rock and provide a worldwide intelligence briefing.

In preparation for his meeting with the DCI, the candidate's staff had prepared extensive reading materials for his review. On the appointed day, the governor met over lunch with his running mate, Senator Albert Gore, and with the outgoing chairmen of the two congressional intelligence committees, Senator David Boren and Representative David McCurdy, who were to participate in the briefing session.

The DCI also had spent considerable time preparing, mindful of the governor's lack of familiarity and experience with the Intelligence Community and its products.[1] Knowing that presidential campaigns often kept candidates too busy for regular briefings, Gates also wanted to make the most of what might be the only opportunity to deal directly with the candidate before the election.

Governor Clinton was a gracious host when the DCI began his briefing in Little Rock on the afternoon of 4 September, and the session proceeded in a relaxed atmosphere. The substantive issues on which the DCI focused included the turmoil in Russia, conflict in the former Yugoslavia, and developments in Iraq, North Korea, China, and Iran. He stressed the problem of proliferation of weapons of mass destruction. There was some discussion of foreign economic espionage directed against the United States and relatively brief treatment of a half-dozen Third World issues ranging from hunger in Africa to prospects for Cambodia.

The governor listened attentively and asked probing questions, primarily on proliferation, Iraq, and the situations in Bosnia and Russia. On nonsubstantive matters, which were discussed only briefly, the DCI was heartened when Governor Clinton expressed his support for a strong and capable US intelligence service. Responding to an allusion by the DCI to intelligence budget stringencies, Clinton turned to Boren and McCurdy and joked, "Is this your doing?"

The others were actively involved as well. Senator Gore, in particular, had a number of questions, and Boren and McCurdy drew on their experiences to highlight various aspects of the intelligence business.

Following that meeting, no further briefings were provided to Governor Clinton until after the election on 3 November. This was not surprising; experience with other candidates in preceding years had shown that such briefings have been difficult to arrange or politically awkward during the period of the heaviest campaigning and presidential debates.

Establishing a "Permanent" Presence

Like other Americans, Agency officials followed the campaign and watched the polls carefully but took no steps to establish a CIA presence in Little Rock until after the election had been decided. This left senior managers

---

[1] Robert Gates, interview by the author, McLean, Virginia, 12 April 1993. Subsequent references to the Gates briefing come from this interview.

somewhat anxious about whether a field facility could be set up in time to provide the highest quality intelligence materials to the president-elect should he want them immediately. As it turned out, this was not a problem; it was a full week before the confusion of the postelection period dissipated and Agency officers could discuss the practical aspects of intelligence briefings with the president-elect's team. In the interim, the DCI reconfirmed President Bush's approval for the establishment of an Agency outpost in Arkansas.

A team drawn from CIA's Offices of Communications, Security, Current Production and Analytic Support (CPAS), and Logistics discreetly established an Agency office in Little Rock in the days following the election. The DCI asked the author, as the Agency's deputy director for intelligence, to head the team and to elicit from Governor Clinton and his staff agreement that he should receive daily intelligence briefings from CIA. Although this was accomplished smoothly, at the time I had more than a few apprehensions. We were aware that staff members in some previous transitions, including at least a couple at very senior levels, had worked vigorously to thwart undertakings such as we were about to propose.

On 11 November, I met with Berger and Nancy Soderberg of Governor Clinton's staff to make our pitch. The meeting was held in downtown Little Rock in a hastily commandeered office in the building into which the transition team was moving that very day. Berger and Soderberg could not have been more receptive. They were not familiar with the Intelligence Community or its range of products but were interested in ascertaining what kinds of support could be provided Governor Clinton and key staffers in Little Rock and Washington.

The PDB Briefing Process

During the presidencies of George H. W. Bush and Bill Clinton, the Agency's practice was to print the PDB in the early morning hours and have briefers present it personally to presidentially designated recipients at the opening of business. Having the briefer present when the PDB was read allowed Agency officers to answer a large proportion of questions on the spot. More involved questions and requests for additional information were brought back to analysts at Headquarters, with written or oral answers provided the following day. This system provided the Agency a firsthand and timely method of keeping abreast of policymakers' interests and a reliable means of protecting the security of the PDB.

CHAPTER 6

We described the functions of the various agencies and the products normally provided to the president. Our discussion naturally focused on the PDB, including an explanation of how the president received it from an Agency briefer each day and how the Agency responded to follow-up questions. We recommended that the Agency also provide the governor a daily supplement to the PDB, inasmuch as the regular publication would still reflect the interests of President Bush and its focus would not necessarily correspond with the needs of Governor Clinton.

Berger and Soderberg were shown copies of that day's PDB and a proposed supplemental current intelligence publication. We also showed them the *National Intelligence Daily* and other selected materials, noting that the publications they had before them had been printed earlier that morning in a hotel room in Little Rock. They were clearly impressed with the quality of the books; the installation in Little Rock of secure communications equipment for receiving high-quality color computer graphics from CIA Headquarters proved well worth the effort.

Berger undertook to discuss the issues related to intelligence briefings with Governor Clinton and promised to get back to us promptly. In fact, the next day Soderberg called our advance command post to indicate that Governor Clinton did indeed want to receive the PDB and a briefer, at least for a trial period, to see what kinds of information it contained and what his schedule permitted.

On 13 November, 10 days following the election, we had our first session with Governor Clinton in the book-lined study of the Governor's Mansion. Senator Gore was at the Mansion for other meetings and joined us. Our introductory exchange was a bit awkward as we all fumbled around deciding where best to sit to go over the materials we had brought. We settled on a large round table in the corner of the study. After offering a brief but friendly welcome, our two new customers immediately read every word of that day's PDB, obviously intrigued to see what it contained.

Much of the discussion concerned procedures related to the PDB. The president-elect wanted to be sure he could receive briefings whenever they could be fitted into his schedule. We assured him that he could but suggested a fixed time, preferably an early morning session, as the most likely to be satisfactory on an ongoing basis. We informed the governor that the PDB in the recent past had been provided also to the vice president, the national security advisor and his deputy, the chairman of the Joint Chiefs of Staff, the White House chief of staff, and the secretaries of state and defense, but that in the future the distribution list would be his to control. Governor Clinton replied that he wanted Senator Gore to begin receiving the PDB immediately and asked that we provide it to other cabinet-level recipients once they were named, assuming this was agreeable to President Bush. I took the opportunity to wonder aloud whether it would not make sense to provide the PDB also to the secretary of the treasury, given the steadily growing importance of economic issues. The president-elect thought for only a moment, declared this to be a very good idea and ordered that immediately after the inauguration we should begin regular briefings of the secretary of the treasury as well.

The governor was interested in our suggestion that he receive a personalized supplement. After some discussion, he indicated he would accept in it some material chosen by us to elaborate items discussed in the main PDB. However, he underscored that he wanted the supplement to focus primarily on specific issues requiring early policy action. He opined off the cuff that his list of topics would surely include proliferation issues, Haiti, Bosnia, and Somalia. Senator Gore suggested we include items on global environmental issues.

Berger was charged with drawing up a list of topics to be covered in the supplement. In fact, such a list proved unnecessary, because the staff quickly observed that the issues the governor had identified received virtually daily treatment in the regular PDB. Occasionally, in the weeks to come, the staff was to request that a specific topic be treated in the supplement, and we readily complied.

The discussion of our preparing materials directly related to policy decisions prompted me to volunteer at the first meeting that CIA saw its proper role as providing intelligence reports and analysis, including exploration of the likely ramifications for the United States of pursuing given courses of action. Experience had shown, however, that we should not be in the business of formulating or advocating policy options. In the back of my mind were memories of the policy buzz saws—particularly regarding Latin America and the Persian Gulf—the Agency had walked into during the 1980s. To our relief, Governor Clinton and Senator Gore both understood immediately and agreed with our understanding of the proper role of intelligence. At no time were we to have any problem avoiding policy entanglements.

On the substantive side, both Clinton and Gore had comments on many of the items in the PDB that first day. Various pieces prompted stories of world leaders they had met and countries they had visited. Like all of our readers, they found the graphics—the maps, charts, and imagery—to be especially useful. The fact that the session went on for approximately an hour was flattering but prompted well-founded fears on our side that our chief problem in Little Rock would be scheduling our briefings. It was a continuing challenge to fit the intelligence briefings into the governor's always-hectic schedule.

CHAPTER 6

At this session Governor Clinton was again a gracious host, as he had been when the DCI visited, welcoming us and inquiring about our arrangements in Little Rock. On learning the Agency had set up its operation in a modest motel near the airport, the governor expressed surprise. I half-jokingly responded that we thought it important to impress a new president with our frugality given CIA's limited budget. He took this in good humor, and after laughing appreciatively sat back and said, "Well, I am impressed."

Following the session with the governor, we had an opportunity to talk with Mrs. Clinton as we were departing the Mansion. When she remarked that she was aware of substantial adjustments being made at CIA to deal with the changing international situation, we volunteered that the Agency occasionally had provided support to her predecessors and would be pleased to provide her also with written material and/or briefings to prepare for foreign trips or visitors. She expressed gratitude for the offer and indicated she would follow up through the national security advisor.

Substance of Discussions

The daily intelligence briefings continued almost without interruption from 13 November to 16 January 1993, when both the governor and the briefing process relocated to Washington. Throughout that period, we made a point to provide Governor Clinton exactly the same material that was being shown to President Bush in Washington. This included, in addition to the PDB itself, drafts of national intelligence estimates and selected raw intelligence traffic—including Directorate of Operations reports, State Department cables, and NSA traffic. However, it quickly became apparent that the governor's primary interest was in studying the PDB.

Three subjects were addressed with great frequency in the PDB. First among these was Russia. At the time, the United States and Russia were still putting the finishing touches on the START II agreement. Debate was under way in the press and the Congress about how much additional aid the United States should provide Russia, and there was much discussion of a possible Russian-American summit, possibly one that would include president-elect Clinton. As background to these issues, there were the worrisome daily developments in Moscow as President Yel'tsin and the Russian Congress fought over their conflicting visions of Russia's political and economic future. Coverage of these subjects resulted in the publication of more than 50 PDB articles on Russia that the governor studied during the transition period.

The other two topics that received extensive treatment were Somalia and Yugoslavia. Our policy-level readers had a great appetite for understanding events on the ground in Somalia while discussions proceeded in the executive branch, the press, and the Congress about whether and how the United States should become involved. Clinton obviously knew that he would inherit the Somalia problem whether or not President Bush introduced US forces. Similarly, there were numerous intelligence items reporting on the situation in the former Yugoslavia, and here, too, the governor read with special care, aware that he would be called on to make decisions concerning the level of any US involvement in the conflict there. Clinton seemed throughout to value our efforts to keep him abreast of these developments, and he came to them already well informed. These were two foreign policy problems he had raised in the campaign; he had obviously done his homework, particularly regarding the policy aspects of each.

The next tier of items in terms of the frequency with which they were addressed in the PDB included Iraq, GATT talks in Europe, Haiti, and the Israel-Lebanon situation. During this period, Iraq was relatively calm, although Washington and Baghdad were still jockeying over what was acceptable behavior in terms of the placement of Iraqi air-defense weapons and US overflights. This testing continued throughout the period, and we all were mindful that Iraq's actions might be designed in part to elicit some statement or sign of the attitudes of the incoming Clinton administration.

Concerning Europe, the United States was in the process of negotiating certain intractable agricultural issues with the European Community (EC)—particularly France. This discussion was all but certain to be incomplete at inauguration time. In Haiti, a ragtag fleet of new boats was being built as Haitians prepared to flee their country in the belief the new US president would be more welcoming than the outgoing Bush administration. And in the Middle East, Israeli, Palestinian, and Lebanese leaders were conducting an angry war of words over the fate of the Palestinian expellees then camped on the Lebanese border.

Of these second-tier problems, Governor Clinton clearly was most interested in Haiti. It, too, had been among the foreign policy issues he had highlighted during the campaign. The Iraqi, European, and Israeli issues all were of interest but were fundamentally different in the sense that Governor Clinton obviously did not believe they would require fundamental policy decisions immediately.

A few items in the PDB led to interesting discussions about the relationship between intelligence reporting and appropriate follow-up in the policymaking and law enforcement communities. Sometimes this included discussion of actions that might be taken by the president himself. When he read one piece on the possible transfer of missiles between two countries, for example, the

CHAPTER 6

governor initiated a discussion about actions a president might take in response to such a report. Such occasions permitted us to explain the mechanisms through which the acquisition of intelligence information results in concrete operational accomplishments in the areas of proliferation, narcotics, or other sanctions enforcement.

Unlike the situation in some previous presidential transitions, there was in 1992 a very close congruence between the subject matter presented in the intelligence reporting and the international developments receiving the most attention in the US press. With minor variations, the same issues received the most prominence during the campaign and, to a lesser extent, in the presidential debates.

In fact, during the presidential debates of 1992 there was very little focus on international events. The first debate, held in St. Louis on 11 October, had included some discussion of three high-priority issues: Bosnia, Iraq, and Somalia. The governor's interest obviously continued at a high level as these subjects were discussed subsequently in the intelligence reporting. There were, however, certain other issues raised in the St. Louis debate that turned out to receive almost no coverage and were of little day-to-day interest, including the international politics surrounding the question of US defense commitments and troop levels in Western Europe and the next steps in arms control.

The subsequent two presidential debates, held in Richmond on 15 October and in East Lansing on 19 October, included almost no discussion of foreign affairs. There were some exchanges on global economic issues and the new world order, including the opening of foreign markets to US exports. In East Lansing there was a brief exchange on Iraq. These discussions, however, concerned overall policy direction and did not translate into concrete interest on the governor's part in follow-up intelligence reporting.

To our pleasure, and occasionally to our embarrassment, Governor Clinton read the PDB carefully no matter what might be next on his schedule. We frequently made suggestions that he might want to concentrate on certain items and skip others if he was in a hurry, but he seldom accepted these invitations. On one memorable day the hurried governor was busy putting on his necktie and drinking a Diet Coke when we met for our session. He said he would not have time to read the book and asked that I simply tell him what was important. I gave him two-sentence summaries of a half-dozen items and one longer article in the PDB. When I finished this staccato account I expected him to depart, but he said, "Well, that sounds interesting," seized the book, and sat down and read the whole thing. He had tied his necktie.

Certain aspects of the PDB grabbed the attention of Governor Clinton as they had captured the attention of previous readers over the years. As mentioned earlier, chief among these were the graphics, which he always looked at first. Also, he was obviously interested in the "Weekly Leadership Notes," a feature of the PDB at that time that described briefly what the president's counterparts around the world would be doing during the coming week. Finally, like his predecessors, Governor Clinton reacted well (charitably, actually) to our occasional attempts at humor; he, too, suggested that more humor would be welcome.

Not everything worked. One item that President Bush had found useful, for example, had been a looseleaf notebook the Agency had assembled containing page-size maps of virtually every place of interest in the world. President Bush would regularly open his desk drawer, pull out this collection of maps and refer to it while reading or discussing the PDB. In one of our early sessions with Governor Clinton, we presented such a map notebook to him. He received it with thanks, but that was the last we ever saw or heard of it.

Similarly, we were a bit discouraged, although not altogether surprised, to find that the supplement was only a limited success. I thought analysts in the Agency did a fine job of preparing perceptive background articles pegged to issues treated briefly in the PDB and in providing in-depth material on issues we knew to be high on the Clinton agenda. The first of the supplements, for example, included articles on reform in Russia, the economic outlook for East Asia, the crisis in Angola, and Bosnian Serb flight activity. The second supplement addressed the politically charged issue of detention camps in Bosnia, included biographic material on the three presidential candidates in South Korea, and discussed the background on the fighting in Lebanon. Such material was made available to the governor for a period of days, but it was clear that, while he was interested in principle, he simply did not have time to go through this material unless it was related to a high-priority issue that had to be addressed immediately.

When it became clear that the supplement was not being read and we found ourselves holding it over from one day to the next, we experimented with a much reduced version in which we provided a single page of material on only one or two background issues. These, too, proved of limited utility.

What did turn out to be of use was an art form created in Little Rock by John McLaughlin, CIA's director of Slavic and Eurasian analysis, who spelled me for two-week periods in delivering the briefings. McLaughlin was in Little Rock during a period when the governor's schedule forced postponement of several briefings until noon or even afternoon. By this time, the wheel of international events had turned enough that the morning PDB was lagging behind press reports that were by then available to us and the governor. As a result, McLaughlin began typing up one-page summaries of developments since the

CHAPTER 6

John McLaughlin and President-elect Clinton relax after one of the briefings during the pre-inaugural period.

PDB was published, and we found that these were of interest to governor Clinton. His interest derived from the fact that he was using the briefing process as a useful supplement in preparing for his frequent press conferences. Whenever the PDB briefing was delayed well into the day, we prepared these updates and used them instead of the formal supplement, which was gradually phased out.

Unlike some of his predecessors, Governor Clinton during the transition did not receive any comprehensive briefings on the organization of the Intelligence Community or on sensitive collection programs involving human assets or technical collection techniques. Neither did he receive a comprehensive briefing on covert action programs before the inauguration. As a result, we found ourselves during the PDB briefings occasionally providing explanations of Intelligence Community programs that grew naturally out of the substantive issues discussed in the PDB. This gave us, for example, opportunities to brief on US imaging systems and to describe NSA and its product. On a couple of occasions we provided brief accounts of specific covert action programs, an awareness of which was essential to make sense of the day's PDB.

In retrospect, this probably was a good way to introduce a new president to sensitive covert action and collection programs; that is, tying the fact of a program to its intelligence payoff. Earlier experience had shown that comprehensive briefings on these programs sometimes were overwhelming and did not stick with the recipient. Obviously, after inauguration, any president should still receive a general overview briefing from the DCI and/or the deputy director for operations. In expressing his views on this subject, former President Bush was decidedly of the opinion that a president-elect needed to be briefed on any sensitive programs that had the potential to blow up on him, but otherwise should be spared the details until in office.[2]

Other Opportunities To Help

To underscore the unique relationship between the United States and Mexico, several presidents-elect have made a point of meeting with the president of Mexico during the transition period before holding meetings with any other foreign leader. Governor Clinton was no exception and scheduled a meeting with President Carlos Salinas in Austin, Texas, on 8 January 1993. We had assumed such a session would occur and had prepared a fair amount of material on economic issues—especially the North American Free Trade Agreement—as well as Mexico's political situation and bilateral narcotics cooperation. As it turned out, the governor's own staff had prepared him extremely well on NAFTA, so our material on that subject was largely unneeded.

The day or two before Governor Clinton's departure for Texas to see President Salinas proved to be most hectic. Fearing this, we had worked with his staff to prepare a package of one-page pieces that supplemented the briefing books he had already received. In the discussion in the Mansion before departure on 8 January it was clear he had read the Agency's material carefully. This included specifically the material on the narcotics problem, which obviously was high on the governor's agenda.

The biographies the Agency had prepared of Mexican leaders with whom the governor would be meeting were also of high interest. CIA had found that high-level policymakers welcomed short videos on foreign leaders. In addition to passing along factual information, the videos effectively showed speaking style, body language, emotional intensity, and so on. The Agency had produced a video on President Salinas, and the day before the departure

---

[2] George H. W. Bush, interview by the author, Kennebunkport, Maine, 6 May 1993. Subsequent references to Bush's comments come from this interview.

CHAPTER 6

for Texas we had an opportunity to show it to Senator Gore, who in turn recommended it enthusiastically to Governor Clinton.

Having no confidence we would find an opportunity for Governor Clinton to watch this video in traditional VCR format, we had acquired a minivideo machine, a Sony Watchman, and created a small tape version. Time ran out in our briefing, so Governor Clinton and his traveling companions took the video machine with them so that he could watch it en route to Austin. Berger jokingly remarked that he had heard each new administration receives a free video machine from the CIA. It was returned the next day.

The meeting with President Salinas gave us a welcome opportunity to demonstrate how the Agency could be useful in preparing a president for meetings with foreign leaders. To our satisfaction, when we saw Governor Clinton the next day following his return from Texas, he volunteered that he had found President Salinas and the Mexican approach at the meeting to be "exactly as you had predicted."

We also provided material for use during the many telephone calls the president-elect made to world leaders. The first such instance involved Korean President Roh Tae Woo whom, by coincidence, Governor Clinton was to telephone the first day we saw him in Little Rock. Agency officers provided similar information to assist the governor in making contact with perhaps a dozen other world leaders as well.

The most interesting conversation for which we were able to support Governor Clinton was the one he had with President Boris Yel'tsin on 4 January 1993. Before the call, the governor's aides and we had discussed with him what Yel'tsin presumably wanted from him and the points he was likely to raise during the call. In fact, there were no surprises. The items discussed, as were later reported to the press, included START II and its ratification, Ukrainian support for the treaty, issues of economic reform in Russia, cooperation between the United States and Russia on Bosnia, and the timing of a future meeting between Presidents Yel'tsin and Clinton.

Although it is hardly satisfying to hear only one side of a conversation, particularly one that is conducted through an interpreter, it appeared to be helpful that we were able to sit in the room with the president-elect during his discussion with Yel'tsin. Following that fairly lengthy conversation we were able immediately to go over some of the points Yel'tsin had made. Our discussion served, I believe, to clarify certain of the inherently ambiguous points that had come up. In fact, during that immediate follow-on session and over the next two days, we continued to furnish Agency materials that provided context to the points Yel'tsin had made, especially those related to arms control issues.

McLaughlin had the sad task of helping Governor Clinton with some other telephone calls as well. These were the ones he made to the families of US personnel who were casualties in Somalia. McLaughlin acquired the facts needed to place the calls and, at the governor's request, coordinated with the White House to be sure that calls from the president-elect did not interfere in any way with calls being made by President Bush.

We had been asked to provide substantive and logistic support of a different nature at an earlier point when the vice chairman of the Joint Chiefs of Staff had visited Little Rock. On 4 December, Adm. David Jeremiah, accompanied by Assistant Secretary of State for Political/Military Affairs Robert Gallucci, visited Little Rock to explain the plan for US involvement in Somalia. This visit had been expected but was firmly scheduled only at the last minute. The afternoon before, the White House, through the DCI, had contacted us requesting that the CIA team in Little Rock make the supporting arrangements for Admiral Jeremiah's visit.

The visit went very well, although with much less elaborate logistic support than is usually provided for a flag-rank officer. Agency personnel from the Office of Communications and the Office of Security handled all the arrangements and served as escort officers. They rented a van to transport the expected large number of briefing boards, cleared the military team with the Secret Service, and transferred the admiral and his supporting staff to the Governor's Mansion and back to the airport. Once at the Mansion, they introduced Admiral Jeremiah and his team to the Clinton staff.

The briefing itself was attended not only by Governor Clinton but also by Senator Gore and by Warren Christopher, who had not yet been designated secretary of state. Other Clinton aides were also present. Inasmuch as we had spent almost a month at that point briefing Clinton daily on the situation on the ground in Somalia—and as I had just finished the morning PDB update—Dave Jeremiah devoted relatively little time to describing the current situation and turned instead to a discussion of planned US actions.

As always, Jeremiah provided an informal and to-the-point briefing, which Governor Clinton and the others obviously appreciated. I was relieved to have it occur, because a certain amount of frustration was building among the Clinton staff, who sensibly wanted to know what Somalia operation they would inherit. Gallucci clarified issues related to the policy side of the US involvement. Knowing he would assume responsibility for an ongoing project, Governor Clinton asked about the expected duration of the operation, the conditions under which US forces would be withdrawn, and where things stood regarding the formation of a UN-controlled follow-on force that would relieve the US

CHAPTER 6

units. Governor Clinton's own predictions about how long US forces would be required to stay in Somalia ultimately proved to be right on the mark.

Later in December, McLaughlin and the rest of the group then in Little Rock had a full and exciting day when Governor Clinton named his national security team. While McLaughlin was waiting for his late-morning appointment on 22 December, the national security appointees entered the Mansion's reception area. This gave him and the governor's aides an opportunity to caucus with the appointees in an informal roundtable discussion of the latest events in Serbia, Russia, and the Middle East in preparation for the day's press conference.

During the press conference, the appointments of Warren Christopher, Les Aspin, Tony Lake, Madeleine Albright, Jim Woolsey, and Sandy Berger were announced. Following the press conference, Agency officers had a welcome opportunity to meet the DCI-designate, brief him on the international situation, and show him quickly around the facility that had been established in Little Rock.

As luck would have it, about the time the personnel announcements were made, Little Rock Airport became completely fogged in and none of the appointees was able to depart the city as anticipated. The stranded group all assembled for dinner that evening with one exception—the DCI-designate. Christopher indicated the next day that the group had been curious about Woolsey's whereabouts, joking that "those CIA folks" must have spirited him away. We dispelled the mystery surrounding the DCI-designate's disappearance. It had been important for him to get to California the next day, so one of our communications officers had rented a car—at Woolsey's expense—and driven him to Dallas so he could catch an early morning flight to California.

Great Support Made It Work

Immediately after the election, two representatives of the Office of Communications had been sent to Little Rock to find office space for our support operation. They quickly located what turned out to be a perfect setup in the Comfort Inn, a modest motel approximately a mile from Little Rock Airport. There was an even more modest restaurant, a Waffle House, adjacent. The location facilitated the regular turnover of personnel and provided convenient access to the Governor's Mansion, which was a five- to ten-minute drive from there.

From a security point of view it was an ideal arrangement; we were able to rent a group of rooms that allowed us to control the space above, below and on each side of our command post. The center of our operation was an apartment formerly used by the motel manager, who had earlier installed a "panic alarm" hooked directly into police headquarters. The apartment contained a large living/dining room, which we converted into office space, and two bedrooms, one of which was used as an office for the senior briefer and the other as a refuge for the person who caught the overnight shift. Finally, the facility had a kitchenette that made it much more habitable for all concerned. Coming from Washington, we were impressed that the cost of our individual rooms was $38.50 per night. We paid twice that for the apartment. The motel staff could not have been more supportive or discreet. Initially, they presumed that we were with the Secret Service, an impression we soon corrected.

Our security officers took pains to get to know the Secret Service detail in Little Rock. This was time well spent; its members were eager to give us any backup security assistance we might need at the command post and were most helpful in facilitating our access to the Governor's Mansion. Their help was all the more necessary when we accompanied the Clintons to California and South Carolina.

At the time we established our operation, the press in Little Rock was eager for news of the president-elect's every activity. This made us apprehensive that press attention to our presence could force our relocation to secure quarters. As a result, we investigated the possibility of operating from Little Rock Air Force Base. The commanding officer was eager to have us locate there and was prepared to offer every assistance. Our security and communications officers visited the base and were given a tour of the proposed facilities. Secure storage, office space, and communications were available to us.

The problem was that the air base was several miles beyond the city of North Little Rock on the other side of the Arkansas River; the drive to the Governor's Mansion would have been considerably longer. Moreover, although some quarters might have been available, we would not have been able to stay nearly as close to our command center. In the motel we could simply walk out of one room and into another to receive secure calls, faxes, and so forth. With this convenience in mind, we kept the air base as a fallback possibility, but we were never forced to use it.

It was three weeks before the press became aware of, or at least paid any attention to, the fact that the CIA was present in Little Rock and was providing intelligence briefings to the president-elect. In the early days of our operation the governor's staff had been happy to follow our suggestion that we simply make no public announcement about our operation. At a later stage, however, there was discussion in the press about how Governor Clinton was preparing to take on the international responsibilities of the presidency. At that point, the governor's team confirmed publicly that he was receiving regular briefings from the Agency and was seeing all intelligence material available to President Bush.

CHAPTER 6

It took a few days for the press to get the story straight. Initial inquiries came from the *Los Angeles Times* on the first of December. On the second, the *Arkansas Democrat Gazette* made reference to "daily written briefings from the Administration and briefings by telephone." A day later, the *New York Times* came closer, reporting that "the Central Intelligence Agency has set up an office in Little Rock from which to deliver a copy of the *National Intelligence Daily* to Mr. Clinton. Mr. Clinton also receives a fifteen-minute oral briefing on security matters every day that aides say is the same one that Mr. Bush gets at the White House." Later, on NBC's morning news program, the governor's spokesman, George Stephanopoulos, explained that the president-elect was fully informed about foreign policy issues because the "CIA briefs him daily."

The press kept a vigil on the side street from which all traffic entered and exited the Governor's Mansion and on many occasions filmed our comings and goings. Nevertheless, we were not pursued or otherwise bothered and were successful throughout in protecting our identities and location. Keeping a low profile, however, meant we made little use of the bar in the Capital Hotel downtown; it was the gathering place for visiting politicos, but was also the hangout for all the reporters.

If the Office of Communications had found it easy to acquire a secure and inexpensive location from which to operate, they were challenged a good deal more in establishing the communications links to Washington. The problem came from the fact that we needed to install in Little Rock an unusually capable system that allowed us to transmit a quantity and quality of material significantly greater than anything we had previously done for VIP support on the road. In normal circumstances, traveling PDB recipients in 1992 received a black and white document transmitted via a rather basic secure fax system. As a result of work that was already under way in Washington, it was clear that we had the hardware and software capability to deliver a very high quality version of the PDB to Governor Clinton in Little Rock. The system had never been field-tested, however, so we needed to be sure we had a reliable and redundant capability. The equipment that was installed allowed us to input text at Headquarters and immediately receive and edit it at the other end. It also allowed us to transmit very high quality color graphics, maps, and imagery.

Over and above the PDB operation, we were able with this capable communications system to send large numbers of documents in both directions to support the briefing operation on a real-time basis. This capability was invaluable in enabling us to answer questions and provide background material to Governor Clinton and his aides. Over time the Agency team became sufficiently adept at using the new equipment that it could replicate the process in California when Governor Clinton traveled there over the Thanksgiving holiday and at Hilton Head, South Carolina, where he spent several days after Christmas.

In large part because of the hard work of our people at Headquarters, we were able to publish a book indistinguishable from the one published by the Agency's printing plant. Personnel in Washington put in countless hours of overtime to provide 24-hour support of all kinds. Their mastery of the digitized color graphics process was but one critical contribution. All who participated in this operation thought it set a standard for future VIP on-the-road support.

Looking back, we flinched to discover that our undertaking in Little Rock was by no means inexpensive, even though the cost of hotel rooms was a modest $38.50 per night. Substantial expenditures were made for personnel rotation and accommodations, computer equipment and communications lines, and per diem expenses. By inauguration day, we had incurred expenses in excess of a quarter million dollars.

What Was Accomplished

By any quantitative measure, the Agency succeeded in the primary purpose of providing intelligence briefings to help the president-elect become well informed about international developments. President-elect Clinton read hundreds of intelligence reports on current developments relating to US interests. A large proportion of these reports addressed subjects that were of high priority to him personally, including Bosnia, Somalia, and Haiti. One cannot know precisely how valuable this intelligence reporting may have been, but we did observe with satisfaction that he read the material daily and carefully.

Beyond the PDB briefings, the Agency provided a great deal of ad hoc support. This material was used to prepare for meetings and telephone calls to foreign leaders and in other policy deliberations. On a more pedestrian level, the Clinton team turned to the CIA for help with such things as acquiring safes for secure storage and arranging for the establishment of secure communications between Little Rock and Washington. At varying times we functioned not only as representatives of the Intelligence Community but as surrogates for the State Department, the Joint Chiefs, the Department of Defense, and the General Services Administration.

At no time did we seek or receive any systematic feedback from Governor Clinton on the assistance we were providing, but he was appreciative throughout the transition period. And we have some independent accounts of his reactions. Former President Bush recalls, for example, that when the Clintons visited the White House after the election, the governor "went out of his way to tell me the briefings were useful and he planned to continue them." Bush added that Governor Clinton "told me the CIA information made a big difference on Haiti. He said that the Agency's intelligence made an impact on him and was influential in the decisions he subsequently took."

Immediately after the election, Bush had delegated to Scowcroft the job of dealing with the Clinton team regarding the intelligence briefings. During the Clintons' visit to the White House, however, Bush underscored how useful CIA's daily briefings had been to him and urged the president-elect to continue to receive them when in office. Bush says he also stressed the need to limit the distribution of the PDB. "I told him you had to control and limit access so that the Agency could put everything in the book."

From the Agency's institutional point of view, establishing the practice of regular briefings of the president and senior national security officials met an important goal of the Little Rock operation. However, once he was in office, President Clinton after a few months discontinued the practice of receiving daily PDB briefings. After US forces were killed in Somalia in the Black Hawk Down incident, the briefings were restored and over the years were often attended by the DCI. Throughout Clinton's two-term presidency, intelligence reports regularly reached National Security Advisors Tony Lake and Sandy Berger, and the president. The products of the Intelligence Community may have had more impact than the briefers themselves.

CIA employees felt their efforts rewarded when President Clinton spoke of this briefing process during a visit to the Agency's Headquarters in Virginia on 4 January 1994, after almost a full year in office. The president observed:

Intelligence is a unique mission. Nobody knows that better than those of us who have the honor to serve in the Oval Office. When President Truman autographed the photo of himself that hangs in this building, he wrote, "To the CIA, a necessity to the president of the United States, from one who knows." Every morning, the president begins the day asking what happened overnight. What do we know? How do we know it? Like my predecessors, I have to look to the intelligence community for those answers to those questions. I look to you to warn me and, through me, our nation of the threats, to spotlight the important trends in the world, to describe dynamics that could affect our interests around the world.

The Little Rock undertaking also enabled Agency personnel to meet a large proportion of the people who were to become prominent in the Clinton administration. Senior Agency briefers established at least some relationship with all those who later became key White House figures. We had an opportunity to meet all of those appointed to the top national security posts and the majority of other cabinet-level appointees. Each of the new appointees was exposed to the Agency's role in supporting the president-elect. On one occasion a new cabinet appointee was clearly surprised to see Agency briefers waiting to see the governor and inquired about the frequency with which such briefings were given, asking if they occurred weekly or on some other basis. The questioner was obviously surprised and impressed when told that the Agency briefed each day.

All Agency personnel involved in the Little Rock operation—in Arkansas and at Headquarters—came to have a sense of satisfaction and pride in what they were able to accomplish. Each was also aware, however, of the unique opportunity they had been given and of their good luck that the operation worked out as well as it did.[3]

⌘ ⌘ ⌘

---

[3] Senator Robert Dole, Clinton's challenger in the 1996 election, was not provided a worldwide intelligence briefing. Following the Republican convention, CIA's deputy director for intelligence at the time, John Gannon, proposed in writing to Director John Deutch that Dole should be offered the customary overview briefing. The author contacted Deutch and his chief of staff, Michael O'Neil, both of whom presume the Agency surely would have offered a briefing, but neither of whom remembers having taken any action to arrange it. Deutch and O'Neil both said they had a vague memory that Dole declined a briefing. Senator Dole has no recollection of having been offered an intelligence briefing.

CHAPTER 7

GEORGE W. BUSH: DEMANDING CONSUMER

Governor Bush was "the most interactive 'briefee' I've ever dealt with," wrote CIA Deputy Director John McLaughlin after a four-hour session at Crawford, Texas, in September 2000.[1] Recalling the experience years later, McLaughlin said, "I remember thinking that whoever would be briefing this president better be ready for a ride."[2] Bush had little experience with international affairs but, even as a candidate, was a rigorous questioner who expected a great deal of those dispatched to provide him intelligence assessments of the world situation.

McLaughlin had become responsible for this first intelligence briefing of candidate Bush through a scheduling conflict. The standard practice over the years had been for the DCI personally to brief presidential candidates from each party shortly after their nomination. In mid-2000, the DCI was George Tenet, a charismatic leader who had held the position three years and was conversant with all substantive issues. In any normal circumstances, he would have followed the usual practice and traveled to Texas to deliver a comprehensive, worldwide intelligence overview to the recently selected Republican candidate.

As it happened, the briefing of the governor was scheduled for 2 September. Tenet, however, was centrally involved in extended diplomatic negotiations related to the Israeli-Palestinian peace process and was traveling in the Middle East in early September.[3] As a result, it fell to Tenet's deputy, McLaughlin, to prepare the briefing and deliver it in Texas.

Although Tenet stayed completely out of the process of assembling the briefing team and materials, McLaughlin did receive some guidance. Clinton administration National Security Advisor Sandy Berger counseled, "Don't tell him [Bush] anything sensitive," to which McLaughlin good naturedly replied that he "would use [his] own judgment." Berger understood such briefings had been standard practice since the candidacies of Dwight Eisenhower and Adlai Stevenson and had personally helped make arrangements for President-elect

---

[1] John McLaughlin, "Governor Bush Briefing," 2 September 2000.
[2] John McLaughlin, interview with the author, Washington, DC, 28 September 2011.
[3] George Tenet, *At the Center of the Storm* (New York: Harper Collins, 2007), 73.

CHAPTER 7

Clinton to receive his briefings. At the same time, he was known in 2000 to have limited enthusiasm for the process and came across as wanting to keep the Bush briefing low-key. This understandable dilemma—and exchanges similar to this one—had occurred in a great many transitions, with the outgoing administration not sure which candidate would accede to office and thus very protective of sensitive and classified information, but with its intelligence officers on the hook to provide the best and most useful available information to candidates who might soon be in the White House.

The briefing was held in a casual setting on a Saturday morning in the living room of the modest, original Prairie View home on Bush's ranch at Crawford. In addition to the governor, campaign advisers Condi Rice, Paul Wolfowitz, and Josh Bolton attended. Rice and Wolfowitz asked a number of substantive questions and requested occasional clarifications to highlight a particular point or ensure an area they were interested in was sufficiently covered. All the briefers observed and later remarked, however, that the governor was clearly in charge "from moment one."

From the Intelligence Community side, the team included, in addition to McLaughlin, three senior analysts and managers with expertise in Latin America, East Asia, and the Middle East. McLaughlin himself was a longtime expert in European and Russian issues. The plan was for McLaughlin to deliver a comprehensive overview of the international situation using a series of desktop tent graphics that he would display and flip over as he progressed. The three experts would then join him in fielding questions during a discussion period. Governor Bush listened politely to the first few sentences, then made clear with his preemptive questioning that he was not taken with this painfully systematic approach.

Similarly, the governor was not intrigued by a briefcase the Middle East expert had brought along—one modified to show how easily terrorists could conceal and disperse biological or chemical agents. Such show-and-tell devices usually intrigued individuals and groups being briefed, but the governor gestured to the effect of "get that out of here" and wanted to settle down to serious discussion. He did focus carefully on various satellite images and charts that helped illuminate threats such as worldwide missile proliferation.

There was ample time in this extended session with Governor Bush to discuss all principal threats to the United States and key international players, both states and personalities. Not surprisingly, in 2000 these subjects included countries of perennial interest to the Intelligence Community such as China, Russia, and North Korea; the range of active and potential trouble spots in the Middle East and South Asia, notably Iraq, Iran, and the Israeli-Palestinian dispute; the Balkans, especially Kosovo and Serbia; and a number of Latin

American countries where US interests might be compromised by foreseeable possible developments.

The terrorist threat to the United States was an important element of the briefing. At this time, more than a full year before 9/11, the discussion had a worldwide focus. The Middle East specialist explained his assessment that the next president would face a terrorist attack on US soil, and there was discussion of what certain scenarios could look like. In his memoir, President Bush recalled that he "had received my first briefing on the [al-Qa'ida] terrorist network as a presidential candidate."[4] Much of the discussion addressed a particularly high-stakes variant of terrorism—the possible proliferation to terrorists of weapons of mass destruction by rogue states.

During the briefing Bush took care to explore information about world leaders with whom he anticipated he would be meeting as president. One briefer recalled that this discussion involved "much granularity," with the governor in several instances offering his views of a given leader. He was interested in standard biographical details, but also in gaining less tangible insight into key leaders. The governor's focus on personalities made an strong impression with a second briefer—"That's when he lit up," the briefer recalled. President Bush was very much a people person, and while working knotty issues throughout his time in office, always maintained personal contact with counterparts abroad.

Interactive and sure of himself, Bush was an active questioner and participant throughout the morning, to put it conservatively. In addition to exchanges on key countries, regions, and leaders, he entered into discussion on a variety of military, proliferation, weapons, and big-picture economic issues. Intentionally or not, on some issues he helped the briefers calibrate their presentations by sharing information on countries he had or had not visited and explicitly indicating when information was new to him.

CIA briefers in Crawford were frank to acknowledge areas of importance in which reliable intelligence information was insufficient to draw definitive conclusions. On a couple of occasions during the extended discussion, they could see that Bush was surprised the Intelligence Community did not know more on a given issue. One briefer was concerned the governor might wonder if the briefers were "pulling their punches," adding they certainly did not hold back. It was clear Bush would want "fine-grained human intelligence" when in office.

During the briefing, the issue of intelligence entanglement with policy matters did not arise in any significant way. The governor expressed his views and noted areas where he anticipated policy decisions would be needed. But even on one or two issues where his questions could have been construed as asking

---

[4] George W. Bush, *Decision Points* (New York: Crown Publishers, 2010), 134.

CHAPTER 7

for policy advice, he readily settled for relevant intelligence information devoid of any recommendations on actions that might be taken. He did ask specifically about the role of DCI Tenet in the ongoing Middle East peace process. This was, indeed, an almost unique situation in Agency history, one that Tenet has termed a "semidiplomatic function." His very close involvement with the Israelis and Palestinians at the end of the Clinton presidency was understood at the time as building capabilities and trust to facilitate negotiations rather than as a policymaking role in the negotiations themselves.

At the outset of the session, Governor Bush had asked the team about their areas of expertise and how their jobs and challenges had changed since the end of the Cold War. At the end, he discussed his expectations of intelligence should he be elected and the importance of deploying intelligence capabilities to identify opportunities, prevent conflict, and protect the United States. Overall, the briefers felt satisfied they had been able to cover most of the considerable ground they had come prepared to discuss. In keeping with the Agency's preference to keep its officers out of the limelight, McLaughlin declined Bush's invitation to join him when he met with reporters immediately after the briefing.

During the preelection period in which Governor Bush received his one worldwide briefing, a similar briefing was offered to the Democratic presidential candidate, Al Gore. Not surprisingly, he declined. As sitting vice president, Gore for eight years had been receiving daily intelligence updates in the form of the PDB, as well as more in-depth briefings at meetings of the NSC and otherwise, as requested. At the time President Clinton approved the plan to offer a worldwide briefing to Governor Bush, however, he requested that a similar briefing be offered also to Joe Lieberman, the Democratic candidate for vice president. Senator Lieberman accepted the offer, and was briefed by Martin Petersen, CIA's associate deputy director for intelligence for strategic plans. Petersen found Lieberman to be most gracious and appreciative.

Senior officers of the Intelligence Community have always been eager to brief candidates of both parties, with the same material, to make clear the process is completely nonpolitical. Despite such efforts, however, the IC and its assessments have sometimes become political footballs in presidential campaigns. In the historic debate on international affairs between Vice President Nixon and Senator John Kennedy in 1960, for example, the candidates engaged in testy exchanges on the so-called missile gap between the United States and the USSR, and on Soviet economic strength. On both of these issues, the candidates cited intelligence assessments and public statements of DCI Allen Dulles to buttress their positions. From the point of view of the IC, no good can come of such a development.

In 2000, the international situation was generally calmer than it had been in many earlier transitions and was destined to be in the next one. On the hopeful side, reformers that year had won control of the Iranian parliament for the first time since the Islamic revolution; North and South Korea signed a peace accord; Serbian President Milosevic was voted out of office; and democracy seemed to have matured in Mexico, as Vicente Fox's election as president ended decades of one-party rule. The immutable problem areas of the Middle East endured, notably renewed, serious clashes between Israelis and Palestinians and the need to contain Saddam Hussein. But in a reflection of the times, as the campaign went on, leaders of IC agencies were deliberating how to scale back their budgets and manpower to meet the stringencies of the post-Cold War "peace dividend" period.

The Presidential Debates

The first of three presidential debates between Al Gore and George Bush was held on 3 October at the University of Massachusetts in Boston. The second was at Wake Forest University in Winston-Salem, North Carolina, on 11 October, and the last at Washington University in St. Louis on 17 October. There was one vice-presidential debate between Joe Lieberman and Dick Cheney, held 5 October at Centre College in Danville, Kentucky. Domestic issues dominated all the debates, but the moderators ensured there were some exchanges related to international affairs. Intelligence issues arose only indirectly or by implication.

The first foreign affairs question posed in the debate in Boston was how to deal with President Milosevic of Serbia, who was clinging to power despite having lost the election. Gore and Bush sought to distinguish their positions from one another, including on the matter of whether Russia could help solve the problem, and whether it would be appropriate to use force in such a situation. Fortunately for the IC, the two candidates agreed more than they disagreed, and the substantive intelligence record on the Balkans was a very strong one, so there seemed to be no temptation on anyone's part to bring intelligence issues into the exchange.

Bush and Cheney offered forceful critiques of US actions and the situation in Iraq. On October 5 in Danville, Cheney charged that the US government "no longer knew what was happening in Iraq, in particular, whether that government was reconstituting its programs for building weapons of mass destruction." Cheney at this time offered no explicit criticism of intelligence related to Iraq, but the implication was clear, especially in light of extensive reviews of intelligence performance on Iraqi WMD programs before and after the first war with Iraq in 1990–91, when the US-led coalition drove Iraqi forces out of Kuwait and destroyed them.

In his second debate, Governor Bush echoed Cheney's points, saying, "We don't know whether he [Saddam Hussein] is developing weapons of mass destruction." And in the third debate in St. Louis: "The man may be developing weapons of mass destruction, we don't know." Again, these were not explicit criticisms of the IC, but they drew attention to a key area where available intelligence did not meet the needs of policymakers.

Senators Gore and Lieberman defended the defense policies of the Clinton administration on Iraq and a range of other issues, such as troop strength, combat readiness, and weapons acquisition practices. Gore during the debates twice referred to his service on the House Permanent Select Committee on Intelligence as well as his experience on the Senate Armed Services Committee and on the NSC.

By virtue of not having been mentioned by name even once, the IC and the CIA emerged almost unscathed from the presidential debates of 2000, although the several references to the inadequacy of information on Iraq were embarrassing.

Postelection Briefings

Within a few days of the election, presidents-elect customarily have chosen to begin receiving daily intelligence briefings, in which they receive exactly the same publication—the *President's Daily Brief*—that is prepared for the incumbent president right up to Inauguration Day. Every president since Harry Truman has recognized the need for his successor to be up to speed on international developments from the moment he takes the oath of office, so these briefings have been approved in all cases. The president-elect may also task the briefers for additional information, in the form of answers to specific questions or additional supplementary papers.

CIA was in position immediately to provide briefings to the president-elect, whichever candidate that might be. If Gore was elected, he would continue to be briefed in Washington. If Bush was elected, he would be briefed in Austin by the Agency's most senior analyst, Winston Wiley, the deputy director for intelligence, or one of his two deputies, Jami Miscik or Marty Petersen. These briefers were supported in Austin by a four-person team that included a mid-level analyst, communications officer, graphics expert, and information technology specialist. Such a team was in place in Austin on Election Day, with equipment and real-time connectivity that gave them access to the full range of intelligence information they would have had at their desks in Washington.

President elect George W. Bush and Associate Deputy Director for Intelligence Marty Petersen before a briefing in Austin, Texas.

Everyone was surprised when 7 November 2000 came and went with no president-elect. The uncertain outcome of the election in Florida, owing to the "hanging chads," resulted in a month's delay before briefings could begin. Ever resourceful, the support teams—which rotated through Austin roughly every 10 days—used this period to practice the process of receiving the electronic PDB from Washington and sorting through voluminous raw reports and finished intelligence products from several intelligence agencies to assemble the morning package that would be briefed to Bush should he become president-elect. The teams found this to be time well spent. As one of the "Austin analysts" put it, "We were trying to get smart on the whole world."

In fact, presumably anxious about the impact of the extended delay or foreseeing the legal outcome, President Clinton ultimately approved briefings for Bush even before the Supreme Court resolved the election. The CIA was surprised to get the word indirectly, when White House Chief of Staff John Podesta on 30 November announced the president's decision on the *Today* show. The following day, Miscik met with the Secret Service to coordinate

CHAPTER 7

access to Governor Bush, and on Sunday, 3 December, with the governor's future chief of staff, Andy Card. Miscik recalls that the latter made clear the Agency, in its briefings, would need to prove its worth and could take nothing for granted simply because Bush's "Dad had been DCI."[5]

Wiley provided the first briefing, on 5 December at the Governor's Mansion. Governor Bush greeted him with an unexpected question, "Are you a direct report to George Tenet?" Wiley was able to answer that he was. He and others felt reinforced in their judgment that it was best to have the briefings of a newly elected president conducted by a very senior manager and analyst who has worldwide expertise and experience supporting the policy process, but is not himself or herself a political appointee identified with the outgoing administration.

The briefings of the governor almost always began exactly at 8:00 a.m., or a few minutes early, and lasted 45 minutes to an hour. Andy Card met the briefers downstairs at the Governor's Mansion and escorted them to the governor's office. Often, the future national security advisor, Condi Rice, or her deputy, Steve Hadley, would attend also. Wiley found that Bush was an attentive, curious listener and an active questioner. Wiley conducted the first several briefings in December, then turned the process over to his deputies, returning for the last few briefings in Texas before President-elect Bush and his team moved to Washington at the end of the first week in January.

Even senior officials encounter unexpected problems. The first day Wiley was to brief Bush, he and the support team at 3:00 a m. were printing the PDB with a fancy, massive color printer, installed for the occasion, when the ceiling collapsed. Water was everywhere; apparently condensate from the air conditioning system that had accumulated and then leaked through the flat roof above them. Fortunately, the deluge just missed the printing and other communications gear. Cleaning up the mess in the middle of the night distracted everyone and dispelled some of the anxiety of preparing to brief the man who looked likely to become the next president.

Marty Petersen was the senior briefer in Austin on the day the Supreme Court decided the outcome of the election. The next morning, he greeted Bush with, "Good morning, Mr. President-elect." Bush beamed. Petersen found that Bush read the PDB carefully and that he sought supplementary material, including raw intelligence reports, international press reports, and the publications of several intelligence agencies. The president-elect regularly received and studied imagery and other graphics. As he had with other briefers, Bush asked Petersen a lot of questions.[6]

---

[5] Jami Miscik, telephone interview with the author, 8 December 2011.

The briefers soon found that the president-elect had an excellent memory and it was important to build continuity into the material they were presenting. Miscik recalls Bush, seeking clarification on one matter, saying, "A week ago you told me X...." She also remembers telling Bush on one occasion that she needed to correct the record regarding what she had told him two days earlier. She was pleased that the president-elect commented approvingly on the Agency's determination to keep the record straight.

Anticipating the transition briefings, CIA prepared a book that contained contributions from leadership analysts in all Agency geographic analytical components. Provided to both candidates, it provided biographical and other information on foreign leaders, including their past experience traveling to the United States. The book included a list of points the foreign leaders could be expected to raise in their calls of congratulations to the president-elect. Bush put this book to use on a number of occasions when he received calls following his election. He was, moreover, a heavy user of the Agency's standard leadership profiles of foreign counterparts, reading more than 30 of them during the transition.

A review of PDB items delivered to the president-elect during a random 30 days of the transition period reveals a wide geographic distribution of subjects addressed. The greatest proportion of pieces devoted to a single region, 25 percent, related to the Middle East. Most of these analyzed developments in the Israel-Palestinian peace process and Iraq.

East Asia and Latin America were also followed closely, each comprising 17 percent of total items. Of the East Asian pieces, two-thirds focused on China and most of the remainder on North and South Korea. The Latin American pieces assessed developments in several countries across the region. Thirteen percent of PDB items related to Russia, which, along with China, was the single country with the most coverage. Europe, other than Russia, accounted for another 13 percent, with most of these focusing on the Balkans.

Fewer pieces concentrated on international economic and energy issues, and fewer still, in this pre-9/11 period, on South Asian countries and international terrorism.

From the start, President-elect Bush seemed to have confidence in his briefers and the CIA. Petersen observed that while he was in Bush's office, for example, the president-elect would often take phone calls regarding obviously sensitive matters. Petersen would offer to leave the room, but Bush invariably signaled him to stay seated, explaining on one occasion, "I can trust you guys." While the relationship of briefer to a president-elect is always a formal

---

[6] Martin Petersen, interview with the author, Reston, Virginia, 21 September 2011.

one, Bush was "warm, friendly, and engaged," according to Petersen. The latter reported that one of his most unexpected opportunities arose suddenly one morning when it fell to him to help the president-elect extract the family cat from the Christmas tree.

Vice President-elect Cheney

During the transition, the vice president-elect was based in Washington. He received his first briefing on 5 December, just as Bush did. CIA adopted the practice of having Cheney briefed by one of the rotating senior briefers who was not that week in Austin. This helped provide continuity and exposed the briefers to the interests and requirements of both officials. Cheney was often briefed in the car during his morning drive from home to the transition office. As both his home and this office were in McLean, Virginia, the short drive put a premium on thinking through how best to use the limited available time.

The vice president-elect had long experience in government and an equally long memory. It was not uncommon for him to request of the briefers that he be provided national intelligence estimates or other materials that he remembered from his time as secretary of defense as addressing a particular subject. Cheney wrote in his memoir:

> *I had spent time on intelligence issues throughout my career, beginning when I was Ford's chief of staff, then when I served on the House Intelligence Committee, and, of course, as secretary of defense. But when I became vice president, I had been away from it for eight years, and I felt it was important to get up to speed.*[7]

When in office, Vice President Cheney was a regular reader of the PDB and other materials. His briefer met with him early every morning, normally at the vice president's home. Briefers found him to be a most careful reader, but more contained and reserved than Bush. In his morning PDB sessions, he generally asked fewer questions and engaged in less discussion than the president. On other occasions, however, the vice president was among the most forceful questioners of intelligence analysts.

The vice president's copy of the PDB normally included the entire package the president received, but also additional material. As Cheney has written, "The second section—'behind the tab,' we called it—contained responses to questions I'd asked or items my briefers knew I was interested in." The vice president usually attended the president's PDB sessions and would sometimes

---

[7] Dick Cheney, *In My Time* (New York: Simon and Shuster, 2011), 315.

draw on his supplementary material in Oval Office discussions or ask the briefers to share the material with the president. Concerning the makeup of the briefing book generally, the former vice president wrote, "In my experience, intelligence was an absolutely crucial element for those in policymaking positions, and if the briefers thought it should be in the PDB, it should go in."[8]

Covert Action Briefing

Senior intelligence officials have never been of one mind regarding the best time to brief incoming presidents and other senior executive branch officials on covert action programs and other very sensitive operations. One line of reasoning is that it is best to hold off on such briefings until the new president and administration have their feet on the ground, unless urgent developments dictate otherwise. The alternative perspective is that it is impossible to foresee what might happen on a president's first day in office and that they should at least have been alerted to the existence of all such programs in case sudden developments force them to make policy or military decisions involving those programs.

In recent transitions, it has been done both ways. Clinton, for example, did not receive such a briefing during his transition. Carter did. With George H.W. Bush the issue did not arise, as he came to the presidency directly from the vice presidency, where he had been aware of all such programs for eight years, and before that in other capacities, including DCI.

In this case, a decision was made to brief President-elect George W. Bush on a broad range of CIA foreign intelligence, counterintelligence, and covert action activities shortly before inauguration. On 11 January 2001, Director Tenet and Deputy Director for Operations Jim Pavitt provided the president-elect, the vice president-elect, Andy Card, and Steve Hadley an extended overview of these programs at Blair House. As he was the Agency officer with primary responsibility for operational activities, Pavitt did most of the talking. Pavitt recalls, "The briefing was a tour d'horizon of what we were doing…all of it. President-elect was engaged, listened carefully, and asked good questions."[9] Tenet has written, "We told them our biggest concerns were terrorism, proliferation, and China. I don't recall Iraq coming up at all."[10]

---

[8] Ibid., 314–15.
[9] James Pavitt, communication with the author, McLean, Virginia, 6 October 2011.
[10] Tenet, *At the Center of the Storm*, 136.

CHAPTER 7

Strong Supporting Cast

The substantive briefings and related materials provided to President-elect Bush during the transition were made possible by the support of a great many Agency officers behind the scenes. CIA's analytical arm, the Directorate of Intelligence (DI), had begun planning the process almost a year ahead. The deputy director for intelligence at that time was John McLaughlin, who had been one of two senior officers providing briefings to President-elect Clinton in Little Rock during his transition. McLaughlin was, thus, particularly mindful and well informed about the logistical, communications, and security issues that needed to be resolved well in advance if the briefings were to succeed.

In December 1999, the DI Corporate Board approved an ambitious initiative to create a system that could provide electronic, online dissemination of the PDB and other materials to the Agency's most senior consumers at any location. Such a system was needed to meet the Agency's responsibility to provide all its consumers real-time intelligence, but the urgency was reinforced by knowledge that a transition would be occurring in less than a year's time. In the early months of 2000, concern also mounted that the DI needed to determine what real estate would be required if the Republican candidate would be supported from a remote location (the assumption was that Vice President Gore would be the Democratic candidate, briefed in Washington). Any such location would present issues involving physical security, communications bandwidth, and coordination with the Secret Service. Mid-level DI officers were identified and assigned responsibility for beginning work in all these areas.

In February 2000, McLaughlin named a coordinator of preliminary work on transition planning, and in May he asked Marty Petersen, the third-ranking officer in the DI, to assume overall responsibility for transition activities. McLaughlin formalized the roles of other officers already working on IT system development, operational and security issues, coordination, and the preparation of substantive material. Petersen held weekly meetings of these officers to ensure corporate awareness and proper coordination as they worked to implement their goals. He included representatives of the Agency's administration and operations directorates in these sessions. Looking back on that period, Petersen stressed that the keys to success were to start early; get the support piece right, as "that can kill you"; and pave the way for timely assistance from relevant nonanalytical components, for example, needed approvals from the operations directorate related to the sourcing of raw intelligence reports to be shown to the president-elect.

As early as late May, when it had become clear Governor Bush was very likely to become the Republican nominee, DI officers visited Austin to look into real estate options and travel routes for the briefers. The team arranged for secure office space within a reasonable driving distance of the Governor's Mansion. The DI's senior officer responsible for security matters contacted and consulted with the Secret Service well in advance of the election in order to pave the way for seamless cooperation immediately after Election Day. At the appropriate time he also made contact and contingency arrangements with the governor's own staff. By the time briefings began in December, this officer had made multiple trips to Austin, and he stayed in the city for the first week of briefings to ensure everything worked as planned.

The most suspenseful part of the preparations was the challenging IT effort to provide the PDB online and ensure that the analysts and briefers in Austin would have all the capabilities they had on their desktops in Washington. In January 2000, the DI named a program manager for the new presidential intelligence dissemination system.[11] That officer was charged with creating a modernized system second to none, yet cautioned that the effort in Austin "will be the briefing of your lifetime.... We want to impress him as best we can...the briefing cannot fail." From the outset, all involved were concerned these considerations might prove mutually exclusive.

The program manager worked closely with In-Q-Tel to provide managers with options on how to proceed. Founded in the late 1990s, In-Q-Tel was a unique innovation for CIA. Although funded by the Agency, it is an independent, nonprofit, private corporation that undertakes to harness the best of private sector technology to meet Agency operational and programmatic needs. Inevitably, there have been some successes and some failures. This time had to be a success.

In-Q-Tel in 2000 provided some dramatic possibilities for technologically enhanced briefings. The most memorable, in the judgment of the program manager, was an iPad-like system in which the briefer could immediately bring up virtually any relevant intelligence information (albeit with a click rather than a touch of the screen). In-Q-Tel's proposed options were carefully considered by officers representing analysts and briefers who would be using the new system. Not surprisingly, given the very high stakes involved, the prospective users "were very uncomfortable with the most far-reaching and untested approaches."

The dissemination system delivered by this program was a substantial improvement over existing capabilities for briefing senior consumers while they were traveling and proved reliable when deployed. It included some powerful web-based tools developed by In-Q-Tel. In the end, however, the

---

[11] The quotes in the following paragraphs concerning the IT initiative come from an interview with the program manager, an Agency officer under cover, in Herndon, Virginia, 27 September 2011.

CHAPTER 7

technology used was, in the view of the program manager, "far more limited and fundamental than many of the options—it was not all that avant garde or different." While many of the capabilities developed were not used in 2000, they were, for the most part, introduced into Agency IT services over the next 10 years. "Our ideas got leveraged."

From the point of view of Agency analysts working in Austin, the important thing was that—for the first time in a transition briefing effort—they had computer workstations with full Headquarters capability and adequate bandwidth to meet their needs, including instant messaging. They could receive the PDB electronically (rather than by fax), and they had full access to all Agency databases. Their other equipment included secure telephones and cell phones, secure and nonsecure fax machines, and a desktop publishing capability with a "big, fancy" printer. IT professionals rotated through Austin throughout the period of the briefings to ensure everything functioned properly.

The DI selected four experienced analysts to serve in Austin, helping the briefer prepare for the morning sessions with the governor. The analysts typically were in Austin for 10-day, solo tours of duty, overlapping a day or two with the colleague who would relieve them. The analysts were chosen for their versatility and initiative rather than their areas of expertise, which varied widely. Although the days in Austin were demanding, the analysts reported that they enjoyed and were challenged by the work, which forced them to become knowledgeable about developments worldwide. Looking back on the experience, one of them commented that after the job in Austin was finished, "it was very hard to go back to our narrow accounts."

The analyst reported for work sometime between midnight and 3 a.m. each day to begin sorting through the large volume of intelligence reporting. The basic PDB was the centerpiece of the presentation to the president-elect. There were also press reports from around the world, individual reports from human assets, satellite imagery, communications intercepts, and a wealth of publications from all US intelligence agencies, ranging from leadership profiles on foreign leaders to multiagency NIEs. The governor obviously would not have time to read great quantities of such material, so the task was to identify specific items that related directly to that day's PDB, were otherwise responsive to a particular request or need, or enabled the briefer to make helpful, supplementary oral comments.

A big part of the analyst's work throughout the day was to follow up on questions the governor or his aides raised in the morning briefing. The briefer could answer some on the spot, but often the answer would be provided the following morning in the form of written material prepared by analysts in Washington, or with an oral answer made possible by information acquired from intelligence databases in the 24 hours since the last briefing. The analyst, graphics specialist, and communications officer were all involved in sorting and researching information and preparing responsive material for presentation at the next session. The daily deadline was to get the briefer on the road in time to arrive at the Mansion well before the 8:00 a.m. scheduled start time, as the governor was often ready to begin a few minutes early.

CIA officers at Headquarters were eager to assist the team in Austin—sometimes too eager, in fact. The virtually limitless communications capability presented the analyst and briefer in Austin with a challenge. They were sent a great deal of material and were tempted or needed to access a huge amount themselves. Some material, including many of the most sensitive, "raw" reports from the Directorate of Operations, came to the Agency's Operations Center only in paper form, rather than electronically. The Operations Center therefore tended to use the secure fax to forward various materials to Austin, to the point that the fax pipeline and the analysts were both overwhelmed. When interviewed about their experience and recommendations, the analysts, while grateful, diplomatically noted that Headquarters, and the Operations Center in particular, might have exercised more selectivity and discretion in what was sent to the Agency's support operation in Austin or wherever it might be the next time around.

The president-elect was briefed almost exclusively in Texas during the transition period. There was one important exception, however, when he asked that he continue to receive briefings while visiting Boca Grande Island, Florida for a two-day family gathering Christmas week. The Agency learned of this requirement at the last minute, with the result that briefer Jami Miscik and her supporting colleagues had to stay in a hotel that was a 45-minute drive from the briefing site. On Christmas Day, Miscik and an analyst conducted a trial run, both to familiarize themselves with the route and to try out a portable suite of communications equipment that was much less capable than the sophisticated system they had been using in Austin.

The briefing team was in suspense the early morning hours of 26 December. The download time for the PDB and associated background material was greater than they had anticipated, and they learned by telephone that the president-elect wanted to receive his briefing earlier than even he usually required. In the end, the PDB was received less than an hour before Miscik needed to depart the hotel for the briefing site. The package was assembled, and she reached the president-elect's hotel in time to hear him ask, as he arrived, "Is the CIA here yet?"

One unique aspect to the Florida trip was that Miscik on 26 and 27 December briefed President-elect Bush and former President Bush at the same time.

CHAPTER 7

She recalled thinking that the last person in that situation would have been President John Quincy Adams's intelligence briefer.

Bush's two briefings in Florida and one in Washington during a stopover on his indirect return to Texas were a harbinger of things to come, as the briefer during the Bush presidency would accompany him wherever he traveled. The requirement for briefings while on the road, especially during a family holiday at Christmas, also seemed to signal that the president-elect had come to value and rely on the briefings.

When Governor Bush relocated to Washington at the end of the first week of January, analysts who had served in Austin continued to support the briefer who met with the president-elect. From the beginning of the transition, analysts who were back in Washington (rather than serving in Austin that week) would support the briefer who was meeting each morning with the vice president-elect. Ironically, the analysts found it was harder to do their job in Washington than in Austin. While in Washington, they were "super executive assistants" with a variety of tasks that diluted their efforts to support the briefers. They also observed tension between the long-established PDB staff working with the incumbent administration and themselves. Preparing the range of materials necessary to support properly both the outgoing and incoming administrations created a lot of work for everyone.

All the supporting cast in Austin found they became caught up in "duties as assigned" that were largely unpredictable. It fell to them, for example, to install a secure telephone in the Governor's Mansion, a secure phone and fax in the president-elect's home in Crawford, and safes for secure storage in the mansion and in a second building on the ranch. When the transition briefings in Texas were completed, Agency officers recruited a Secret Service counterpart to help them remove one of the safes to an Agency location.

Impact of Austin

President-elect Bush was provided transition briefings in Austin until 6 January 2001 and was then briefed in Washington right up to Inauguration Day. Deputy Director for Intelligence Wiley used the occasion of the last briefing in Texas to introduce Michael Morell, a senior DI officer who would be taking over briefing responsibilities in Washington and would continue as briefer to President Bush after inauguration. The pre-inauguration briefings in Washington were usually at the Madison Hotel, a setting that Wiley recalled as vastly different from Austin, primarily because of enhanced security—the corridor of the hotel through which the briefers accessed the office of the president-elect was "full of security forces in combat gear." [12]

In their final session in Austin, Governor Bush expressed to Wiley his appreciation for the briefings he had been provided, pronouncing them "great, and helpful." It was what he said next, however, that really stuck in Wiley's mind. The president-elect said, "When I am sworn in, I expect I will be getting the good stuff." CIA knew it had work to do, believing it had been giving him "the good stuff" all along.

Within a week of his return to Washington from Texas, Wiley sent a message to all hands in the Directorate of Intelligence. He reported President-elect Bush had very high expectations regarding the intelligence support he would be receiving from CIA as president and had indicated he would be approving distribution of the PDB only to a few senior cabinet members and White House advisers. Wiley informed his workforce that he would be making a number of fundamental changes to the PDB.

Immediately after Inauguration Day, Director Tenet announced to the Agency workforce that changes would be made to presidential support. "I know that we are off to a strong start with President Bush," he wrote, continuing with an admonition that the Agency should "step up the quality of our support." The director noted that the DI would be taking the lead in implementing improvements to the PDB process, but would rely more than ever before on input from the other directorates. Jim Pavitt added that the DO saw the PDB as a key way it supported the president and his advisers, and that the directorate was prepared to shed more light on the sourcing of intelligence reports because it would increase confidence in the reliability of the information.[13]

In fact, senior CIA officers understood well that the "good stuff" the new president really wanted was what one of them called the "blood and guts" of operations. Historically, CIA had run very sensitive pieces in the PDB, but these almost always were analytical items that did not include operational or programmatic details. Clearly, with the new president wanting such information and willing to limit sharply the distribution of the publication, more such explicit information would need to be included. Wiley also made a number of other changes, the thrust of which, as he put it, was to "break the binding on the book" and make the PDB briefing "an event rather than a book."

---

[12] Winston Wiley, interview with the author, McLean, Virginia, 5 October 2011.
[13] "Agency Announces Changes to Presidential Support," *What's News at CIA*, No. 829, 23 January 2001.

CHAPTER 7

President Bush as a Customer

During his eight years in office, President Bush continued to be actively engaged in the PDB process—his briefings really were events. In the week following his inauguration, Director Tenet and the president's briefer, Michael Morell, met every day with the president, vice president, chief of staff, and national security advisor in what were described at the time as "highly interactive sessions." Initially, in addition to the White House team, PDBs were delivered only to the secretaries of defense and state and to the Joint Chiefs of Staff. This limited dissemination enabled to Agency to include very sensitive operational information as the new president wanted. By the end of Bush's tenure, however, the list of PDB recipients had grown to 20.

After the initial launch, there was a brief time when Tenet did not attend every PDB session. Tenet had confidence Morell would handle the job well, and he did not want it to appear, as a result of his daily appearances at the White House, like he was lobbying to keep his job as DCI on a permanent basis in the new administration.[14] However, the president soon informed Morell that he wanted the director there every day. The briefer was highly knowledgeable about the contents of the PDB, as well as the raw intelligence and analytical considerations that undergirded the day's pieces. He normally introduced the pieces and answered questions. Tenet's contribution, as he has described in his memoir, was "to provide color commentary and the larger context." The director would also "pull back the curtain" and explain to the president how CIA and the Intelligence Community had acquired the intelligence. President Bush undoubtedly became significantly more knowledgeable about the sources and methods of the IC than any previous president, with the exception of his father, George H. W. Bush, who carried into his presidency such knowledge gained during his time as DCI.

To facilitate this free flowing discussion and meet the president's needs, the Agency each day provided Bush with intelligence tailored to his schedule right up to the last minute. This included late-breaking intelligence reports, numerous maps and charts, imagery, and information on operational developments interspersed among the more traditional analytical pieces. The compilation of material was put together with a greater flexibility of format and writing style, clearly leading with the most important items, of whatever length, and greater transparency regarding the source of the material, whether human or technical. Even during the Bush presidency, however, CIA protected absolutely the true names of human sources—those were never included in the PDB.

---

[14] Tenet, *At the Center of the Storm*, 137.

President Bush received an intelligence update every day. As he put it, "Six mornings a week, George Tenet and the CIA briefed me.... On Sundays, I received a written intelligence briefing."[15] His Agency briefer traveled with him wherever he was, which was unprecedented. This daily contact and close relationship enabled the briefer immediately to refer any questions the president might have to Agency colleagues for quick follow-up. It also ensured the contents of the book, and the supporting material, would be as relevant and timely as possible. Periodically throughout his eight years, Bush's chief of staff or national security advisor would work with the DNI or CIA to focus the PDB even more closely on what one of them called the "president's rhythms."

In these efforts to focus the PDB, no one attempted to tell the IC what to say substantively; rather, it was guidance to ensure certain high-priority subjects would be addressed in the PDB at a time when the information would be most useful to the president. For example, for a period the president held twice weekly video conferences with the US commanding general and ambassador in Iraq. It was requested that on those mornings the PDB should include the latest intelligence on Iraq. On the off days, the proportion of the book devoted to other areas and issues would expand, along with the time to discuss them.

In addition to his daily PDB sessions, or as an extension of them, President Bush in early 2007 began a practice of receiving more in-depth briefings directly from CIA and IC experts in selected countries, regions, or functional areas. These sessions, which came to be known as deep dives, were nominally bounded by a specific, planned length of time, but if the president was interested, they would go on longer. The president would often begin by questioning the briefer or briefers about their backgrounds, including the time they had worked on their account, their language expertise, residence in their area of responsibility, and the like. He did this so consistently that before long the Agency started giving him prepared biographies of the briefers for upcoming deep dives. The president obviously wanted to confirm that he was hearing from individuals who really knew their subject. Usefully, he would often characterize his own experience or inexperience with a given subject, which would help the analysts calibrate their presentations.

The vice president, senior White House and NSC aides, and sometimes the secretaries of state and defense would sit in on the deep dive briefings, either in person or via video conference. Generally, the White House aides liked the briefings because they were of interest to the president and were useful to him. Others had reservations, because the president took seriously what he heard in these sessions and would sometimes make what turned out to be quite firm

---

[15] Bush, *Decision Points*, 153.

CHAPTER 7

decisions about courses of action based on the briefings but before the normal interagency policy process had a chance to run its course.

On one early occasion the president was briefed by two analysts in a session at Camp David that was planned for 30 minutes, but which as a result of his extended questioning lasted 90 minutes. Not long after this briefing, the president, according to DNI Michael McConnell, said, "As long as I am president, we will keep doing these."[16]

Intelligence and Politics

In his memoir, President Bush explained he had initially intended to nominate Donald Rumsfeld, veteran of previous Republican administrations, to be DCI. As events unfolded, however, Rumsfeld was selected to be secretary of defense. With no obvious alternative candidate for CIA, Bush decided to postpone resolving the matter definitively, and instead leave George Tenet in the job for an indefinite period. President Bush, in his memoir, explained his thought process:

> *I had great respect for the Agency as a result of Dad's time there. Retaining Bill Clinton's CIA director would send a message of continuity and show that I considered the Agency beyond the reach of politics. I had been receiving intelligence briefings as president-elect for a few weeks when I met the sitting director, George Tenet. Tenet...obviously cared deeply about the Agency. As George and I got to know each other, I decided to stop looking for a replacement. The cigar-chomping, Greek-to-the-core director agreed to stay.*[17]

In his memoir, Tenet wrote, "In my heart I wanted to stay because I felt the job was unfinished." He recounts it was at the conclusion of the briefing of Bush on Agency operations (on 11 January) when the president-elect asked him to stay behind to discuss the matter of his continued service. "Why don't we just let things go along for a while and we'll see how things work out?" he remembers Bush saying. "I gathered from that I was neither on the team nor off it. I was on probation." Tenet explained also that while he would not be a member of the cabinet in the Bush administration, he would soon find he had extraordinary access to the president. "Being in regular, direct contact with the president is an incredible boon to a CIA director's ability to do his job."[18]

---

[16] VADM Michael McConnell, interview with the author, Herndon, Virginia, 26 October 2011.
[17] Bush, *Decision Points*, 84.
[18] Tenet, *At the Center of the Storm*, 136–37.

The president and the DCI were alike in many respects and bonded closely. Their daily contact during the PDB briefings—and shared burden to protect the country from additional terrorist attacks in the wake of 9/11—ensured the director's relationship with the president and senior White House staff was initially strong despite their different party backgrounds. Unfortunately, however, events unfolded in such a way that Tenet's relationship with the White House deteriorated seriously before the end of Bush's first term.

Several intelligence-related issues—including public statements by the administration and the IC about Iraqi WMD, the reported acquisition from Niger of raw materials for Iraq's nuclear program, and alleged cooperation between Iraq and al-Qaʻida—became highly charged politically and caused growing disaffection with the Agency on the part of some senior officials. In such circumstances, the nuances or even essential facts of the issues become irrelevant. When any intelligence matter seriously embarrasses the administration, the head of the CIA, as captain of that ship, is held responsible. By July 2004, Tenet had concluded that trust had been broken between him and the White House. He informed the president's chief of staff, "It's time to go," and, after seven years in the job, resigned.[19]

Porter Goss succeeded Tenet as DCI and assumed responsibility for the daily intelligence briefings. Goss was to be the last DCI. As a result of perceived weaknesses in the structure and functioning of the IC related to the events of 9/11, Congress and the Bush administration created the cabinet-level post of director of national intelligence. In April 2005, John Negroponte was appointed the first DNI and responsibility for the daily briefings thus fell to him. Goss continued as director of the CIA and, like his successors, attended Oval Office sessions, albeit less frequently, to discuss Agency operational matters. Negroponte, in turn, was replaced in February 2007 by Michael McConnell, who carried on the briefings until the end of Bush's second term.

Kerry and Edwards Briefed in 2004

President Eisenhower, running for reelection in 1956, established the practice of approving intelligence briefings for his challenger. Most challengers have accepted. Stevenson (1956), Carter (1976), Reagan (1980), and Clinton (1992) were briefed. McGovern (1972) accepted a briefing offered by Henry Kissinger, which was to be followed by CIA briefings, but Kissinger's briefing and thus the series were cancelled as McGovern dealt with the political fallout from the withdrawal from the race of his running mate, Senator Eagle-

---

[19] Ibid., 486.

ton. Senator Mondale (1984) declined to be briefed. Senator Dole (1996) apparently was not offered a briefing.

CIA has always taken seriously the opportunity and obligation to brief challengers, knowing the process is a nonpartisan one that should favor neither side and that an incumbent president has access to the full range of intelligence information. Beyond that, almost half of those who have challenged an incumbent president in the period the Agency has existed have been successful, making it all the more important for them to receive the government's best information about developments abroad as soon as practicable.

In 2004, the George W. Bush administration followed the well-established tradition and approved briefings for Senators John Kerry and John Edwards. Each candidate received two briefings. Presidential candidate Kerry was briefed on 1 September in Nashville and on 25 September in Boston. Vice presidential candidate Edwards was briefed on 31 August in Wilkes-Barre, and on a second occasion at his home in Washington, DC.

Acting Director of Central Intelligence John McLaughlin conducted both of Kerry's briefings and Edwards's first. McLaughlin had been serving as acting director since Tenet's resignation in July. In addition to having just served four years as DDCI, McLaughlin had been centrally involved in the briefings of President-elect Bill Clinton and candidate George W. Bush and was ideally suited for the task. Deputy Director for Intelligence Jami Miscik conducted the second briefing of Edwards; earlier she had been heavily involved with briefing President-elect George W. Bush.

Agency components provided inputs to an inch-thick package of written material that McLaughlin studied to formulate his briefing for Kerry and Edwards. From that, McLaughlin distilled a briefing that was literally worldwide. His approach, he stressed, was to construct a briefing "that would answer the question, what does he really need to know to be president?"[20] It was also intended to respond to seven pages of questions that had been received from the Kerry/Edwards campaign.

Not surprisingly, three years after 9/11, the briefing highlighted the global war on terrorism, with a focus on al-Qa'ida and other groups, political Islam, and terrorism-related developments in Afghanistan and Pakistan. It also focused on the political situation and insurgency in Iraq, and on states of proliferation concern such as North Korea, Iran, and Libya.

The briefing provided the IC's assessment of developments in countries and regions of longstanding high intelligence interest—Russia, China, and the

---

[20] McLaughlin interview, 28 September 2011.

Middle East—and trouble spots in a half dozen selected states in Africa, Latin America, and East Asia. Finally, it addressed a few transnational issues, including energy security. Even the distilled version of the briefing was substantial—it lasted two hours.

Referring to the subject of Iraq, Senator Kerry informed McLaughlin and the analysts who accompanied him that he wanted the briefing "with the bark off." He asked to hear "exactly what you would tell President Bush." McLaughlin felt he provided the same objective assessment of developments that the Agency had been providing the administration, recalling, "At that time, we [CIA] were not all that popular in the White House [concerning CIA's assessment of Iraq]."

Overall, the briefers found Senator Kerry in both sessions to be "more inclined to be briefed than Edwards or Bush," meaning Kerry would hear them out while they made their points rather than moving immediately to discussion or questions. At the same time, while the senator was very friendly, even gracious, he asked well-informed, probing questions. One of the experts accompanying McLaughlin recalled Kerry asked very specific, hard questions, almost like an interrogation. He felt the session was challenging and rewarding, but intense, saying there "was not a 10-second period that was wasted time." Kerry's highly professional and systematic method of questioning obviously reflected his years of service on the Senate Foreign Relations Committee.

The briefings of Senator Edwards were considerably more relaxed than those of Kerry, and did not run as long. CIA briefers were pleased the first session occurred at all, as they heard Edwards tell his staff as he approached the briefing room at the hotel, "I know I have to do this, but I will get it over with quick and we can go for pizza." In the event, Edwards gave the briefing team a generous amount of time, and the session, although conversational, was interactive and substantive. Edwards's staff participated more fully in the back and forth than did Kerry's, where one accompanying staff member limited his role to asking a few questions to clarify particular points.

Looking back on the briefings of the challengers in 2004, McLaughlin remarked that he "felt very good about the briefing of Kerry in terms of the substance and our relationship with him." He felt the briefing of Edwards was "less thorough" than he wanted it to be.

The presidential debates leading up to the election of 2004 began only days after the second intelligence briefings of Kerry and Edwards. Debates between President Bush and Democratic challenger Kerry were held on 30 September at the University of Miami in Coral Gables, Florida; on 8 October at Washington University in St. Louis; and on 13 October at Arizona State University in

CHAPTER 7

Tempe. There was one debate between Vice President Dick Cheney and John Edwards, held 5 October at Case Western Reserve University in Cleveland.

Inevitably, in light of the intervening events of 9/11, intelligence issues featured more prominently in the debates of 2004 than they had in 2000. The umbrella topic of the first debate was foreign policy and homeland security. Bush referred to the intelligence on Iraq that had contributed to his decision to go to war to remove Saddam Hussein. Kerry said he had accepted the intelligence reporting on the threat from Iraq and supported the president's authority, and displayed an awareness of what had been reported in more recent Intelligence estimates on Iraq.

In the second debate, Bush was more pointed in saying, "We all thought there were weapons there [in Iraq]. I wasn't happy when we found out there were no weapons, and we've got an intelligence group together to figure out why." The president in the first debate underscored his intention to "reform our intelligence services to make sure that we get the best intelligence possible," and, later in the debate, his plan to "strengthen our intelligence gathering services."

In their one debate, the vice president and Edwards had a direct exchange on another controversial issue related to Iraq. In answer to the first question asked in the debate, Cheney charged that Saddam Hussein "had an established relationship with al-Qa'ida. Specifically, look at George Tenet, the CIA director's testimony before the Committee on Foreign Relations two years ago when he talked about a 10-year relationship."

Edwards countered, "Mr. Vice President, there is no connection between the attacks of September 11th and Saddam Hussein. The 9/11 Commission has said it. Your own secretary of state has said it. And you've gone around the country suggesting that there is some connection. There is not. And in fact the CIA is now about to report that the connection between al-Qa'ida and Saddam Hussein is tenuous at best." Later in the debate, Edwards cited his service on the Senate Select Committee on Intelligence and the travel to the Middle East he had undertaken while on the committee as a reason he had "a very clear idea of what has to be done to keep this country safe."

These exchanges regarding the CIA, its director, and specific intelligence issues were the most explicit such references in a presidential debate since the debates between Nixon and Kennedy in 1960. In general, they reflected the dissatisfaction with the IC that was felt by many in Congress and the administration as a result of the events of 9/11 and the WMD issues associated with the start of the war with Iraq. Within six months of the presidential debates of 2004, the White House and Congress disestablished the position of DCI and created the post of director of national intelligence.

George W. Bush restructured the Intelligence Community more fundamentally than any president since Truman in 1948. By a significant margin, he also made more use of the IC to provide information on international developments than any previous president. He almost never missed his daily PDB briefing, acquired unprecedented knowledge about IC sources and methods, devoted a great deal of time to focused, in-depth briefings, and became uniquely informed about intelligence operations.

⌘ ⌘ ⌘

CHAPTER 8

Concluding Observations

Through 10 transitions from 1952 to 2000, the Intelligence Community has provided intelligence support to the presidents-elect. This support, endorsed by each of the sitting presidents, has been designed primarily to acquaint the incoming president with developments abroad that will require his decisions and actions as president. A second goal has been to establish a solid working relationship with each new president and his advisers so the IC could serve him well, once in office.

The IC has been generally, but not uniformly, successful in accomplishing these goals. Overall, it has proved easier to help the new president become well informed than to establish an enduring relationship. Both aims have been met better in recent transitions than during some of the earlier ones. One key variable is that the IC in recent years has made a much more organized and concerted effort to provide intelligence support to the president-elect and the national security team.

The background and attitudes the president-elect brings with him obviously are powerful variables in determining the extent to which the IC's effort will succeed. Ironically, prior familiarity with the Intelligence Community and experience with foreign developments—or lack thereof—do not by themselves predict much of anything. In the period under review, Presidents Reagan, Clinton, and George W. Bush, for example, were by any objective measure the least experienced in foreign affairs at the time of their election, yet by Inauguration Day each had absorbed an immense amount of information. Once in office, their dramatically different operating styles dictated the nature of their equally different relationships with the CIA and the IC.

At the other extreme, Presidents George H. W. Bush and Eisenhower provide clear cases of individuals who had had long experience with intelligence and foreign affairs before their election. Here too, however, their management styles, personal interests, and backgrounds determined their different relationships with IC after inauguration—informal and close in one case, formal and aloof in the other. The Agency had provided good substantive support to each during the transition.

CHAPTER 8

In the three cases where the CIA's relationship with the White House was to prove the least satisfactory—or the most volatile, a different but equally challenging matter—the president either brought a grudge with him or quickly became disillusioned with intelligence. President Nixon felt the CIA had cost him the 1960 election; President Kennedy was immediately undercut and disillusioned by the Bay of Pigs misadventure; and President Johnson was alienated by the Agency's negative assessments on Vietnam. In each of these cases the relationship was not helped by the fact that CIA had not succeeded in providing good intelligence support to, and establishing ties with, any of the three before their inauguration.

The obvious but sometimes elusive key for the IC, and particularly its director, is to grasp each new president's needs and operating style and accommodate them during the transition and beyond. Individual proclivities aside, however, some generalizations can be offered about how the IC can best approach its unique mission of providing substantive support during presidential transitions. Most of the evidence suggests that the Community has learned from its past experiences and built on them.

Patterns of Support

In looking at the intelligence support provided the early postwar presidents before their inauguration, it is necessary to set aside President Truman, who came to office before the creation of the modern IC, and Johnson, whose elevation to the presidency came suddenly amid extraordinary circumstances that one hopes will never be repeated. Concerning the others, it is notable that each of them—Eisenhower, Kennedy, and Nixon—received intelligence briefings both in the preelection period and during the postelection transition. Kennedy and Nixon received few briefings; Eisenhower was given somewhat more, including several presented by the DCI. However, not one of the presidents-elect during the 1950s and 1960s read the Agency's daily publications or met with a CIA officer for daily updates during the transition. Only Kennedy received a briefing on covert activities and sensitive collection programs before being sworn in.

During the first 25 years of its existence, CIA enjoyed no significant success in its efforts to establish a close and supportive relationship with each president. The reverse was true: these relationships went downhill after Truman. He had received intelligence information at the weekly meetings of the National Security Council, read the Agency's daily and weekly intelligence publications, and received in-depth weekly briefings from the DCI. His successor, Eisenhower, was perhaps the best at using the NSC as a vehicle for receiving intelligence, but he did not read the publications regularly and did not routinely see the DCI for separate intelligence briefings. Kennedy, Johnson, and Nixon also received intelligence information at NSC meetings, although they relied less on the formal NSC system. Once in office, these three presidents did read a daily intelligence publication, which took a different form for each. However, no president through the early 1970s read the daily publications with the assistance of a briefer, as has generally been the custom in more recent years.

No DCI during the Agency's early decades was able to replicate on a continuing basis the relationship that Bedell Smith had established with Truman. During the early Johnson years, John McCone attempted to restart regular briefings of the president, but Johnson became impatient and ended them before long. The third DCI to serve under Johnson, Richard Helms, saw that an alternative approach was needed and managed to establish an excellent relationship with the president by providing him intelligence at the famous Tuesday luncheons and via short, highly pertinent papers. But even Helms could not sustain his access or influence with Nixon. During Nixon's years in office, the relationship between the president and the CIA reached the lowest point in the Agency's history.

The presidents who have come into office since the mid-1970s have, during their transitions, received more intelligence information on developments abroad and on the activities of the US Intelligence Community than their predecessors did. Like their predecessors, they all received worldwide overview briefings from the DCI, DNI, or other senior officers. Unlike their predecessors, however, they also read the PDB throughout the transition. With some variations in how it was done, each of them met daily during the transition with an officer of the IC, who provided oral briefings to supplement the PDB. Almost all of this group—Carter, Reagan, George H. W. and George W. Bush—were given in-depth descriptions of covert action and sensitive collection programs during the transition. Clinton did not receive such a briefing; outgoing DCI Robert Gates decided to use his one briefing opportunity with Clinton to concentrate on substantive issues and to leave discussion of sensitive activities until after the inauguration. Ford was aware of such programs from his service as vice president.

Once in office, all recent presidents received intelligence at meetings of the NSC and read the PDB regularly. Distinguishing them from their predecessors, however, was the fact that most recent presidents, with the exception of Reagan, while in office have read the PDB with a briefer in attendance. Usually, a briefer from the IC was involved, although for a portion of Ford's presidency and with Carter the national security advisor was with the president as he read the book and IC officers were not present on a daily basis. For most of the Ford and Clinton presidencies and during both Bush presidencies, IC briefers were

CHAPTER 8

in attendance when the president was in Washington. Briefers also accompanied George W. Bush when he traveled.

The single most critical test of whether the IC is properly supporting the US policymaking process is the effectiveness of the intelligence support provided the president. Overall, the level of that support deteriorated somewhat during the IC's first 25 years but improved and strengthened during the period between the early 1970s and 2008. To a substantial extent, this positive trend resulted from the leadership of one man, George H. W. Bush. Bush ensured that full intelligence support was given to Presidents Ford, Carter, and Reagan, and his own presidency was a high point in terms of the CIA's relationship with the White House. He saw to it that President-elect Clinton and his national security team received extensive intelligence support during the transition and encouraged his son, George W. Bush, to receive the PDB daily. The latter, in 2008, directed that extensive support be provided his successor, Barack Obama.

What the Presidents Recommend

Interviews with four former presidents eliciting their opinions on why the system of intelligence support worked better during some transitions and administrations than others unearthed one immediate, common, and obvious reaction: each president is different. Ford, in particular, stressed that point, asserting that "the backgrounds and circumstances of the various presidents are so different that there can be no one formula for future support. Eisenhower or Ford or even Kennedy were so much more familiar with intelligence than a Clinton or a Reagan." Ford went on to underscore that "the Intelligence Community has to be prepared to be flexible to accommodate the different experiences."[1]

Carter had some of the most concrete advice on how the CIA ought to go about establishing its relationship with each president-elect. As a start, he urged the Agency to "give a new president-elect a paper on what previous presidents had done regarding intelligence support. Let the next incumbent decide—show them the gamut of material."[2]

In discussing how presidents and times change, Carter noted that, if he were in the White House in later years, he would have welcomed computerized intelligence support in the Oval Office. Pleased to hear that the Agency had

---

[1] Ford interview, 8 September 1993. Subsequent observations by Ford also come from this interview.
[2] Carter interview, 23 June 1993. Subsequent observations by Carter also come from this interview.

been experimenting for some time with a system for making real-time intelligence available via a computer terminal on the desk of senior consumers, Carter volunteered, "If I was in the White House now I would welcome it. I feel comfortable with computers and would use it, not as a substitute for the other support, the PDB and the briefings, but in addition to it." He explained that when a question arose about developments in a particular country he would "like to have access to something where I could punch in a request for the latest information."

The IC's experience indicates that a critically important variable in establishing a successful relationship is the approach taken by the DNI (formerly DCI). Comments of the presidents who were interviewed reinforced that impression. During every transition, the director has been involved personally in providing at least one, and in some cases many, briefings. In those cases where the relationship was established most effectively, the common factor was that the director succeeded in bringing the institutions of the IC into the process so that intelligence professionals could assist him and carry the process forward after his role diminished or was discontinued. In one form or another, this has been accomplished with each of the presidents elected since the mid-1970s.

When the institutional link between the IC and the president was not properly established, it was usually because the director attempted to handle the relationship singlehandedly. Two cases show that this can happen in quite different ways. DCI Allen Dulles, for example, chose to support the incoming Kennedy administration almost entirely on his own, giving three briefings to Kennedy and involving only one other CIA person. Those briefings reportedly did not impress Kennedy, and the relationship between the two men, complicated immensely by the Bay of Pigs fiasco, unraveled within months.

In the case of Nixon, Helms was involved in one briefing immediately after Nixon's selection as the Republican nominee and in a perfunctory discussion at the White House after his election. Unfortunately, the handoff of responsibility from the DCI to the CIA career officers positioned in New York to provide support did not succeed in its fundamental purpose. Nixon was never seen personally, and he read very little Agency material. Given his deep suspicions of the CIA and Henry Kissinger's determination to monopolize all contact with the new president, it is doubtful that the relationship could have been handled any better. The Agency's inability to establish a satisfactory relationship at the outset continued throughout the Nixon presidency—arguably, to the detriment of both the president and the Agency.

While vigorous and effective action by the head of the IC clearly is a determining factor in establishing the Community's institutional relationship with a

CHAPTER 8

new president, it does not follow that such involvement solidifies the position of the DCI or DNI himself with the new president or administration. Directors who were the most involved in transition support activities included Smith with Eisenhower, Dulles with Kennedy, George H. W. Bush with Carter, and Turner with Reagan. Sadly, each was disappointed with the role he was given, or not given, by the incoming president.

Generally, directors of the IC retained from one administration to the next are not destined to succeed. All in this category were dismissed or resigned prior to the end of the term of the president who kept them on. Dulles, for example, was very successful serving under Eisenhower but lasted only a few months with Kennedy. McCone served successfully under Kennedy but quickly wore out his welcome with Johnson. Helms was among the Agency's most successful directors during the Johnson years but was later dismissed by Nixon. Colby served in particularly difficult circumstances under Nixon, only to be dismissed later by Ford.

The two most recent cases in which a director was held over, those of William Webster and George Tenet, illustrate a larger point as well. Webster was appointed by Reagan and served successfully in a rather formal relationship with him. Webster had a fairly extended period in the George H. W. Bush administration as well, faring better than any predecessor to that time who had been extended from one administration to the next. On the other hand, he never established with Bush and his key White House aides the close relationship that his successor, Robert Gates, enjoyed as a result of his prior service as deputy assistant to the president for national security affairs. Tenet, likewise, had an excellent relationship with President Clinton, who appointed him as his third DCI, and, initially, with George W. Bush and his staff as well. Politically charged intelligence issues soured the relationship, however, and Tenet resigned in frustration near the end of Bush's first term.

It is often suggested that for each of the directors who was obliged to resign there was a single explanatory cause. For Dulles, the argument goes, it was the Bay of Pigs; for McCone, the Agency's independent analysis of the war in Vietnam; for Helms, the failure to cooperate on the Watergate coverup; for Colby, his failure to alert the White House in advance of the public exposures of the Agency's misdeeds, and so on. A more careful analysis, however, indicates that every director encountered serious difficulties of one kind or another, including some that were an embarrassment to the White House. Most of these problems, however, did not lead to the DCI's dismissal.

Each of the former presidents interviewed underscored that it is of the highest importance for a president to have an intelligence director in whom he has confidence and with whom he feels comfortable. Opinions were mixed regarding the best background or qualifications, whether a nominee should be an intelligence professional or an outsider, and concerning the importance of the candidate's political background. Recalling his nomination of Gates, George H. W. Bush explained, "It helped that Gates had been a professional, but I picked him because he did such a good job sitting right here [on the deck of the Bush home at Kennebunkport, while serving as deputy national security advisor]. Actually, I had known Bill Webster better over the years socially, from tennis and so on, than I had Bob Gates."[3] With the unique perspective that came from having been CIA director as well as president, Bush refused to be pinned down on the issues of whether a CIA professional should hold the director's job and whether there should be a turnover of directors at the end of each administration. Rather, he suggested, "There should be no set rule. It would be good for the Agency to know that one of their own could be [director]. We should never feel like the torch has to pass [at the end of an administration]."

Like Bush, Ford had no strong feelings on the question of whether a director should continue in office from one administration to the next. He pointed out that he "had inherited one and appointed one. You need the right person that you are comfortable with. I worked well with both Colby and [George H. W.] Bush." Ford underscored repeatedly that he had the highest confidence in Colby's handling of the Agency's intelligence collection and analytic activities, but he concluded midway through his term that he simply had to appoint a different director to defuse tensions with Congress over the CIA's past activities. Ford was most charitable in his characterizations of Colby, euphemistically referring to his "resignation" and noting, "I offered him the job of ambassador to Norway, but he declined."

All of the former presidents interviewed, with the exception of Reagan, expressed the feeling that the individual selected to run the IC should be apolitical. Carter, for example, volunteered that, although Bush had proved to be a very capable director of the Agency, his selection had been ill advised because of his role as chairman of the Republican Party—"he was too political." Without, ironically, discussing his own initial choice of Kennedy political adviser Theodore Sorensen to serve as DCI, Carter stressed that the man who did serve as CIA director in his administration, Stansfield Turner, had been a career military officer without any political ties who was also experienced in using intelligence.

More than one of those interviewed was critical of, and used as an example, the selection of William Casey as CIA director. Bush, who like Helms was a forceful advocate of the need to keep intelligence and policy separate, volun-

---

[3] George H. W. Bush interview, 6 May 1993. Subsequent observations by Bush also come from this interview.

teered, "Casey was an inappropriate choice. We would be having a cabinet discussion of agriculture and there would be Casey. That shouldn't be—the DCI should not enter into policy discussions."

Kissinger wrote that Nixon also believed that the job of CIA director should not be a political plum and that this led him to retain Helms rather than appoint a new director. Nixon's decision was made against a backdrop in which his two predecessors, Johnson and Kennedy, had retained a CIA director from the previous administration. Kissinger records Nixon retained Helms despite Nixon's reservations about CIA as an institution and his lack of comfort with Helms personally. Nixon's discomfort allegedly derived in part from the fact that Helms moved in Ivy League and Georgetown social circles.[4]

On 15 November 1968, Nixon offered Helms the job of CIA director apparently in large part because outgoing President Johnson had twice recommended him to Nixon. The most recent occasion on which Johnson had commended Helms had been four days earlier, on 11 November, when Johnson, Nixon, Helms, and others had met in Washington at the White House.

The inescapable lesson from the history of the IC—albeit a lesson that neither presidents, DCIs, or DNIs are eager to draw explicitly—is that it works better when a new president appoints his own director. In the intelligence business innumerable delicate actions are undertaken that have the potential to embarrass the US government and the president personally if they are mishandled or if misfortune strikes. In these circumstances the president must be comfortable with his director, trust him implicitly, be associated with him politically, and, above all, give him routine access.

The alternative thesis argues that some things are more important than a close relationship with the president. According to this view, appointing a career intelligence officer as director and routinely carrying over a DCI or DNI from one administration to the next is the best way to protect the IC's nonpolitical status and operational and analytical integrity. Appealing as this notion is to professionals, history does not treat it kindly. The incidence of occasions in which the IC has become embroiled in politically stupid or even illegal actions does not correlate with whether its leader was a political appointee or an intelligence professional.

The relationship of trust between president and director occasionally derives from close personal or professional associations in the past, witness the cases of Ford and Bush, Reagan and Casey, and Bush and Gates. Alternatively, there have been several cases where the president did not personally know well the individual he appointed as DCI, but was willing to accept the assurances of

---

[4] Henry Kissinger, *White House Years* (Boston: Little, Brown, and Co., 1979), 11, 36.

others that the nominee would serve with distinction. Such cases included Kennedy and McCone, Johnson and Helms, Carter and Turner, Clinton and Woolsey, and Bush and Tenet. Some of the cases where there had been no close past association worked well, but several did not.

Keeping Out of Politics

Perhaps the most challenging of the political issues with which the IC must grapple in establishing and sustaining its relationship with a new administration is how to support the president without being drawn into policymaking. It frequently takes some time for a new administration, and for a new director, to understand that the IC's proper, limited role is to provide policymakers relevant and timely raw intelligence and considered, objective analysis, including analyses of the probable ramifications of different US courses of action. Experience has shown that the IC should not take the additional step and become involved in recommending policy.

Not infrequently, IC directors during transition periods have been offered tempting opportunities to go beyond the bounds of proper intelligence support into policy deliberations. DCI Smith reportedly was highly alert to these potential pitfalls and held to a "strict constructionist" view of his responsibilities. When Eisenhower, not wanting to rely solely on the US Army's analysis of how the war in Korea was going, called for a CIA briefing that virtually invited a different interpretation and policy involvement, Smith—an experienced general officer and once Eisenhower's chief of staff—was very careful to stick to the facts and make no recommendations.

The line between intelligence and policy was not respected so carefully by those providing support to the two following presidents. The written record leaves little doubt that IC analysts' independent assessment of developments in Castro's Cuba was not solicited by or offered to Kennedy when he began his deliberations leading up to the Bay of Pigs operation. Not even the informal assessments of the working-level operations officers were included in the presentations given the new president and his team. CIA's senior managers, including Allen Dulles and Deputy Director for Plans (Operations) Richard Bissell, perceived an obligation to devise and execute a program that would "do something" about Castro. Some consciously proceeded against their better judgment of the probable outcome but, ironically, did not want to let down either Eisenhower, who was pressing for action, or Kennedy, who had committed himself to their program.

Johnson presented a temptation of a different sort to the DCI he retained from the Kennedy period. The president found that John McCone would give him independent assessments of the course of the war in Vietnam. McCone's candor and outspokenness led Johnson to solicit from him advice on what should be done regarding the conflict and concerning the assignments of diplomatic personnel—matters that were not properly part of McCone's responsibilities. Flattered by the new president, McCone offered advice going beyond his brief in a manner that soon put him at odds with his counterparts in other government departments and, before many months had passed, with the president himself.

The lesson that Dulles and McCone had been burned by their involvement in policymaking was not lost on Helms, who served as DCI for the bulk of the Johnson and Nixon presidencies. More than any previous director, Helms was careful to limit his role to providing intelligence while staying out of policy discussions. He also recognized and stressed the need to get intelligence facts and analysis to the president at a length and in a form that was digestible.

Kissinger has written perceptively of the challenge an intelligence director faces in walking the fine line between offering intelligence support and making policy recommendations. Probably more than any other national security advisor, he was sensitive to the reality that an assessment of the probable implications of any US action can come across implicitly or explicitly, intended or not, as a policy recommendation. He wrote in *White House Years*, "It is to the Director that the assistant first turns to learn the facts in a crisis and for analysis of events, and since decisions turn on the perception of the consequences of actions the CIA assessment can almost amount to a policy recommendation." Of Helms, he said, "Disciplined, meticulously fair and discreet, Helms performed his duties with a total objectivity essential to an effective intelligence service. I never knew him to misuse his intelligence or his power. He never forgot that his integrity guaranteed his effectiveness, that his best weapon with presidents was a reputation for reliability.... The CIA input was an important element of every policy deliberation."[5]

The Arrangements Make a Difference

Through the Bush transition in 2000, CIA alone handled the briefings of presidents-elect. The Agency made efforts to include analysis from the other agencies, but success was limited and uneven, dependent wholly on the determination of the senior briefer on the scene. That briefer always received unquestioning support from CIA but there was in place no institutional supporting framework to introduce information from the Community into the mix.

---

[5] Ibid., 37, 487.

CONCLUDING OBSERVATIONS

From the earliest years, comments by the presidents-elect or their senior staffs revealed that they were aware of this problem. Eisenhower, for example, lamented that he was not receiving regularly both Army operational assessments and CIA information on the situation in Korea. Kissinger, speaking for Nixon, at one point insisted—without result—that information and/or personnel from the State Department accompany the Agency's daily support. In 1992 one of the first questions the Clinton staff raised with the Agency's representative in Little Rock related to how the various agencies of the Intelligence Community worked together and whether the CIA officer would be including their information in his briefings.

The intelligence units of the policy agencies, notably the Departments of State and Defense, during transitions historically had concentrated on helping their departments prepare for their incoming secretaries, rather than focusing specifically on the new president. It was not until the ODNI assumed responsibility for transition briefings in 2008 that the several agencies making up the IC became meaningfully involved in the process.

Concerning more basic logistics arrangements, CIA's experience over the years had indicated that the system works best if the briefing support team was in place in the city where the president-elect had set up his offices. The CIA attempted to do this from the outset but had mixed results. During the Eisenhower transition, for example, the support operation established in New York City was never utilized by Eisenhower himself and provided relatively minimal support to his senior assistants, notably Sherman Adams. Because Kennedy spent much of the transition period in Washington, albeit with extended stays at Hyannisport and Palm Beach, there was no separate team set up specifically to support him. Provision of daily intelligence had been approved by outgoing President Eisenhower, but a satisfactory system to provide continuous support was never established with the incoming Democratic president. This clearly was a missed opportunity to establish a good relationship with Kennedy and his senior assistants, many of whom were unfamiliar with and suspicious of the Agency.

In the cases of Nixon and Carter, support operations were established that succeeded in making intelligence available on a daily basis. Retrospectively, however, it may be that the officers who supported the Nixon transition in New York were too junior to gain the necessary entree. Nixon never received the Agency's representatives, although Kissinger did so frequently. Carter personally received an Agency officer each day, but he was more a courier than a substantive expert.

The system has worked best when the CIA and the IC have made available to the incoming president—on a continuous basis and on the scene—an experienced senior officer who can engage in some substantive give and take on the spot. The two contrasting cases where a vice president moved up to the presidency in midterm provide an instructive example of the benefits of having established a familiar relationship for the discussion of substantive issues one-on-one. Ford had been receiving daily briefings from a senior member of the PDB staff for many months before his accession to the presidency. This compared favorably to the difficult situation where Johnson, as vice president, had been specifically denied the president's daily intelligence publication and had received no regular briefings. He had been sent a copy of a less sensitive daily intelligence publication, to which he paid little attention.

In recent transitions—for Reagan, George H. W. Bush, Clinton, and George W. Bush—the IC dispatched more senior officers who were experienced in supporting policymakers and were familiar with the full range of substantive issues about which the president-elect would be reading each day. In fact, in a great many of the daily sessions, the president-elect would simply read through the PDB with few if any questions. On other occasions, however, he would ask follow-up questions about subjects treated in the written material or, less frequently, ask for an update on issues not discussed at all in the publication. In each of these cases it proved valuable to have senior officers in place who could elaborate on the material presented. Occasionally they explained IC collection programs or the way the material related to covert action efforts under way.

Fortunately, modern technology has provided a solution to what had been a problem in several early transitions: communications links with bandwidth sufficient to transmit securely the most timely and relevant intelligence information to the president-elect wherever he may be. Now it takes only the installation of a portable computer and printer in a hotel room to provide printed material on-site that is literally indistinguishable from that which the president receives in Washington. This communications capability permits the support team to draw on the full resources of the IC in Washington and around the world to provide text, high-quality imagery, and graphics.

By the time anyone reaches the presidency, that individual has long-established work habits that are not going to change. The military approach of Eisenhower or the highly disciplined styles of Truman, Carter, or George W. Bush, for example, were vastly different from the more relaxed and less predictable approaches of Kennedy, Reagan, or Clinton. The job of the intelligence director and his representative is to accommodate each person's style. Flexibility is critical on matters ranging from the scheduling of appointments to the presentation of the substantive material, where the length, level of generality, and subject matter must be within parameters suitable to the incoming president.

The IC must provide support not only to the incoming president but also to his senior assistants. This does not mean subordinates should be shown the most sensitive material prior to inauguration, a practice successive outgoing presidents have made clear is not acceptable. Nevertheless, designees to cabinet posts and other close aides to the president-elect have intelligence needs and can be shown a full array of less sensitive materials. The IC in the past has sometimes served these individuals well and on other occasions has ignored them. Meeting this responsibility in a prompt and well-organized way helps establish a better relationship with an incoming administration. Other things being equal, it is obviously easier to accomplish this if the outgoing president and national security advisor are sympathetic to the need for a smooth transition, as George W. Bush and Steve Hadley were in 2008. It is easier still if the transition is between two presidents of the same political party.

In the preelection period, it has proved feasible and desirable to provide intelligence briefings to candidates from both or even multiple political parties. For the most part, this has been done; it certainly should be continued. For various reasons intelligence support was not provided to a few major-party candidates over the years. For example, Barry Goldwater declined the Agency's offer. George McGovern and Walter Mondale displayed only limited interest and when scheduling difficulties arose, the prospective CIA briefings fell by the boards. Robert Dole apparently was not offered a briefing. All of those who have been elected to date have accepted and benefited from the proffered intelligence support.

Material That Was Welcome

Whether in the preelection period, during the transition, or once in office, presidents almost without exception have concentrated on the current intelligence that related directly to the policy issues with which they were grappling. Similarly, they were also the most interested in oral briefings that related to those same issues. Written items or briefings were welcome if they were concise, focused, and accompanied by graphics or imagery that helped get the point across quickly. The best received briefings were those delivered by experts who were obviously masters of their subject—in recent years, typically the NIOs. Worldwide overviews provided by intelligence directors were politely received but on a few occasions were judged to have repeated material available in the newspapers.

The substantive topics addressed in the material presented to a given president-elect are obviously a function of contemporaneous international developments and, therefore, vary significantly with each incoming administration. There have been some nearly constant themes, however, such as developments in Russia, China, North Korea, and the Middle East that are subjects the IC knows it will be called on to address during each transition. North Korea's Kim Il-song and his family were probably the only foreign leaders whose activities were the subject of intelligence reporting over the whole period under review.

IC officers are well advised to be acutely conscious of the issues debated in the election campaign. Presidents-elect typically are well informed on such high-profile issues; in those areas they require only continuing updates and help in sorting the vital nuggets from the torrent of information they will receive. The IC's greater challenge with a new president is to provide useful intelligence on important issues that have not been highlighted in the campaign. On a continuing basis, roughly 60 percent of the items covered in the PDB are not addressed in the newspapers. This body of information, in particular, is likely to be unfamiliar to a prospective president.

With virtually every new president, the IC has experimented with offerings of supplementary written intelligence to elaborate issues raised in the PDB. Only two presidents-elect have clearly welcomed such supplementary material and read it thoroughly when it was offered. Those two were otherwise quite different individuals: Eisenhower and Reagan. Other presidents who were presented such background material, especially Nixon and Clinton, showed no sustained interest. Supplementary material should be made available to, but not pushed on, a president-elect who is already overburdened with reading material and short on time.

The staff aides who support the president on security issues showed a deeper interest in the extra information. The best known of them, Kissinger, once told Helms, "You know the most useful document you fellows turn out is that *Weekly Summary* that you put together. That's much more valuable than the daily stuff. That I can sit down on a Saturday morning and read and bring myself up to date and I think it's a good publication."[6]

As a result of the presidents' preference for material that can be digested quickly, it has always been a challenge to interest them in longer analytic studies and the Intelligence Community's formal national intelligence estimates. As a rule, presidents have read carefully only those studies or estimates specifically urged on them by the DCI or the national security advisor because they related directly to a policy matter of high, ongoing interest. Otherwise, the IC has found the most success when it has gisted the findings of longer papers and integrated a summary into the PDB. Indeed, the Agency has been told by national security advisors that the PDB was the only publication on

---

[6] Helms interview, 21 April 1982.

any subject that they could be absolutely confident their principal would read on any given day.

From the IC's perspective, there are clear advantages to having a new president come into office well informed not only about developments abroad but also about covert action and sensitive collection programs. Ford, Carter, Reagan, George H. W. Bush, and George W. Bush all were well briefed on such activities. Eisenhower, Kennedy, and Clinton entered office with limited familiarity with the Agency's sensitive activities. Two others, Johnson and Nixon, had no up-to-date knowledge of those programs when they took office.

Familiarity with sensitive programs does not necessarily result in support for them. Carter, for example, ordered a halt to some of the Agency's sensitive undertakings within weeks of taking office. A president's early awareness of such programs is, nevertheless, essential for him, the country, the IC, and the CIA. He needs to be in an informed position to defend and support these often politically charged activities or to change them if necessary to ensure their consistency with his overall foreign policy objectives. If the Bay of Pigs fiasco taught nothing else, it was that administration policy should drive covert action; covert action projects should not drive policy or color the intelligence provided.

There has been an almost unbroken pattern over the years in expanding the support provided a new president and his team in areas beyond daily intelligence. Beginning with the Nixon transition, his key staff aides—Kissinger and Eagleburger—were provided significant quantities of material for their own policy-planning purposes. For Clinton, the Agency provided background material for use by the president- and vice president-elect and their senior staffs for telephone calls with foreign leaders, speeches and press conferences, and internal policy deliberations. The key to success in these efforts, as with intelligence generally, is to stick to the facts. The new team must know that the IC is neither defending policy for the old administration nor creating it for the new one.

There has never been any doubt that the PDB, right up to Inauguration Day, is designed to address the interests of the president in office. Realistically, however, as the time for the turnover draws closer and as the incoming president is reading the PDB with care, the inevitable and probably appropriate tendency is to select and address substantive items in a way that meets the needs of the new president as well as the outgoing one. Fortunately, in practice this usually amounts only to adjustments on the margin.

The IC's experience in providing intelligence to 11 presidents—through 10 quite different transitions—has led many of its officers to appreciate the wisdom President Truman displayed in a speech he gave on 21 November 1953:

CHAPTER 8

> *The office of President of the United States now carries power beyond parallel in history. That is the principal reason that I am so anxious that it be a continuing proposition and the successor to me and the successor to him can carry on as if no election had ever taken place.... That is why I am giving this president—this new president—more information than any other president had when he went into office.*[7]

President Truman was the first and the most senior of the intelligence briefers to be involved in the more than half-century series of briefings from 1952 to 2004. Truman personally had provided an intelligence overview to General Eisenhower on 18 November 1952. In his speech at CIA three days later he said, "It was my privilege...to brief the man who is going to take over the office of President of the United States." It has been the IC's privilege as well, many times.

⌘ ⌘ ⌘

---

[7] *New York Times*, 22 November 1952, 1, 10.

INDEX

A

Aaron, David, 92, 95, 102, 107
Adams, Sherman, 19, 187
Afghanistan, 101, 112, 117, 172
Africa, 132, 173
Agnew, Spiro, 61
Albright, Madeleine, 125, 144
Algeria, 34, 35
Allen, Richard, 65, 66, 67, 112, 121, 122
al-Qa'ida, 153, 171, 172, 174
Ames, Robert, 112
Amory, Robert, 19, 22
Anderson, John, 113
Anderson, Martin, 65, 66, 67
Angola, 90, 96, 126, 139
Arab-Israeli conflict, 69, 101
Aspin, Les, 144
Attorney General, 57

B

Balkans, 152, 155, 159
Ball, George, 53
Bay of Pigs, 6, 40–42, 44–46, 48, 178, 181, 182, 185, 191
Beatty, Ed, 19
Becker, Loftus, 23
Belgium, 34
Bentsen, Lloyd, 125
Berger, Samuel (Sandy), 131, 133, 134, 142, 144, 148, 151
Berlin, 34, 35, 69, 71
Biddiscomb, John, 104–105
Bissell, Richard, 40–42, 185
Black Hawk Down incident, 148
Bolton, Josh, 152
bomber gap, 22

Boren, David, 132
Bosnia, 129, 132, 135, 139, 142, 147
Bowles, Chester, 45
Brezhnev, Leonid, 81, 101
Brzezinski, Zbigniew, 107, 109, 118
Bundy, McGeorge, 22, 48, 50, 53, 58, 66
Bush, George H. W., 5, 123, 124–129, 135, 139, 141, 147, 165, 168, 177, 179, 182, 183, 191
    as DCI, 83–85, 87, 89, 90, 91
        concerns about politicization of intelligence, 97
        resignation, 102
    briefing preferences, 125
    intelligence interests as vice president, 117, 121
    operational, covert action briefing, 161
    preelection briefings, 124, 131
    promotion of presidential intelligence support, 97, 111, 115, 118, 119, 120, 121, 124, 129, 180
Bush, George W., 155–156, 160, 175, 177, 179, 182, 189, 191
    briefing preferences, 153, 168–169
    intelligence support during presidential travel, 166, 169
    operational, covert action briefing, 161
    postelection briefings, 156–159, 162–166
    preelection briefing, 151–154

C

Cabell, Charles, 25, 35
Cambodia, 80, 96, 120, 132
campaign politics, 13, 96, 113
    intelligence as an issue, 29, 61, 63, 96
Card, Andy, 158, 161, 168
Carter, Billy, 105
Carter, Jimmy, 87–110, 113, 116, 118, 120, 131, 171, 179, 183, 191
    briefing preferences, 91, 102, 107, 179
    evaluation of PDB, 105, 107
    interest in satellite photography, 94, 104
    operational, covert action briefing, 98–100, 161
    postelection briefings, 97–103
    preelection briefings, 87–95
        feedback and follow-up, 93

    restrictions, 91, 94
  recommendations on improving presidential briefings, 180–181
Casey, William, 116, 117, 126, 183
Central America, 116, 126
Central Intelligence Bulletin, 65
Central Intelligence Group (CIG), 7
Chavez, Dennis, 45
Cheney, Dick, 155, 160–161, 166, 168, 169, 174
Chile, 96
China, 14, 17, 25, 34, 35, 69, 75, 89, 92, 94, 105, 129, 132, 152, 159, 161, 172
Christopher, Warren, 143, 144
Church Committee, 83
CIA Operations Center, 69, 165
CIA print plant, 147
Clifford, Clark, 47, 64
Clifton, Chester, 48, 49, 56
Clinton, Bill, 3, 5, 120, 131–148, 152, 157, 162, 171, 177, 179, 182, 190, 191
    briefing preferences, 148
    intelligence and policymaking, 135
    operational, covert action briefing, 140, 161
    postelection briefings, 133–138
    preelection briefings, 131–132
Clinton, Hillary, 135
Colby, William, 74, 75, 76–77, 79, 81, 83, 93, 182, 183
communications, see logistics and communications
Conger, Clifton, 55
Congo, 34, 35
Corscadden, Paul H., 65, 66, 67, 68, 70
Countdown for Decision, 37
covert action, 5, 21, 24, 29, 31–32, 43, 53, 91, 100, 112, 117, 120, 140, 161, 188, 191
Crowe, William, 126
Cuba, 6, 30–32, 34, 35, 40–42, 43, 47, 55, 61, 90, 116, 120, 185
    covert action, 31, 32, 36
        also see Bay of Pigs
Cuban missile crisis, 50
Current Intelligence Bulletin, 9, 19, 48, 50
Current Intelligence Weekly Review, 9
Current Production and Analytic Support (CPAS), 133
Cutler, Robert, 21
Cyprus, 26
Czechoslovakia, 61, 69

D

Daily Summary, 8
Davidson, Meredith, 9, 16–18, 23
Davis, Dixon, 119, 120, 121
DCI presidential briefings, 9, 29, 75, 148, 151, 178, 179, 181
    Bush for Carter, 98–100, 103
    Bush for Carter (preelection), 90–94
    Colby for Ford, 82
    Dulles for Eisenhower, 20–21
    Dulles for Kennedy, 42–44
    Gates for Cinton (preelection), 131–132
    Gates for George H. W. Bush, 127
    Helms for Nixon, 61–64
    McCone for Johnson, 52, 54–55, 56
    McCone for Kennedy, 50
    Smith for Eisenhower, 16–19
    Smith for Truman, 9
    Tenet for Bush, 168–169
    Turner for Carter, 109
    Turner for Reagan, 114, 117–118
    Turner for Reagan (preelection), 111–113
    Webster for George H. W. Bush, 127
DDI-New York, 65–71, 97
deep dive briefings, 169–170
Department of Defense, 9, 23, 38, 57, 94, 109, 147, 168
Department of State, 9, 20, 23, 57, 70, 76, 94, 109, 113, 136, 147, 168
Department of Treasury, 57, 135
Deutch, John, 149
Diamond, Douglas, 116
Diem, Ngo Dinh, 53
Directorate of Intelligence, 167
    efforts to upgrade intelligence support, 162–166
Directorate of Operations, 136, 165, 167
Directorate of Science and Technology, 104
Djibouti, 92
DNI presidential briefings, 179
Dobrynin, Anatoly, 101
Dole, Robert, 95, 149, 171
Dominican Republic, 43, 59, 61
Donovan, William, 18

Dukakis, Michael
    preelection briefings, 125
Dulles, Allen, 20, 20–22, 29, 32, 36–38, 42–44, 46, 48, 50, 63, 154, 181, 182, 185
    and Kennedy preelection briefings, 34–36
    relations with Kennedy, 48
Dulles, John Foster, 18, 20, 26

E

Eagleburger, Lawrence, 68–69, 70, 72, 73, 191
Eagleton, Tom, 171
East Asia, 159, 173
economic espionage, 132
Edwards, John, 173
Edwards, Sheffield, 18
Egypt, 15, 90, 92, 95
Eisenhower, Dwight, 3, 7–23, 32, 34, 37, 43, 44, 46, 47, 48, 73, 151, 177, 178, 185, 187, 190, 191
    briefing preferences, 20–23
    intelligence support during presidential travel, 23
    postelection briefings, 16–20
    preelection briefings, 14–16
    tensions with Truman during transition, 11–13
Eisenhower, John, 23
Eisenhower, Mamie
    participation in intelligence briefings, 17
Eizenstat, Stuart, 87, 91, 92, 94, 95, 97
Elder, Walter, 51, 57
European Community (EC), 137
Evans, Rowland, 102

F

family jewels, 82
FBI, 66
Fitzgerald, Jennifer, 97
Foley, Edward, 45

Ford, David, 87
Ford, Gerald, 5, 39, 76–84, 88, 99, 102, 107, 179, 183, 191
    briefing preferences, 77–78
    decision to stop PBD briefings by CIA, 83
    operational briefings, 79
Foreign Broadcast Information Service (FBIS), 67
Fox, Vicente, 155
France, 14, 34, 35, 69

G

Gallucci, Robert, 143
Gates, Robert, 125, 127, 131–132, 179, 182
Gates, Thomas, 37
General Agreement on Tariffs and Trade (GATT), 137
General Services Administration, 147
Germany, 129
global economy, 139, 159
global energy, 104, 112, 159, 173
global environment, 135
Glomar Explorer, 79–80
Goldwater, Barry, 63, 189
    preelection briefings declined, 57
Goodpaster, Andrew, 21, 23, 37, 40, 43, 48, 70, 73
Goodwin, Richard, 30, 32
Gore, Albert, 131, 134, 142, 143, 154, 155, 162
Gore, Albert, Sr., 35
Goss, Porter, 171
Gray, Gordon, 21, 22, 44
Greece, 92
Guatemala, 43

H

Hadley, Steve, 158, 161, 189
Haig, Alexander, 77, 122
Haiti, 61, 129, 135, 137, 147, 148
Haldeman, Robert (H. R.), 65, 67

Hamilton, Lee, 125
Harper, John, 100
Helms, Richard, 61, 61–64, 73, 74, 179, 181, 182, 186
Hendrickson, Melvin, 14–16
Hodges, Luther, 45
Hoover, J. Edgar, 40
Horn of Africa, 101
Humphrey, Hubert, 63
Hungary, 25
King Hussein, 35
Hussein, Saddam, 155, 174

I

India, 25
In-Q-Tel, 163
intelligence and policymaking, 18, 37–40, 54–56, 94, 116, 135, 137, 153, 183, 185–186
Intelligence Community
    greater role in transition briefings, 186–189
Intelligence Review, 57, 58
intelligence sources, 117, 120, 191
    gaps, 153
    human, 5, 32, 79, 98, 101, 117, 127, 140, 164, 167, 168
    technical, 5, 24, 32, 37, 43, 53, 55, 75, 79, 88, 94, 95, 98, 107, 117, 140, 164
intelligence support for first ladies, 136
Iran, 14, 15, 24, 34, 112, 126, 132, 152, 155, 172
Iran hostage crisis, 110, 113, 117, 119, 120, 121
Iraq, 90, 112, 132, 137, 152, 155, 161, 171, 173, 174
Israel, 26, 114, 119, 137, 152, 154, 155
Italy, 21

J

Japan, 14, 15
Jeremiah, David, 143
Johnson, Lyndon, 32, 34, 50–59, 61, 63, 64, 68, 71, 178, 185, 191

briefing preferences, 52, 55, 59
covert action briefing, 53
Joint Chiefs of Staff, 20, 21, 23, 38, 46, 51, 57, 70, 76, 106, 147, 168
Jordan, 26, 35

K

Kampuchea, see Cambodia
Kefauver, Estes, 26
Kennedy, John, 6, 20, 68, 79, 154, 174, 178, 185, 187, 191
    1960 presidential debates, 29–32
    briefing preferences, 22, 47, 49
    dissatisfaction with intelligence briefings, 48
    postelection briefings
        Cuban covert action, 40–42, 44–46
        restrictions, 43, 44
        worldwide intelligence operations, 42–44
    preelection briefings, 34–36
        Cuban covert action, 31–33, 36
        feedback and follow-up, 35
        intelligence systems, 37
        missile gap, 36–40
        restrictions, 32, 34, 37
Kennedy, Joseph P., 45
Kennedy, Robert, 35, 63
Kerr, Richard, 119, 120, 122
Kerry, John
    preelection briefings, 172–173
Kessler, Martha Neff, 114–115
Khan, Aga, 35
Khan, Sadruddin, 35
Khrushchev, Nikita, 35, 48
Kissinger, Henry, 61, 67–72, 78, 79, 81, 82, 83, 89, 171, 181, 184, 186, 187, 191
    critique of PDB, 68
    efforts to control flow of intelligence, 68, 70, 71, 73, 77
Knoche, Henry, 100, 102, 103, 107
Korea, 16, 71, 73, 92, 94, 95, 155, 159
Korean War, 11, 14, 15, 17–18
Kosovo, 152

Kuwait, 156

L

Lake, Tony, 144, 148
Laos, 35, 43
Latin America, 152, 159, 173
Lay, James, Jr., 20, 21
leaks, 47, 57
Lebanon, 89, 90, 92, 101, 120, 137, 139
Lehman, Richard, 49, 57, 65, 87–88, 89, 91, 94, 97, 101, 104, 105–106, 112, 114, 119
Libya, 90, 92, 95, 126, 172
Lieberman, Joe, 154, 155
Lodge, Henry Cabot, 53–54
logistics and communications, 5, 14–15, 16, 19, 25, 65, 66, 88–89, 104, 134, 142, 143, 144–147, 156, 158, 162–166, 187, 188
Lopez-Portillo, José, 122

M

Maddox, Lester, 63
Malaysia, 25
Manhattan Project, 7
Mayaguez seizure, 80, 81
McCarthy, Eugene, 63
McCone, John, 50, 50–53, 59, 63, 179, 182, 185
    and Vietnam policy, 53–56
    resignation, 56
McConnell, Michael, 170, 171
McCrory, Ray, 90
McCurdy, David, 132
McFarlane, Bud, 124
McGovern, George, 171, 189
McLaughlin, John, 139, 143, 144, 151, 154, 162, 172–173
McMahan, Knight, 25–27
McNamara, Robert, 51, 53, 56
Medaris, John, 37

Meese, Ed, 111, 114
Mexico, 34, 116, 120, 141, 155
Middle East, 114, 173, 190
Miller, Herbert, 22
Miscik, Jami, 156, 157, 159, 165
missile gap, 30, 36–40, 154
Mitchell, John, 65, 70
Mondale, Walter, 90–91, 92, 93, 95, 97, 100, 103, 106, 107, 124, 171, 189
Morell, Michael, 166, 168
Morgan, Edward P., 34
Morocco, 120
Mossadeq, Mohammed, 24
Moyers, Bill, 59
Mozambique, 92
Murphy, Daniel, 100

N

9/11, 153, 174
Nasser, Gamal Abdel, 25
National Intelligence Council, 112
National Intelligence Daily (NID), 76, 122, 134, 146
National Intelligence Digest, 10
national intelligence estimates (NIEs), 16, 38–39, 66, 70, 81, 136, 160, 164, 190
national intelligence officers (NIOs), 87, 112, 114, 189
National Security Council, 22, 32, 39, 44, 48, 55, 72, 74, 79, 107, 109, 154, 156, 169
    venue for presidential briefings, 20–22, 55, 74, 81, 178
NATO, 69
Negroponte, John, 171
Nigeria, 69
Nixon, Richard, 29, 31, 32, 61–67, 73–76, 154, 174, 178, 179, 181, 184, 187, 190, 191
    1960 presidential debates, 29–32
    briefing preferences, 68–72, 75
    distrust of CIA, 73
    postelection intelligence support, 65–67
        security, 65
    preelection briefings, 61–63

Noriega, Manuel, 126
North Africa, 14
North American Free Trade Agreement (NAFTA), 141
North Korea, 132, 152, 172, 190
Novak, Robert, 102
NSA, 136, 140
nuclear proliferation, 172
nuclear testing, 34

O

O'Neil, Michael, 149
Obama, Barack, 180
Office of Communications, 133, 143, 144, 146
Office of Current Intelligence (OCI), 9, 49, 65, 68, 78
Office of Logistics, 133
Office of National Estimates, 21
Office of Security, 18, 66, 133, 143
OPEC, 101
Operations Advisory Group, 101
Osborn, Howard, 65
Oswald, Lee Harvey, 52

P

Pakistan, 96, 112, 120, 172
Palestinian issues, 114, 121, 137, 152, 154, 155
Panama, 126
partisan politics, impact of, 12–13, 172
Pavitt, Jim, 161, 167
PDB briefers, role of, 76–79, 84, 104–105, 106–109, 119, 120, 121, 122–123, 124, 125, 127–128, 159, 160, 164–166, 168–169, 179, 186
Persons, Wilton, 43
Petersen, Martin (Marty), 154, 156, 158, 162
Peterson, David, 76, 79, 83, 106, 107, 109
Pforzheimer, Walter, 47
Philippines, 120
Pike Committee, 83

Podesta, John, 157
Poindexter, John, 123
Poland, 62, 101, 116, 119
politicalization of intelligence, 22, 40, 63, 92, 97–98, 124
Powell, Jody, 89, 103
Powers, Francis Gary, 29, 37
President's Daily Brief (PDB), 5, 50, 56–59, 65, 68, 83, 99, 104–110, 131, 135, 138, 154, 156, 160, 188
    and press reporting, 105, 107, 139
    feedback and follow-up, 59, 76, 78, 104, 108–110, 123, 127, 128, 137, 164
    graphics, 135, 139, 147
    real-tim delivery, 181
    real-time delivery, 162–166
    recipients, 107, 122, 126, 134, 148, 167, 168
    scheduling, 134, 135, 139, 164
    security, 123, 127, 168
    storage and handling, 67, 72, 78, 109, 127, 166
    supplemental material, 5, 104, 105, 120, 134, 135, 139, 158, 161, 164, 190
    tailoring content and format, 68, 72, 105–107, 122, 128, 139, 168, 169, 190
    Weekly Leadership Notes, 139
President's Intelligence Checklist, 47–50, 54, 56–58
    recipients, 49, 51, 57
    tailoring content and format, 49
presidential debates, 29–31, 63, 88, 95–96, 113, 138, 154, 155–156, 173–174, 190
    intelligence as an issue, 126, 155, 174
    intelligence issues, 155
presidential feedback and follow-up, 9, 10, 17, 21–22, 35, 48, 49, 57, 121, 129
    also see under President's Daily Brief
presidential visits to CIA Headquarters, 148
    John Kennedy, 46–47
press coverage, 19, 41, 89, 112, 146
proliferation, 132, 135, 161

Q

Qadhafi, Muammar, 106
Quayle, Dan, 126
Quemoy and Matsu, 30, 91

also see Taiwan Straits

R

Raborn, William, Jr., 59, 64
Reagan, Nancy
    interest in intelligence briefings, 119
Reagan, Ronald, 5, 111–124, 131, 171, 177, 179, 182, 190, 191
    briefing preferences, 116, 119–121, 122–124
    distrust of daily intelligence briefings, 118
    operational, covert action briefing, 117–118
    postelection briefings, 114–122
    preelection briefing, 111–113
Rhodesia, 89, 90, 92, 95, 101
Rice, Condoleezza (Condi), 152, 158, 168
Rockefeller Commission, 83
Roh Tae Woo, 142
Rosen, Kenneth, 65, 67, 70, 73
Rostow, Walt, 64
Rumsfeld, Donald, 83, 170
Rusk, Dean, 50, 51, 53, 57, 61, 63
Russia, 15, 16, 25, 29, 34, 35, 61, 69, 81, 87, 89, 92, 93, 94, 101, 104, 112, 116, 119, 120, 129, 132, 136, 139, 144, 152, 159, 172, 190

S

Sadat, Anwar, 115
Sakhalin and Kuril Islands, 25
Salinas, Carlos, 141, 142
Sanford, Terry, 45
Saudi Arabia, 112
Schlesinger, Arthur, Jr., 30, 45
Schlesinger, James, 74, 79, 83
Scoville, Herbert Jr., 22
Scowcroft, Brent, 78, 79, 80, 83, 87, 95, 126, 129, 131, 148
Secret Service, 18, 66, 103, 105, 143, 145, 157, 162, 166
security, 14, 18, 19, 55, 66, 144, 147, 162, 166
    clearances for presidential staff, 16, 42, 65, 69

Serbia, 144, 152, 155
Sheldon, Huntington, 20, 21, 23, 46, 48, 49
Shultz, George, 123
Singapore, 25
Situation in Vietnam, 65
Situation Summary, 9, 10
Smith, Bromley, 51, 52, 57, 59
Smith, R. Jack, 52, 57, 65, 67
Smith, Walter Bedell, 7, 11, 12, 16, 16–20, 24, 109, 179, 185
Soderberg, Nancy, 133, 134
Somalia, 92, 120, 129, 135, 136, 143, 143–144, 147, 148
Sorensen, Theodore (Ted), 31, 45, 48, 98, 107
Souers, Sidney, 10
South Africa, 89, 95, 110
South Asia, 159
South Korea, 89, 139
Soviet space program, 35
Special Group, 36
SR-71, 43, 53
START II, 136, 142
Stephanopoulos, George, 146
Stevenson, Adlai, 3, 10, 11, 17, 151, 171
    preelection briefings, 23–27
        feedback and follow-up, 24, 26
        not shown communications intelligence, 24, 26
Stimson, Henry, 7
Stoertz, Howard, 39, 40, 90
Stokes, Louis, 125
Strategic Arms Limitation Talks (SALT), 81, 88, 90, 91
strategic weapons, 34, 36–39, 69, 70, 81, 87, 90, 93, 95, 115, 119, 126
Suez Crisis, 25–27
Sununu, John, 126
Symington, Stuart, 38, 40
Syria, 35, 90, 114

T

Taiwan, 34, 35, 91
Taiwan Straits, 34, 90
Taylor, Maxwell, 42

Tenet, George, 151, 154, 158, 161, 167, 168–169, 170–171, 172, 174, 182
terrorism, 153, 159, 161, 172
Tibet, 43
transition teams, 114, 133
    relations with, 19, 37, 65–67, 95, 102, 121, 133–135, 147, 187–189
Truman, Harry, 3, 7–9, 23, 48, 109, 131, 156, 178, 191
    briefing preferences, 9
    tensions with Eisenhower during transition, 11–12
Turkey, 92
Turner, Stansfield, 107, 109, 111–112, 114, 116
Twining, Nathan, 38

U

U-2, 29, 36, 43
Uganda, 90
Ukraine, 142
United States Intelligence Board, 70
US Congress, 23, 39, 46, 54, 77, 83, 90, 93, 136
    Armed Services Committee, 156
    House Defense Appropriations Subcommittee, 39
    oversight committees, 125, 131, 156, 174
    Senate Aeronautical and Space Sciences Committee, 50
    Senate Foreign Relations Committee, 40, 80, 102, 173
    Senate Preparedness Committee, 35, 38
USSR, see Russia

V

Valenti, Jack, 58
Vance, Cyrus, 61, 109
Venezuela, 43
Vietnam, 21, 43, 53–56, 62, 64, 71, 96, 182, 186

W

Wallace, George, 63

Watergate, 75, 76
weapons of mass destruction (WMD), 153, 155, 171, 174
Webster, William, 123, 125, 127, 182, 183
Weekly Review, 65
Weekly Summary, 8, 190
Weinberger, Caspar, 122
Wheeler, Earl, 64
White House Communications Agency, 104
White House Situation Room, 65, 76, 80
Whitman, John, 94, 95
Wiley, Winston, 156, 158, 166
Wolfowitz, Paul, 152
Woods, Rose Mary, 67, 68, 72
Woolsey, James, 144

Y

Yel'tsin, Boris, 136, 142
Yugoslavia, 15, 62, 96, 132, 136

www.ingramcontent.com/pod-product-compliance
Lightning Source LLC
Chambersburg PA
CBHW082119230426
43671CB00015B/2741